Conversations

with

Abner Mikva

Final Reflections on Chicago Politics,

Democracy's Future, and a Life of

Public Service

SANFORD D. HORWITT

Foreword by
SENATOR DICK DURBIN

 University Press of Kansas

Published by the University Press of Kansas (Lawrence, Kansas 66045), which was organized by the Kansas Board of Regents and is operated and funded by Emporia State University, Fort Hays State University, Kansas State University, Pittsburg State University, the University of Kansas, and Wichita State University

Library of Congress Cataloging-in-Publication Data

Names: Horwitt, Sanford D.
Title: Conversations with Abner Mikva : final reflections on Chicago politics, democracy's future, and a life of public service / Sanford D. Horwitt.
Description: Lawrence, Kansas : University Press of Kansas, [2018] | Includes index.
Identifiers: LCCN 2018027418
 ISBN 9780700627387 (cloth : alk. paper)
 ISBN 9780700627394 (ebook)
Subjects: LCSH: Mikva, Abner J. | Legislators—United States—Biography. | Judges—United States—Biography. | United States. Congress. House of Representatives—Biography. | Illinois. General Assembly. House of Representatives—Biography. | Legislators—Illinois—Biography. | Jewish politicians—United States—Biography. | Obama, Barack—Friends and associates. | Chicago—Politics and government—Anecdotes. | United States—Politics and government—Anecdotes.
Classification: LCC E840.8.M525 H67 2018 | DDC 328.73/092 [B]—dc23.
LC record available at https://lccn.loc.gov/2018027418

British Library Cataloguing-in-Publication Data is available.

Printed in the United States of America
10 9 8 7 6 5 4 3 2 1

The paper used in this publication is recycled and contains 30 percent postconsumer waste. It is acid free and meets the minimum requirements of the American National Standard for Permanence of Paper for Printed Library Materials z39.48-1992.

For democracy's next generation:

Lila Grace Horwitt
Vivienne Marie Horwitt

Jordan Mikva Cohen
Rebecca Mikva Cohen
Jacob H. Mikva
Keren Mikva Rosenberg
Benjamin Mikva Pfander
Samantha Mikva Pfander
Sarah Mikva Pfander

CONTENTS

A photograph gallery follows page 102.

Democracy is a verb. That was Abner Mikva's mantra and one of the countless pieces of wisdom he imparted to the people whose lives he touched. Abner Mikva was—and is—my hero. He was always my North Star for integrity in public life and a paragon of both progressive values and independence from party orthodoxy. In an era of cynicism and disappointment, Abner's record of public service is proof that the good guys can win without selling their souls.

Ab's final reflections with his friend Sandy Horwitt about his rich experiences and the road ahead are a timely gift to all of us who care about our democracy.

Ab Mikva was a patriot in every sense. He served his country in uniform in World War II and later served in all three branches of the US government. He was a Supreme Court clerk, an Illinois state legislator, a member of Congress, a federal appeals court judge, and a counselor to President Bill Clinton. He was also a mentor to so many—including a promising young Chicago community organizer named Barack Obama.

Ab Mikva was the pol "nobody sent." In 1948—an election year—Ab, then a twenty-two-year-old law student, was fired up about the top of the ticket in Illinois: Adlai Stevenson for governor and Paul Douglas for Senate. So he walked into the 8th Ward Regular Democratic Organization and said he wanted to help.

Dead silence.

Then a cigar-smoking ward committeeman barked: "Who sent ya, kid?"

Ab said: "Nobody sent me."

To which the committeeman replied: "We don't want nobody nobody sent." This was the old machine's way of saying scram. That would have broken many young people's political spirit. Not Ab Mikva. Instead of giving up, he found himself in the Illinois house at the age of thirty—kicking off a forty-year career spanning nine presidents. And how did Ab characterize his years in public life? "More years in public service unindicted than anybody else. I did it all. It was fun. I wouldn't trade a day of it."

That's what made Ab special. It wasn't simply the résumé that earned him such great respect. It was his approach to the job. He brought humility, integrity, and fairness to every challenge he faced—combined with an extraordinary sense of humor and a famous ability to get along with others, regardless of their politics.

Illinois and America are better today because he defied the party bosses and rallied thousands to beat them. Ab's Mikva Challenge will continue to create new generations motivated by his life in public service. Ab's spirit lives on in all of us who were inspired by his courage, his wisdom, his profound decency, and his devotion to America and to justice.

Dick Durbin
US Senator
Illinois

Introduction

Abner Mikva saw death coming but not Donald Trump.

My old boss, friend, and liberal icon, a true believer in the lofty possibilities of American democracy, died in Chicago at ninety years old, fittingly, on the Fourth of July. It was two weeks before the 2016 Republican National Convention. Until nearly his last breath, he still wanted to make a difference, to make our world a better place.

In mid-May, despite getting weaker by the day, he had booked a 7:00 a.m. United Airlines flight to Washington, where he was determined to testify at a forum organized by Democratic senators in support of his protégé and friend Judge Merrick Garland, who had been nominated for a seat on the US Supreme Court by Barack Obama, another friend of Ab's. I planned to pick him up at Reagan National Airport, but he called me the night before and said, "Sandy, I've taken a turn for the worse. I'm going into the hospital tomorrow morning." And then, days before he died, we had our last, brief conversation. He told me that he couldn't wait for the Republican convention to start. "I'm afraid Trump may self-destruct before the convention," he laughed weakly.

I said, "Well, I think the Republicans are stuck with him."

"I think they are, too," Ab replied, "and it couldn't be better." He was envisioning a resounding victory by Hillary Clinton, whom Ab liked and respected from his days in the Clinton White House, despite their sometimes rocky relationship.

As it turned out, Ab's customary political perspicacity was off the mark, although not completely; Hillary Clinton won the popular vote by 2.8 million votes, while Donald Trump won a majority in the Electoral College.

Later, I was surprised to discover that when Ab was serving his first term in Congress in 1969, he and his colleagues in the House of Representatives voted overwhelmingly to abolish the Electoral College. The measure had broad bipartisan support because George Wallace's third-party, racist campaign had won 46 electoral votes in 1968, coming close to throwing the election into the House. But a filibuster in the US Senate led by southern Democrats thwarted the historic reform—and forty-eight years later, Donald J. Trump was president.

In my monthly conversations with Ab over the last three years of his life, I recognized that the most important part of his timely story is that, for the last half century, he personified the kind of courageous, hopeful, honorable public service and authentic democratic voice that our country so urgently needs today. As veteran journalist Albert Hunt wrote after Ab's death: "Over the four decades I've been covering national politics, any all-star starting five of politicians would include Abner J. Mikva. . . . If judgment and integrity were the coin of the realm, Ab Mikva was Bill Gates."

This book is mostly about Abner Mikva's end-of-life reflections and insights; it is not a biography. I also have a presence in the narrative that emerged from our conversations about American politics and the law, aging and death, and the generational differences and fortuitous events that shaped both our lives. This is also a story about conversations between two friends catching up and summing up lifetimes of memories while trying to make sense of how it happened and where we are now—the two of us and our country.

I press the red start button on my old cassette tape recorder just in time to capture a savory slice of Abner Mikva's undiminished passion for American politics, justice, and the premium he places on political courage. Never mind that he has just turned eighty-seven, can't see the butter on the other side of the breakfast table, and has trouble breathing after inhaling three packs of Pall Malls every day for thirty years. He is razor sharp and has not mellowed, I'm happy to observe.

It is Wednesday, April 18, 2013, and this is our first conversation about democracy and life. A few months earlier, I had visited my old boss and friend at the apartment he shares with his wife Zoe in a retirement high-rise on North Lake Shore Drive in Chicago. After an hour or so of chitchat, I finally forced myself to ask whether he might be interested in having a series of conversations with me about his thoughts on life, family, aging, and, of course, the state of the Union, politics, and the fascinating characters that have been part of his life: the young and not-so-young Barack Obama, Bill and Hillary Clinton, his former US Appeals Court colleague Antonin Scalia, his prize law clerk Elena Kagan, Chicago's "Boss" Richard J. Daley, and disgraced Illinois governors. Ab has had a unique set of experiences. Since World War II, perhaps no other American has been such a keen participant-observer while serving in all three branches of the federal government and in one of the most notorious rock 'em, sock 'em legislative boot camps, the Illinois state legislature, in the 1950s and 1960s.

I didn't want to sound like I was asking Ab to sit down and talk about his life's lessons before it was too late, but that's what I was thinking. Since I'm not too comfortable facing up to my own mortality, I was uncomfortable even hinting at his. I was also a little concerned about rejection—that, for whatever reason, he might say no. But no sooner had I asked him whether he was interested in meeting monthly with me and suggested that our conversations might turn into a book than he immediately responded with familiar gusto, "Absolutely!"

Like many of the monthly conversations we had over the next three years, our first one started with an impromptu story on that typically chilly April day. We met in the living room of Ab's twenty-fourth-floor apartment with stunning views of two Chicago treasures: Lake Michigan to the east and Wrigley Field to the west. It was four months after a crazed gunman shot and killed twenty schoolchildren and six educators at the Sandy Hook Elementary School in Newtown, Connecticut. In the aftermath, President Obama and a majority of Americans wanted Congress to pass stronger gun control legislation. But even the most modest proposals in Congress were running into fierce opposition by the National Rifle Association (NRA).

This was déjà vu all over again, political kickboxing that Abner Mikva knew all about from firsthand experience. In the 1970s he was the most outspoken advocate in Congress for gun control, including a ban on the sale and manufacture of handguns. When President Carter nominated Ab to be a judge on the US Court of Appeals for the District of Columbia Circuit in 1979, the NRA launched a national anti-Mikva campaign and came very close to derailing the nomination. Ab has never forgotten the weak-kneed Democratic senators who voted against his nomination.

So on this day in his apartment, he wanted to tell me about two letters he had recently sent to Mark Pryor, a Democratic senator from Arkansas. Pryor, who was up for reelection, was described in news accounts as wavering on a vote to send gun control legislation to the Senate floor. Ab and Pryor's father, David, had served together in the House of Representatives in the late 1960s. Ab had liked the elder Pryor and was impressed by his integrity. Ab said his first letter to the son went like this: "Dear Mark, I take the privilege of calling you by your first name because I've known you since you were six years old." That was in 1969, when he met young Mark on the House floor for the opening session of the new Congress and members brought their children with them. It was the first day of Ab's first term. In the letter, he recalled that Mark's father had told him that "'the biggest thing you need to be a good congressman was courage.' As far as I'm concerned," Ab continued, "it still is and always was. I'm sure the gun control legislation is going to be a tough vote but just remember who you are and look in the mirror and you'll do fine. With respect, Abner Mikva." That was last week, Ab told me, his eyes narrowing and his face hardening. I remember the look; he's never been a wimpy liberal. "And then he voted against cloture so he wouldn't have even allowed the bill to come to the floor for a vote. So I wrote him a second letter. This time it was not 'Dear Mark'; it was, 'Senator Pryor, why don't you change your name so that people won't confuse your cowardly act with that of your father.'"

I met Abner Mikva in the winter of 1974. We were both in a place where we didn't want to be. He had been redistricted out of a safely Democratic congressional district on Chicago's South Side and was only temporarily, he hoped, practicing law while gearing up for another congressional race in a Republican-leaning district in the North Shore suburbs. Several years out of graduate school, I was teaching at the University of Illinois in Chicago but wanted to be doing something political. I began volunteering in his campaign a few hours a week, and by the summer, it was my full-time work. I sometimes sat next to another volunteer, precocious college student Merrick Garland. When Ab eked out a victory in November, he was on his way back to a post-Watergate reform Congress, and I was headed to Washington as his press secretary, speechwriter, and sometime legislative aide on a hodgepodge of hot issues from guns to Nazis marching in Skokie, Illinois.

Back then, he was middle-aged and I was practically a kid with a young wife, a two-year-old son, and another not yet born. Now we're both senior citizens. How did that happen? In the course of our conversations, I began to realize how much of a difference one generation made in our lives and just how much each of us is a product of his times. A coincidence that had nothing to do with our first meeting forty years ago is that we were born in the same city, Milwaukee, seventeen years apart, yet a world apart, too. Nothing in Ab's early life, including a dysfunctional family and embarrassing poverty, would have hinted at a remarkable career at the exalted levels of law and politics and his status as a contemporary gold standard for integrity, public service, and liberal ideals. Very few of his stepping-stones were in place or obvious along the way, and neither were mine.

Our conversations, unscripted except for a few topics that I usually wrote down in a notebook, inevitably zigged and zagged from funny old stories to the world we live in now. Along the way, I was surprised at how much I didn't know about Ab's life, then and now: life-altering stories from his youth, political betrayal and moral lapses, his thoughts about Barack Obama and his optimism about the prospects of a Hillary Clinton presidency, his most important legacy, and a healthy view about aging and death. On political and some personal issues, we often agreed, but not always. Learning more about his life and thinking has helped me consider my own in ways I had not intended.

I

From Rags to Respect

About twenty minutes into our first conversation in April 2013, I say, "Ab, when your phone rings and it's a call from the NBC–*Wall Street Journal* poll, and they ask you whether things in our country are generally headed in the right direction or do you feel that things are off on the wrong track, how will you answer?" I wasn't expecting his quick, emphatic response: "Wrong track." Why am I surprised, since a majority of Americans feel the same way? Well, because people who answer "right track" are apt to be, like him, Democrats and devoted supporters of President Obama. Plus, in the years I've known him, Ab's outlook on politics and life has generally been sunny, optimistic. Sunny and smart—very smart—is how I've thought of him for as long as I've known him. But I didn't know him when he was a child growing up during the Depression and struggling in school.

His father and mother's ill-fated union, Ab speculates, began with "a contract marriage in Ukraine, even though they were married here. He didn't like her family and she didn't like his, and they didn't much like each other," Ab tells me over lunch one day. His father, he says, sometimes hit his mother, which is difficult for Ab to admit even now. "But most of the time, as I remember it," he says, "my father and mother weren't talking to each other." Young Abner often played the uncomfortable role of the go-between or messenger for his feuding parents. "You tell your mother . . . ," his father would say to him, beginning in English and sliding into Yiddish. "You tell your father . . . ," his less Americanized mother would reply in Yiddish. Some sixty years later, he realized he was playing the same uncomfortable role, minus the Yiddish, when he was Bill Clinton's White House counsel and Janet Reno was the attorney general. He often acted as a carrier pigeon of angry messages in the bad political marriage between Clinton and Reno.

I tell Ab that his Mikva family discord sounds familiar to me. My first-generation parents were something of a mismatch; I never understood what brought them together. And growing up, I didn't know of a single happy marriage among my Jewish-immigrant relatives; the unions all seemed an ocean away from wedded bliss. My mother's parents, who were about the same age as Ab's parents, came to Milwaukee from the vicinity of the Polish-Russian border and had a rocky relationship. My grandfather would disappear each summer to Michigan, allegedly to seek relief from the misery of his hay fever, but my mother suspected it was also a convenient refuge from the misery of matrimonial warfare. Still, in our two Jewish American extended families, the Mikvas and the Horwitts, divorce was almost unheard of. More than anything, the glue that kept our families from cracking up were the children.

And here is where Ab and I agree with today's conservatives and their contentious celebration of the two-parent family. "The change in family makeup," Ab says, "is no longer only about race. There are an awful lot of single mothers, either by choice or divorce, who are white. And that's not healthy. It just isn't." I mention that about two-thirds of all black kids are growing up in single-parent homes, which is triple the percentage of white kids in single-parent homes. But Ab is right about the trends. And I observe that he and I were much better off, even in our strife-filled families, with our mothers and fathers around. "It made a difference," he agrees.

The Depression made things a lot worse in the Mikva household when Ab turned five and his father lost his job as an insurance agent. "He was fired in 1930, and it changed his life and it changed ours," Ab tells me, his voice still conveying the anguish of those distant, confusing days. "For many years, I thought the word *fired* meant that somebody took a match and put it to somebody's rear end." In his elementary school years, "there was literally no money. I still don't know how we got by. I remember one night—this was a terrible domestic scene—I complained that there wasn't any butter. I said, 'Where's the butter?' My mother said, 'We don't have any.' My father blew up. 'What do you mean there's no butter,' he yelled. And it shook me up." In tough times, when America didn't seem like the promised land, Ab's mother would say bitterly, "*ah broch tzu* Columbus"—a curse on Columbus.

Ab doesn't remember going to bed hungry, but he does remember missing sweets. One day his mother sent him to Berson's, the neighborhood grocery store. I, too, recall going to Berson's years later; my aunts and uncles lived three blocks away. "She sent me to buy ten cents worth of salami, but I copped two cents" for candy, Ab says. "I came home. She looked at the salami and said, 'They cheated you, there's not ten cents worth of salami.' So I had to tell her about the candy. She was very upset. And then I also remember—I think that may have been my only case of shoplifting—they had these little one-cent Hershey bars on the counter. I came in one day and Mrs. Berson was in the back. She said, 'I'll be right out.' So I reached in and grabbed a few and put them in my pocket. She came out, she was glaring at me. She said, 'Did you get enough?' And I said, 'I haven't ordered anything yet.' She just glared at me. Nothing happened, but it embarrassed me enough that I don't think I ever did it again," he recalled.

"How old were you?" I asked.

"Ten, maybe eleven."

Ab's grocery store embarrassment was momentary compared to the full-time humiliation of being on welfare until he was twelve or thirteen. The family's food, his clothes, and his schoolbooks all came courtesy of the Milwaukee County Outdoor Relief Agency. "I don't know why they called it Outdoor Relief, but that's what it was," he says. "We would pick up our food in a coaster wagon. My dad and I pulled the wagon back from the relief station. My mother used an oilcloth to cover the wagon so people wouldn't know." In the winter, Ab avoided wearing the telltale Outdoor Relief blue wool cap. "It had to be well below zero before I put on that cap." For a time, the Mikvas lived in a duplex that was owned by the parents of his friend Newton Minow, and Outdoor Relief paid the rent. Ab says, "It humiliated me that Newt knew that we were on relief."

For a long stretch, school wasn't much of a sanctuary. "Were you always a good student?" I ask Ab in one of our early conversations, expecting him to say yes because I already knew he had been a star at the University of Chicago Law School. "No," he says. "I had a bad second- or third-grade teacher. We had moved from the West Side to the North Side during one of my father's periods of particular poverty. I think he was opening up a beer depot on the North Side. Then I came back to Hi-Mount School on the West Side, but I had broken my continuity. I didn't know anybody and school was very, very unpleasant. There was a teacher who was picking on me. I think she was offended," Ab laughs, "that a white, Jewish student was on relief. The West Side at that time was completely white, about 15 or 20 percent Jewish and mainly middle class. I don't think there were more than three kids on relief at Hi-Mount."

The Mikva family's fortunes improved somewhat in the latter half of the

1930s when Ab's father landed a Works Progress Administration job. But when Ab started junior high school at Steuben, a ten-minute bicycle ride from his family's duplex apartment, he was still feeling insecure. "I would always flunk penmanship, art, and gym, so I really didn't think of myself as very able," he says. But then one day—and he tells me this as though it happened yesterday—"the class was choosing people to write a play. And they nominated people and voted on it. Of course, I was not nominated. And the teacher was very angry. She said, 'Abner is the best writer in this class, how can you not nominate him?' And of course, then they nominated me." I observe that, even after all these years, it still sounds like a fresh story. "You remember it," he says. "The impact is so heavy. I still remember Miss Hardgrove saying, 'He's the best writer in the class.' It had never been said about me, by anybody."

Perhaps because of Miss Hardgrove, Ab's first serious career aspiration was to be a journalist. It says so in his senior-year profile in the Washington High School *Scroll Weekly*. By then, he was the editor in chief of the *Scroll*, but it took some luck to land that position.

Located on Sherman Boulevard in the heart of Milwaukee's old West Side, Washington High School was considered the best in the city, both academically and athletically. I attended Washington High, too, class of January 1961. Ab and I didn't know it then, but this was perhaps the golden age of urban public education. The legendary George Balzer, principal of Washington High in Ab's era, was succeeded by the debonair, charismatic Arlie Schardt in my post–World War II era. Schardt's son, Arlie Jr., told me many years later that it was the pinnacle of his dad's professional life. Washington was a three-year high school with some 1,500 students when Ab was there; by the time I graduated, the school was packed with nearly 2,500 students, including the first wave of baby boomers. In our high school days, the virtually all-white student body, about 15 percent of which was Jewish, came mostly from working-class and modestly middle-class families. If our classmates went to college, they were likely the first ones from their families to do so, as was the case with Ab and me.

From Ab's high school days in the early 1940s and into the 1960s, Washington High was loaded with talent, or so it seemed. Student leadership roles were determined by a mix of merit and popularity, as Ab discovered when he sought the editorship of the *Scroll*. The paper's faculty adviser, Rose Helen Hauer, nominated Ab and three other students, Ab recalls, even though "she complained about me, that I didn't do this, that I didn't do that. In today's language I would have called her a kvetch. I was not her favorite person but, on the other hand, she obviously thought I had talent." Each candidate gave a campaign speech to the student body, which elected the new editor. It was Ab's first losing electoral experience, with a dash of insult added to injury. "I had expected to run second or third," Ab says, "but I finished dead last. Even a guy who had done nothing for the newspaper, a guy named Mel Teski, beat me out. He had a very clever speech. 'T is for truthfulness, E is for enthusiasm, S is for blah, blah, blah.' He ended up third. But the final indignity was the next day when I saw Mr. Balzer in the hall. He stopped me and said, 'That was a wonderful speech you made, taking your name and using the letters like that.'" All was not completely lost, however. The girl who was elected editor graduated the following January, in the middle of Ab's senior year. Miss Hauer, the kvetch, appointed Ab editor in chief of a staff that included his friend Newt Minow as associate sports editor.

Just for fun, and, I guess, because I was a little curious, I went back to our old high school and talked a clerk into digging out our transcripts. When I see Ab the next time, I say: "I have your grades here, but I haven't opened the envelope because it's stamped confidential." He laughs and says, "OK, we'll keep it confidential, but you'll have to read it to me." Our grades were similar, mostly As and some Bs, with a few of Ab's highest grades coming in Latin and typewriting. "I was an excellent typist," he says. "I was the fastest typist in my class."

He also became an excellent speller, thanks to the demanding, uncompromising Miss Hauer. And like her, he had developed a persnickety, zero-tolerance attitude toward misspellings by the time he became a congressman and I was writing speeches for him. So, when I saw a *New York Times* story in the spring of 2013 about a Yiddish word that had been used to determine the winner of the Scripps National Spelling Bee, I couldn't resist putting Ab to the test. We were having breakfast at The Bagel, a deli on North Broadway, just a short drive from his apartment and the default location for many of our conversations. He orders his usual, salami and scrambled eggs, which is a treat after the dreary fare that is the specialty of the kitchen at his retirement complex. I go for the Hoppel Poppel and then pull out a copy of the *Times* article. I say to Ab: "You told me that when you wrote for the *Scroll* you became a stickler for spelling."

"Right," Ab says.

"I've got a word for you."

"OK."

"This was the championship word in the most recent Scripps National Spelling Bee. A thirteen-year-old boy, his name is Arvind Mahankali, spelled it correctly." I say this with the intent of ever-so-slightly needling my very competitive friend. "The word is: 'knaidel.'"

"Knaidel," Ab repeats. "A Yiddish word."

"Right. A dumpling, like the kind of dumpling that's in matzo ball soup. But the thirteen-year-old kid, whose parents are from India, probably doesn't know the difference between a matzo ball and a snowball."

"I would spell it k-n-e-d-e-l," Ab replies. "Or, k-n-e-d-l-e."

"You only get one."

"I would spell it e-l."

"OK, spell it again."

"K-n-e-d-e-l."

"Sorry, no. Here's the correct spelling. It's k-n-a-i-d-e-l. But there's a controversy about the spelling. The YIVO Institute for Jewish Research . . . "

Ab interrupts. "Evo," he pronounces it. "YIVO is an old Yiddish institution."

"Well," I say, "in the *Times* story, according to YIVO, the correct spelling is k-n-e-y-d-l. But the Second Avenue Deli in Manhattan has it on the menu as k-n-e-i-d-e-l, and an eighty-three-year-old bubbe who teaches a Yiddish class in Queens spells it k-n-a-d-e-l. The thirteen-year-old spelled it k-n-a-i-d-e-l and won the spelling bee."

Ab, sounding annoyed and a little peevish, says, "Why would they use a Yiddish word in the spelling contest?"

"I don't know," I say. "But their bible is *Webster's Third New International Dictionary*."

To which Ab says dismissively, "*Webster's* doesn't know borscht about Yiddish."

Ab and I both did well academically, even though our family lives were not child-rearing models by today's standards. As a kid, I don't remember my parents ever reading a story to me. In fact, I don't remember that we had a single book in our cramped one-bedroom apartment, where I slept on a hide-a-bed sofa in the living room for the first ten years of my life. In Ab's case, he was not going to receive much assistance with his homework from his immigrant parents, although his sister Rose, seven years older, sometimes helped. Ab gives a lot of credit to his public school education. "In my case," he says, "school did make all the difference. The school was able to pick up the deficits from family life. But it was an important institution for everybody, not just the dysfunctional families like mine."

Listening to Ab's stories about growing up, I realize that one of our common denominators was that our parents wanted us to do well in school, they expected us to do well, and we knew they loved us. "My mother was probably the most important inspiration for my getting an education," Ab says of his Yiddish-speaking mother who had no formal schooling. "In retrospect, I've always felt guilty about not appreciating my mother more. She clearly loved me unconditionally. Even though she was not educated, she felt it was important that I did well in school."

"As you were growing up," I ask Ab, "how did she express that?"

"She appreciated when I would get good grades. She would be concerned if I—I used to get 'poor' in penmanship, art, and music. And she would say, 'Why can't you do better than that?'"

It was Ab's mother, imagining that the New World could offer new possibilities for her newborn son, who made the strategic selection of his name. "You heard how I got my name?" Ab asks, and then explains how his mother made the choice. "Her grandfather was named Avrum, which is my Hebrew name. That translates to Abraham, but my mother didn't want me to be called Abie. She wanted me to be fully Americanized." Later, I think to myself, maybe she was uncomfortable about the association with *Abie's Irish Rose*, a hit Broadway comedy around the time Ab was born, about a young Jew who marries a Catholic girl. In any event, Ab says that his mother went through a Bible that had "very poor scholarship and she found the name Abner, which she somehow thought would be a good translation of Avrum. But Abner is not Avrum. Abner is Avner, who was a general in David's army. And so whenever I got up in a synagogue as a kid, they'd say, 'So your Hebrew name is Avner.' And I'd say, 'No, it's Avrum.' And they'd say, 'No, it can't be Avrum. Avrum would be Abraham.' I'd say, 'No, I can't be Abraham.' And to this day, if somebody calls me Abe, I have to correct them."

At our breakfast, I've also brought a photocopy of a 1943 issue of the Washington High School *Scroll Weekly*, when Ab was the editor. We look at the masthead, and as I read the names aloud, Ab notices that about half the student editors are Jewish kids. "We had a disproportionate number of smart people, the active people in our class," Ab says. Suddenly he's reminded of an old *New Yorker* cartoon. "This football player is hunkering over a Japanese student who's in the library. She's got glasses on, looks very nerdy, she's writing, and he says, 'What is it that makes you people so smart? Is it the fish you eat? What do you think it is?' And in the last panel she says, 'Well, first of all, I'm Jewish.'"

A generation later, when I was at Washington High, I wasn't part of the Jewish subculture. Virtually all of Ab's friends were Jewish, while most of mine were not. Part of the reason is that I was a serious jock, and my football and baseball teammates had names like Burgardt, Kreuger, Wertz,

Crowley, Tevich, LaPrest, and Hatch. After Friday night football games, we'd go to Picciolo's for pizza, where my Catholic friends would have to skip the pepperoni on those old meatless Fridays. Ab, who was barely five foot nine and weighed maybe 135 pounds, considered himself a little nerdy in high school. He would have loved to be Washington High's quarterback, as I was. He says, "I remember standing outside of the fence at the practice field watching the football players with such admiration." And he still has a bit of a chip on his shoulder about a baseball career that never happened because, he says solemnly, his father never played catch with him, "so I never did learn to play baseball." Perhaps sensing that I am somewhat dubious about his ability to have been a Jewish Willie Mays, he fires off a lawyerly enthymeme. "Now, you were a good baseball player," he says, knowing that I was. "Did you play catch with your dad?" I had to admit that I did. "OK," he says, case closed.

But it wasn't only athletics that set us apart as kids. Ab and I grew up in different neighborhoods and had different Jewish cultural and religious experiences. By the 1940s, the old West Side, which is now called Sherman Park, was the heart of Jewish life for many of Milwaukee's eastern European Jews whose parents and grandparents had emigrated from Russia, Poland, Ukraine, Lithuania, and Romania. This was Ab's neighborhood. My neighborhoods were a few miles away, at first to the north and then on the edge of the city's far western boundary near Mount Mary College, where Jews were an alien species.

Still, Ab might have had gentile friends, but he almost never did. On any block in the slightly less than two square miles that made up the heart of the Jewish West Side, Jews lived side by side with their far more numerous, often German-gentile neighbors. But they tended to be the closest of strangers. When he lived on North Forty-Ninth near Center Street, Ab's Catholic neighbors walked to St. Catherine's Catholic Church on Sunday, his Lutheran neighbors to Mt. Calvary. The religious divisions played out in school. "I remember one time asking a parochial school girl to go out with me," Ab recalls. "She said, 'Oh, I can't. You killed Christ.'" In high school, Ab briefly dated one non-Jewish girl, LaVonne Ketter, whom he recalls fondly. This was very rare; even a generation later, I was one of the few Jews at Washington High who dated gentiles. The tribalism was still intact. Ab says he really liked LaVonne. "Unfortunately, she was a good ice skater and I was a lousy ice skater, so I almost broke my ankles trying to keep up with her. I found out later that she got grief from her parents for going out with me."

As for Jewish culture and religion, our youthful experiences were unusual in different ways. Ab's father, Henry, was unequivocally, passionately, stridently anti-religion. He would often boycott Passover Seders with the family. When his wife tried to keep two sets of dishes for her devout father, who came to the house for Seder, Henry would deliberately use them for every day. "My father came over in 1916 or 1917," Ab says. "It was either just before or during the revolution. Jews were the easiest people to recruit to be revolutionaries because they had reasons to hate the czar and many of them had reason to hate religion because it was so repressive. It was an angry God, a mean God. I still remember my mother used to say to me when she was really unhappy with me, '*gott vet der shtrofen*,' God will punish you. And so it was easy to be an atheist and anarchist. And my father came over happy in both those roles." For young Abner, that meant an odd Sunday school experience. His father, who loved Yiddish music and culture, wanted his son to learn about that culture, so he sent Ab to the Garfinckel Cheder at Fifty-Second and Center Streets. But cheders also taught Hebrew, the biblical language. Ab had strict instructions from his father: "I could go only to learn Yiddish and Yiddish songs and poetry. As soon as they started Hebrew, I would have to get up and walk out. I remember that Mr. Garfinckel used to say, 'Abner, come sit down. Don't listen to that meshugena father of yours.' I knew better. I kept walking."

When I hear Ab's story, I tell him that it reminds me of how my mother learned Yiddish in the 1920s at a local chapter of the national Workmen's Circle. "The Arbeter Ring," Ab says quickly, using the Yiddish name for the socialist workers' organization. Its members consisted of my maternal grandfather and thousands of other secular eastern European Jews who came to the United States in the early twentieth century. Like Ab's father, my grandfather never attended a religious service that I'm aware of, at least not willingly. My father and mother seemed indifferent to religion, with one exception: my father would faithfully say Kaddish whenever someone in the family died. But he never took me to a synagogue, and unlike Ab, I never attended Sunday school to learn about Jewish culture and history. Neither Ab nor I was bar mitzvahed.

For me, lessons about growing up Jewish were largely implicit: I could observe that family was important, that doing well in school was important, and that Jews could expect to be treated unkindly and unfairly because we were different. When our downstairs neighbor banged on her ceiling because I was making a little noise, my father might say, "She doesn't like Jews." When my parents started talking about buying a house, I learned that some neighborhoods were off-limits because NJA—no Jews allowed. I understood at an early age that, as a defense mechanism, many Jews, including my parents and aunts and uncles, thought of themselves as superior to the goyim. But simultaneously, we often felt like underdogs in American society. That may be why my first hero when I was six or seven years old was Jackie Robinson. I'm not sure that I realized at first that Jackie Robinson was black. But by the way adults talked about him, I sensed that he was a courageous underdog. My first phonograph record, which I still have, is *Slugger at the Bat*, featuring Jackie Robinson and Pee Wee Reese, the white, southern Brooklyn Dodgers teammate who befriended Robinson when opposing players and even his own teammates were hurling slurs. On the two-record album, Jackie and Pee Wee encounter a kids' sandlot baseball team and help them win the big game by showing them that the key to victory is color-blind, unselfish teamwork. I listened with hopeful, receptive ears.

In Ab Mikva's last semester of high school in 1943, the senior play was Robert Sherwood's *Abe Lincoln in Illinois*. Ab played Lincoln's law partner Joshua Speed. His classmate, Bill Spankus, played Lincoln. Both Ab and Bill were eager to join the military after they graduated, like virtually all the boys at Washington High. But Ab had to wait until he turned eighteen. Spankus, six months older, didn't have to wait. The next year, on a German battlefield, he died.

Ab tried to enlist in the US Navy Air Corps, he says, "because they took you at seventeen, but I flunked the physics exam." He tells me this one morning while we're talking about how he and his friends could barely wait to fight in the "Good War." We're at The Bagel, and the deli's sound system is pumping out rock-and-roll hits from the 1960s, when my friends and I wanted no part of fighting in Vietnam. A mere generation earlier, kids like Ab were unflinchingly, passionately devoted to the war effort. Ab's Washington High class of 1943 held numerous student-led war savings bond and savings stamp drives and participated in highly organized block-by-block campaigns to collect paper, string, and metal keys for the war effort. Every issue of the *Scroll Weekly* carried stories about these campaigns and how successful they were—90 percent of the student body participated in a savings stamp drive in Ab's senior year. There were frequent updates about teachers who had enlisted and where they were serving. At least one was a woman, Edna Goeden, who had been Ab's English teacher. At his graduation, Ab says, instead of having the valedictorian speak, a panel of students gave speeches about the branch of the armed services they would be serving in. Ab spoke about the US Army Air Corps.

"I enrolled in the army air corps when I was seventeen, but they wouldn't take you until you were eighteen," Ab recalls. "I kept writing letters to the Department of the Army saying please take me right after my eighteenth birthday, and they complied. I got my notice of induction to report on January 25, four days after my birthday." I ask Ab what his seventeen- and eighteen-year-old friends were thinking about as they signed up to go to war. "First of all, it was a good war. It was the last good war and we all felt that we should be there. We had a great feeling of patriotism. I had a few friends who were 4F, who couldn't serve because of some physical problem, and they felt like outcasts. I did not know anybody who tried to avoid service. It was nothing like it was in Vietnam." No, it wasn't. The escalation of the Vietnam War in 1965, when I graduated from college, was built on lies by President Johnson and others. About the only thing I have in common with Dick Cheney, our war-hawk former vice president, is that we both used student deferments from the military draft to attend graduate school rather than fight in Vietnam. At least in my case, I wanted to be in graduate school and I opposed the war. My only regret is that I didn't do more to stop it, like my late friend Curtis Gans, a leader of the dump-Johnson movement. That was a worthy effort, even though the country ended up with Richard Nixon in 1968 and seven more years of war.

After his enlistment, Ab recalls, "I couldn't wait to get overseas."

"Why the army air corps?" I ask.

"I wanted to fly," he says. "It sounded glamorous." But after basic training and a battery of tests for depth perception and certain manual skills, his dream of being a pilot was over. "The saying later on was that all the Jewish kids became navigators because our manual skills weren't that great, but we were smart," he laughs. "So I went to navigator school." By the summer of 1945, he and his unit were on a train heading west and eventually, he thought, to Walla Walla, Washington, which was supposed to be their port of embarkation. "We had already crewed up in Lincoln, Nebraska, and we were on the way to an air base in Tonopah, Nevada. We were going to do our bombing training there and learn to fly together." On the train from Lincoln, however, they got the news of Japan's surrender and the end of the war. "We were all very disappointed. I shudder to think of that. Instead of cheering and whooping it up, we were sad that it was over before we had a chance to get into it."

Unlike his classmate Bill Spankus and the more than 400,000 other Americans who did not survive World War II, Ab Mikva's service to his country was seemingly uneventful. But what happened next changed the trajectory of his life in a way he could never have imagined just a few short years earlier.

While he was in the US Army Air Corps, Ab tells me at breakfast six months after we started our conversations, he began to rethink his career possibilities. "I was really very conscious of not wanting to be poor anymore. We had been poor all my life, and I just wanted to put that behind me." He began to think that working as a newspaperman, an aspiration in high school, was not the ticket to financial security. "I had one friend whose father was a reporter at the *Milwaukee Journal*, and they didn't seem to live very well." One day, Ab and another friend brainstormed about starting a partnership after the war. The friend would be the lawyer, and Ab, who was good with numbers, would be the accountant. But that was a very ambitious career choice because the Mikvas had no money for college. Ab's sister was smart enough to go to college, but after graduating from high school she found a job as a bookkeeper that paid $8 a week. After Ab graduated, he attended the University of Wisconsin Extension in Milwaukee for a semester before being inducted into the US Army Air Corps. An uncle paid the $30 tuition bill. Ab thought that after the war he might be able to attend the extension and get a two-year degree in accounting if he lived at home and worked nights. His mother would have pushed him hard to do it. But going to the prestigious University of Wisconsin in Madison was out of the question and never a consideration—until the GI bill came along and changed the odds of climbing into the middle class for Ab and other veterans from poor and working-class families.

The Servicemen's Readjustment Act of 1944 provided low-interest mortgages, vocational training, and, for more than 2 million veterans, money to attend colleges and universities. "I don't know if you're aware of how fabulous the GI bill was," Ab says to me. "It paid not only your tuition and books, 100 percent, but as a single person I got $90 a month. In those days, 1946, 1947, that was a lot of money."

Suddenly, the young veteran had a free ride to one of the country's great universities. In his first semester at Madison, which is how Badger State residents refer to the University of Wisconsin in the capital, Ab made straight As, he recalls. "Then I learned how to play bridge, sail on Lake Mendota, and date women. So the next year I had Bs in the first semester and Cs in the next one."

Serious romance was not on his mind when one of his roommates, the fun-loving Leonard Zubrensky, persuaded him to go on a blind date. The girl—Jewish, naturally—was a student at the University of Chicago and a friend of Len's girlfriend. Len had heard, he told Ab, that the girl wasn't much to look at but had loads of personality. If it wasn't love at first sight for Ab, it was close. "She's walking down the stairs wearing my jacket, which I had left upstairs in the bedroom," Ab tells me approximately sixty-eight years later. "I had taken off my coat jacket and for some reason she put it on, she was cold or something. I was never that good talking to girls, especially on first dates. She broke the ice. We had a great time."

Contrary to Zubrensky's warning, the petite Zorita Wise was cute, with sparkling brown eyes like marbles; she was also smart and fun, her humor tending to blunt acerbic populism. As their relationship heated up, Ab told Zoe (rhymes with doe) that he was thinking about becoming an accountant. "I wouldn't want to marry an accountant," Zoe deadpanned. "All they do is make money."

"What about law school?" Ab asked later. "Yes," Zoe replied, "that sounds like it would be fun." And that was how Abner Mikva's law career began. Around the same time he met Zoe (or Zoey, as Ab often calls her), he had read *Clarence Darrow for the Defense*, Irving Stone's dramatic biography of perhaps the most celebrated American defense attorney in the first half of the twentieth century. Ab identified with Darrow, a brilliant, tenacious defender of underdogs and civil liberties. But if Darrow's story planted a small seed of interest in the law, it did not blossom until Zoe entered Ab's life.

Ab and Zoe were married on September 19, 1948, the same day I celebrated my sixth birthday. After a brief honeymoon, he started law school at the University of Chicago while she began graduate studies in the university's famed Department of Sociology. When they first started dating, Zoe was an undergraduate at Chicago, and Ab came down from Madison to visit her and sometimes sat in on her classes. After earning a PhB from Chicago, Zoe went back to her family's home in St. Louis, where she studied for a year at Washington University. Ab followed her, enrolling in a special veterans' program at the university. "I went back to getting straight As. I didn't have anything else to do in St. Louis, except to study and woo Zoe." He applied to law school at the University of Chicago and was accepted after only three years of undergraduate work and no college degree. "Had I stayed at Wisconsin with my Cs, I'm not so sure," he says. "But it wasn't as hard to get in then as it is now. They were all short of students; the boys were just coming back." And Ab still had the generous benefits provided by the GI bill, which continued through most of law school.

Ab admits to being worried that he might not measure up once he got to law school. He tells me this one fall day as we sit in an old wooden booth at Jake's Delicatessen in Milwaukee. It is the location of one of my earliest childhood memories. My dad and I would go to the deli late on a Sunday afternoon and take home a pound of sliced corned beef, the pickled tongue he preferred, and, my favorite, the succulently sour, garlic-laden dill pickles. It was called Cohen's in the 1940s, but not much else has changed since then, except for the customers—mostly Jews then, mostly blacks now. It's a delicious time capsule that inevitably evokes memories, and Ab starts reminiscing about his high school education and to what extent it prepared him for law school and beyond. We had driven from Chicago up to Milwaukee earlier that sunny, mid-October day. Ab had been invited to attend the ceremony honoring the newest members of the Hall of Fame at our old high school. Ab is already one of its charter members, along with his old friend Newt Minow, actor Gene Wilder, and former Major League Baseball commissioner Bud Selig. Ab loved the idea of going back to Washington High. "Of all the schools I attended," he says, "the two that had the greatest influence on me were Washington High School and the University of Chicago."

At Washington High, Ab's extracurricular activities, especially his leadership role on the student newspaper, boosted his shaky adolescent self-confidence. He breaks out in a big smile when I show him a photo from his high school yearbook with the caption, "Ab's Family." In it, Ab is at his editor's desk at the *Scroll Weekly*, surrounded by his adoring subordinates and friends. Academically, he says, he received a good, basic education at Washington High in math, Latin, and English, where he learned how to diagram a sentence in the latter. "I still think that I know how to write a sentence better than most people because of those rote learning experiences, but it didn't promote your intellectual powers." He realized this when he sat in on some of Zoe's undergraduate classes at the University of Chicago. "The students seemed to know about philosophers and arcane subjects that I never heard of." So, the summer before law school, he read Plato and Aristotle to catch up. "I was very concerned that I was in over my head. I told Zoe that if I didn't do well, I'd drop out."

To his surprise, he did very well, becoming editor in chief of the law review and finishing third in his class when he graduated in 1951. "I happened to find my calling," he says.

"How so?" I ask.

"It wasn't until I got to law school that I found that professors weren't asking for a numbered answer, they were asking you to think through a problem. It was a fascinating, mind-opening experience"—one he had an affinity for. In law school, he says, "one of the first exercises you have is the professor will give you two cases that come out with opposite results, or with different results. And they say, OK, reconcile it. You can't say A plus B equals C. You have to put yourself in the mind of the judges who wrote the opinions. You have to consider the distinguishing facts. Or you can say that this came about fifty years later and times changed. There is no right answer."

He mentions one of his favorite professors, Harry Kalven, and asks whether I remember the name. I do. Kalven was the eminent First Amendment scholar whose writings I encountered in 1963 when I was an undergraduate at Northwestern University taking a course taught by the unassumingly brilliant Franklyn Haiman. Frank was a PhD, not a lawyer, and he would have a great influence on my life, personally and intellectually. In the fall of 1963 Frank was a trailblazer, teaching what was thought to be the first undergraduate course on the First Amendment in the country. (I was getting ready to go to his one o'clock class on November 22 when I heard on the radio that President Kennedy had been shot in Dallas.)

The First Amendment, of course, is the cornerstone of our democratic society, the embodiment of democratic philosophy and values. It remains astonishing and depressing to me that most young Americans can leave high school and even college with little more than a superficial understanding of the history, theory, and tensions wrapped up in those exhilarating, difficult, and challenging forty-five words. Like American students then and now, I came to Frank's course almost completely ignorant of what the First Amendment was. I say to Ab, "I'm guessing, based on your years at Washington High School and then at Madison and Washington University, that you didn't have a very well-informed understanding of the First Amendment until you had a course from Kalven."

"Right," he says. "What I knew about the Constitution when I came to law school was that it was a document that we trotted out on the Fourth of July. I actually knew more about the Declaration of Independence. I didn't understand at the time why there was any difference between the two. One was a shorthand version of what the lawyers came up with a few years later. And then I met Harry Kalven. He was one of the best teachers I ever had."

But before Kalven, there was another influential professor: the scholarly, bow-tied Edward Hirsch Levi. Around the time Ab started law school, Levi wrote what became a small classic, *The Introduction to Legal Reasoning*. Ab devoured it and became one of Levi's star students—and Levi became Ab's first important mentor. Even though both were Jewish, culturally, they had little in common. Levi's elite German Jewish heritage included a father and grandfathers who were rabbis and philosophers. But Levi, who became dean of the law school in 1950, took a liking to Ab and became his friend as well as his mentor. "I had done very well in law school, and he was very much interested in rejuvenating the national reputation of the law school," Ab says. "It had been a great law school, but during the war it sort of went down. One of the ways he could refurbish it was to get a Supreme Court clerkship for one of the graduates, which we hadn't had for many years. And he almost literally camped out on Minton's doorstep," Ab recalls, referring to Supreme Court Justice Sherman Minton, a former Democratic US senator from Indiana who was nominated to the Court by President Harry Truman. "Minton had been taking his clerks from Indiana and Northwestern. Levi reminded him that Chicago was part of his circuit, too." After a so-so interview with Minton, Ab became one of his clerks in 1951.

2

"We Don't Want Nobody Nobody Sent"

After our first few conversations, I realized that Ab's health was even more precarious than I wanted to admit. Whenever I see a "Mikva Google Alert" on my computer screen, I nervously execute a cowardly click. I do not want to think about the possibility that someday he, or I, might not be here anymore. As it turns out, Ab begins to teach me a little about facing up to mortality as well as about politics and our country.

Today is July 17, 2013, and it's going to be a stifling, hot, humid Wednesday in a not so windy Chicago. When I talked to Ab on the phone the week before, I suggested that we take a ride around his old Hyde Park neighborhood in the morning and have an early lunch at one of his old hangouts, the Valois Cafeteria, a down-home landmark since the 1920s. But a few days before I was scheduled to pick him up at his apartment complex, the Hallmark, I was tipped off by a friend that Ab had recently spent four days in the hospital with heart failure. Because of that, plus his chronic obstructive pulmonary disease (COPD), I assumed that he would postpone our field trip for a cooler, more breathable day.

But there he was at the front door, mahogany cane in hand, ready to go. He is physically diminished, and it seems that this happened to him, and to Zoe, so quickly. A mere five years ago, Ab and Zoe, and my wife Joan and I, were on the Philadelphia mainline, going house to house knocking on doors for Barack Obama in the run-up to the 2008 Pennsylvania presidential primary. A sizable contingent of Chicago friends had made the trip, and our old-style Chicago voter canvassing was preceded by a memorable Seder service in Philadelphia's historic district, led by Ab and Zoe's youngest daughter, Rabbi Rachel Mikva. When you're in your forties and fifties, I used to think, five years one way or the other didn't matter so much. But a bit of hypochondriacal humor, which I try not to think about,

is the not so funny reality: we're all here hanging by a thread. Since 2008 in Philadelphia, Zoe has had a stroke, and Ab's day starts with a dozen pills. "The eighties
are tough," Ab says to me one day. But he refuses to go quietly into the night. As
of this summer, he's still driving his car, slowly, to the grocery store. I ask him if his
children give him a hard time about driving. "Oh, yes, constantly," he laughs. "My
daughter Rachel in particular is giving me a hard time. Her husband borrowed the
car once. We were in the Dunes. He did a couple of thousand dollars' worth of damage backing into a basketball pole."

"Did you have a comment about that?" I ask.

"I just smirked," he says dryly.

I tell Ab that many adult children worry about their parents who are still driving in their eighties, not because the parents are bad drivers but because of their
own anxieties. "It's probably true," he says, about children's motives. "But driving is
a piece of independence that you just hate to give up."

Political independence was Ab's hallmark from the beginning of his electoral career in Chicago, but it was an unplanned career, I discover. A phone
call changed everything. Where better to begin a conversation about South
Side Chicago politics from Mikva to Obama than at the legendary Valois
Cafeteria in the heart of Hyde Park. We're in my trusty old Buick LeSabre,
heading in that direction, on this sultry July morning.

When Ab left Washington in 1952 after clerking for Justice Minton and
returned to Chicago, he took a job at Arthur Goldberg's law firm. At the
time, Goldberg, a future Supreme Court justice, the son of Jewish immigrants from Chicago's West Side, and a growing presence in national legal
and political circles, was also general counsel for the United Steelworkers
of America and the CIO. Representing the steelworkers' union, Goldberg
appeared before the Supreme Court in the most important case during Ab's
clerkship, *Youngstown Sheet & Tube v. Sawyer*. "Goldberg had five minutes to
argue his case," Ab says, "and he did more in five minutes than the government or the steel company lawyers did in a half hour. I was so impressed
that I was determined to go to work for him."

When Ab interviewed with Goldberg, he said he was considering a few
other jobs, including working for Illinois governor Adlai Stevenson, who
was making noises about running for president in 1952. "Goldberg told me
that I had already wasted a year. I had taken a side move from the practice
of law and I should not waste any more time."

"What was the side move he was referring to?" I ask.

"The clerkship," he says.

"You're kidding!" I blurt out.

"It didn't count for that much in Chicago," Ab says, while telling me to turn left onto Fifty-Fifth Street as we meander through Hyde Park. "People like Arthur, who also had a Washington office and was active in the Washington legal community, knew that it was a feather in his cap to have a law clerk in the firm, but it didn't count for that much in Chicago."

Still incredulous, I ask him, "Wouldn't all the big law firms in Chicago be vying to hire a Supreme Court law clerk?"

"No, no," Ab says. "When I first started thinking about a job here, I went to talk with my friend Bernie Meltzer and he urged me to go to a couple of big firms. And I said, 'Bernie, one of them won't hire any Jews.' And he said, 'Yeah, but they might consider that you were a law clerk. Well, anyway, you ought to try.' I didn't think that sounded like a great endorsement."

Actually, Ab forgot to mention, until we met again a few months later, another Chicago job he was interested in. With his clerkship winding down, Justice Minton asked Ab what he wanted to do next. Ab said he might like to be a prosecutor for a while, to which Minton replied that he knew the US attorney in Chicago, Otto Kerner. Kerner's father had been a federal judge with Minton. Ab says to me, "So Minton wrote a note which he gave to me to give to Kerner. It said, 'Otto, this young man has been a very fine clerk and he'd be a great assistant US attorney,' signed Shay. The note was enough to get me an interview with Kerner. He was very pleasant, very good-looking. He said, 'Justice Minton thinks well of you.' I said that I had a good year with him. He said, 'Who's your sponsor?' And I said, 'Well, I guess Justice Minton.' He said, 'No, no. Who's your ward committeeman?' And I said I don't know. That was the end of my interview."

"You blew it," I kid Ab. "How could you possibly think that a recommendation from a mere Supreme Court justice was going to cut it in Chicago?" Really, he should have known better after his first misadventure in Chicago-style politics four years earlier. That episode still ranks as one of the classic Chicago political stories. Over the years, I've heard it many times, told by either Ab or somebody else. But in the retelling, some of the details get rearranged, so as we're driving on the South Side, just south of Hyde Park, the scene of the famous episode, I ask Ab to tell the real, true story.

Growing up in Milwaukee, Abner Mikva was well aware of the city's reputation for clean, open government under socialist mayor Daniel Hoan. Remnants of the admirable German political culture were present when I was growing up a generation later; Frank Zeidler, another socialist, was the mayor then. Milwaukee was the polar opposite of nearby Chicago's patronage-fueled Democratic machine politics. So Ab starts to tells me the story as we're driving: He was advised, "When you come down to Chicago, you can forget any interest in politics. But it is 1948," he says, and two intellectual Democrats, Adlai Stevenson and Paul Douglas, are running for governor and US senator, respectively. "These are really incredible candidates," Ab says. "I'm in law school at the University of Chicago and I'm thinking, 'Hey, Chicago politics aren't so bad after all.' One night on the way home from school I passed the 8th Ward Regular Democratic Organization storefront on Cottage Grove, or maybe it was Seventy-Ninth Street. Right on the window it says, 'Timothy O'Sullivan, Ward Committeeman.' And in the window are posters of Stevenson and Douglas. I walked into the office and said to a woman at a desk: 'Hi, I'm Abner Mikva, and I'd like to volunteer for Stevenson and Douglas.' So I go in to see the ward committeeman. I said, 'I'd like to volunteer in the Stevenson and Douglas campaigns.' He takes a big cigar out of his mouth and says, 'We ain't got no jobs.' And I said, 'I don't want a job, I just want to volunteer for Stevenson and Douglas.' He says, 'We don't want nobody who don't want no job.' And then he says, 'Who sent ya?' And I said, 'Nobody sent me.' And he says, 'We don't want nobody nobody sent.'"

After his year in Washington at the Supreme Court, Ab accepted Goldberg's offer to join the four-person Chicago office of Goldberg and Devoe. The firm also had a small office in Washington. Ab recalls, "In my first financial conversation with Arthur, he said, 'Well, we certainly can meet whatever you're getting on the Court. What is it?' I said, '$5,000 a year.' All the blood drained from his face. 'That's more than a couple of our partners get,' he said. So I got them all increases and I got $5,000 a year. I had one of the best paying jobs of my class."

But within a few years, Ab says, "I was getting restless with the practice of law. I wasn't doing as much union work as I wanted to do. I was doing a lot of commercial stuff that didn't appeal to me. I went to see Ed Levi about a teaching job. But he sensed that I really wasn't that anxious to be an academic and that I didn't have a scholarly disposition." But Levi, Ab's former law professor, had another idea. The Ford Foundation had made a grant to the University of Chicago Law School for a so-called jury project in Wichita, Kansas. A federal judge there, Ab tells me, "had agreed to have us tape-record the jury proceedings in civil cases with the consent of the lawyers and the parties. But the juries didn't know they were being taped." The goal of the project was to get a better understanding of how juries deliberated. "They were fascinating," Ab says. He moved to Wichita with Zoe and their first daughter, Mary, for three months in the spring of 1954. "Every day I would go to the courthouse. It was during the Army-McCarthy hearings, and Zoey was glued to the television set. A sociologist from the University of Chicago and I monitored the jury tapings to make sure that we didn't interfere with the court proceedings and that they were done in a professional manner. For that time, we had very sophisticated recording equipment in the jury room. We taped eight or nine cases. It convinced me that the jury system really works because these jurors did their jobs."

As Ab is talking, I'm thinking that some people, maybe some of the jurors, might not have appreciated the sanctity of the jury room being violated. As it turned out, I wasn't too far off. But it wasn't the jurors who complained; it was the US attorney general and some powerful, conservative, red-baiting US senators who turned the jury project into a front-page scandal. Ab says all hell broke loose when the federal judge in Wichita, "who was a very nice guy and proud of having been part of our project and how well it worked, went to a judicial conference and bragged about it." Soon thereafter, the jury project was denounced by US Attorney General Herbert Brownell Jr. and Assistant Attorney General Warren E. Burger, who would later become chief justice of the US Supreme Court. Burger claimed that the law school had originally planned to conduct "surreptitious eavesdropping" on 500 to 1,000 federal juries.

In October 1955 the Senate's Internal Security Subcommittee held hearings on what was now referred to as the "jury bugging" project by Mississippi senator James Eastland, chairman of the subcommittee. The witnesses, the *New York Times* reported, would include Edward Levi, dean of the University of Chicago Law School; Professor Harry Kalven, head of the jury project; and Abner Joseph Mikva. "They subpoenaed all of us," Ab says. He also admits that he should have listened to Arthur Goldberg's warnings before he went to Wichita. "In retrospect, only one person had been dubious about my doing it, and that was Arthur. He said, 'I know what you guys are going to do will be very circumspect, but it's such a bad time in our country'—McCarthyism and so forth. 'I'm not sure that you're not going to spook the jury system.' But I was twenty-eight years old, anxious to get out of Chicago, and paid him no attention. He was right."

Compared to Levi and Kalven, young Abner was a bit player in the nasty Senate hearings. The University of Chicago was still considered a "pinko institution," Ab says, a carryover from the days when Robert Maynard Hutchins had been its president. And even though Hutchins was now at the Fund for the Republic and was no longer head of the liberal Ford Foundation, the foundation was lumped into the same un-American camp by right-wing conservatives and McCarthyites. The subcommittee aggressively went after Levi and Kalven. As the *New York Times* reported, the subcommittee's general counsel "devoted much of his questioning during the day to attempts to link Dean Levi and Professor Kalven to subversive or Communist causes in the past. He elicited from Dean Levi the admission that he had been a member of the National Lawyers' Guild for a short time more than ten years ago and had signed a letter to the *Chicago Daily News* in 1948 denouncing the House Un-American Activities Committee as a 'spy hunting' group." Ab vividly remembers the chilling, even frightening atmosphere at the hearings. "Levi did a terrible job. He was so nervous and worried about the law school. They uncovered some picture of him with someone who turned out to be a Communist. They flashed that all over. They kept calling him Lev-EYE (instead of LEE-vee). He was beside himself. It turned out to be another witch hunt." In fact, Levi was not a raging leftist; when it came to partisan politics, he was temperamentally and ideologically a dispassionate moderate. A generation later, he was President Gerald Ford's attorney general.

The early 1950s were not only a time of McCarthyism and Communist witch hunts; they were also a period when restless and suddenly prosperous Americans were hunting for new lives in the suburbs. This included my family and, as I discover, Ab's family, too.

Technically, my family didn't quite make it to the suburbs when we moved in 1953 from our tiny apartment to a brand new, seemingly palatial, 1,590-square-foot Tennessee stone ranch-style house where I had my own bedroom. Although our corner house was just within the City of Milwaukee boundary, the neighborhood was new; it still lacked sidewalks and curbs and looked much like suburban Wauwatosa, two blocks away. My parents paid $27,500 for the house, in cash. My father never bought anything on credit. After World War II, he and a partner started a wholesale and retail gasoline and oil business. They caught a wave of postwar prosperity, but it took some years of lobbying by my mother before my cautious father agreed to buy a house. Still, during the last years in our apartment, I didn't think of my family as poor. We were the first among my friends to own a TV set—black and white, of course—and we started to take annual driving trips to Florida that coincided with my school vacations around Easter. Only a generation down the road from Ab's precarious Depression-era childhood, I never felt the sting or stigma of deprivation; nor did I think of government programs as having rescued my family from painful poverty. In later conversations, I began to see how that generational difference affected our thinking.

As for Ab, after Wichita and the Senate hearings on the jury project, he was ready to leave Chicago for the suburbs. I'm surprised to hear this because he has always been identified with the city and its politics. He had acquired a building lot in Northbrook, and a friend who was an architect drew up plans for a new house. "We hadn't started building yet, but the plans were all set," he says. "Zoey was very unhappy about the whole idea. But I was pushing hard because I was clearly unhappy with my job and living in the city. So she reluctantly agreed. But then Victor called me." And that phone call changed everything—not only where the Mikvas lived but Ab's career, too.

Victor deGrazia, a young Hyde Park activist, was a leader of the Independent Voters of Illinois (IVI), a liberal, anti–Democratic machine, good-government group. Ab tells me about the conversation with deGrazia: "He says, 'Lou Silverman and I decided that you would be a good candidate to run for the legislature.' I said, 'Vic, I don't think so. First of all, I've just been subpoenaed to testify in Washington and it will be a big scandal if I run. And secondly, I'm thinking of moving to Northbrook.' He said, 'Oh, you can't move to the suburbs. You have to stay here. Let Lou and me talk with you.' So they came over. It wasn't that hard to talk me into it."

When Ab and I first started talking about his early interest in politics, the only influential experience he mentioned was a high school program on leadership and government called Badger Boys State. It's still around. But he never mentioned the influence of his father, who was clearly interested in politics and world affairs, subscribed to Far Left and Communist publications, and had strong, often angry views about almost everything. Even Ab's mother had some political sensibilities. She was sixteen years old when she first arrived in Milwaukee and soon found a job, through family connections, at the Wienshel pants factory. "A few days after she started working," Ab tells me, "the Amalgamated Clothing Workers called a strike. So she's a good social democrat from Ukraine and goes out on strike. Her cousin, the boss, comes over and says in Yiddish, 'Ida, what are you doing here, you're my cousin?' She's all of four foot eleven and she says, 'No. Today I'm with the Amalgamated, tomorrow I'll be your cousin.'"

By the time Ab arrived at the University of Wisconsin, he was clearly interested in politics. But I am amazed to discover that his first electoral experience after the war was volunteering to *help* Joe McCarthy—yes, that Joe McCarthy—win the Republican nomination for the US Senate in 1946. "He was running against Bob La Follette in the Republican primary," Ab says.

"We were afraid that if La Follette won the primary, he would win the general election. We had a very good Democratic candidate, Howard McMurray." Ab was too young to vote, but he and his friends passed out McCarthy leaflets. They helped McCarthy win the primary, and then McCarthy ended McMurray's political career with a landslide victory. McCarthy's anti-Communist crusade would soon begin.

Ab had never thought about running for office himself until he met with Victor deGrazia and his Hyde Park neighbor Lou Silverman. "I had been active in the IVI," Ab says, "and Zoey and I had supported a couple of local candidates, but the idea of running for office in Chicago seemed totally impossible." His two friends painted a persuasive picture, however. Because of reapportionment, Ab would be running in a new legislative district in 1956 with no incumbents. And with Illinois' cumulative voting system for General Assembly seats, each voter had three votes that could be split among candidates or "bulleted," giving all three votes to one candidate. If Ab became the IVI-endorsed candidate, he might get enough bullet votes to win one of the three seats up for grabs. With a strong base of IVI volunteers available to knock on thousands of doors in the three city wards that made up the new 23rd Legislative District, the scenario was at least plausible. The year before, in 1955, deGrazia had managed the successful, historic, IVI-endorsed campaign of Hyde Parker Leon Despres, who ran for alderman against the Democratic machine candidate. "It sounded doable," Ab recalls thinking.

But turning "doable" into a victory would depend on how inspiring Ab was as a candidate. That's what it would take to get hundreds of IVI volunteers to give up their evenings and weekends to go door-to-door and enthusiastically push Ab's candidacy. The Democratic machine had patronage workers whose jobs depended on turning out the vote, regardless of who the candidate was. And they had the advantage of being able to offer tangible benefits—fixing a parking ticket, getting a neighborhood pothole repaired, or finding a city job for an unemployed husband. The Democratic machine was something of a social services operation. The IVI volunteers were selling a different, loftier kind of good government. They needed to be inspired, as they had been by the brilliant Leon Despres. Like Despres, Ab came to his first campaign with exceptional intellectual and liberal credentials, of course. But he had to learn to sell himself and get his IVI precinct workers excited about him personally. Of medium height and build, he was not a physically imposing presence, but like most good politicians, he could flash a natural, luminescent smile. He also spoke with energy and passion. And he had learned a little about the art of selling as a teenager when he worked at Nisley's, a women's shoe store, in downtown Milwaukee. "You got paid so much an hour plus a commission on each pair of shoes," Ab tells me. "There were the PMs, the premium merchandise. Those were shoes that hadn't been selling and you got a premium, a bigger commission, if you sold them, maybe a dollar or even two dollars. You'd push those shoes, especially to somebody who took a liking to a nice young man."

With deGrazia's and Silverman's considerable help, Ab won the IVI's endorsement, and then the volunteers poured out into the precincts and helped him pull off a historic victory in the decisive Democratic primary. But Ab tells me he was the beneficiary of a little unsolicited Chicago-style vote rigging.

It was something of a tradition in the cumulative voting system, Ab explains, that "the Democratic Party and the Republican Party, in order not to overwhelm each other and to ensure that at least one of their candidates would be elected to the assembly, sort of as a noblesse oblige courtesy, would agree not to put up more than two candidates in the general election. In a Democratic legislative district like mine, the Regular Democratic Organization would put up two candidates for the general election, and so would the Republican Party. When I ran in the Democratic primary there were three candidates—me, and two Regular candidates, Nate Kennelly and Sandy Banks. There hadn't been an independent Democrat elected to the legislature, and certainly not from Chicago, in a long, long time, if ever. And the only reason it happened this time was because we got my voters to bullet their three votes for me. The Regulars had to divide their votes between Kennelly and Banks to get them elected. On Election Day, when the 7th Ward Regular precinct captain started to realize that I was probably going to win, he started urging his voters to bullet for Kennelly. He didn't really care about Banks; he was a 5th Ward candidate. In those days, believe it or not, the precinct captains counted the votes. They were all on paper ballots. Our IVI poll watchers, like my friend Hal Patinkin, would all watch to make sure the Regulars didn't cheat. So the 7th Ward precinct captain is seeing that I am carrying the precinct very heavily because I'm getting all my voters to vote three votes for me. And since it's a Jewish precinct, Banks, who was Jewish, is doing pretty well too, and Kennelly is falling behind. Pretty soon the Regular precinct captain starts reading off—the ballot says Kennelly and Banks, but the captain calls out, 'one and a half for Kennelly and one and a half for Mikva.' He looks at my friend Hal, who just smiles. And then he reads another ballot that has three votes for Banks but he calls out, 'one and a half for Kennelly, one and a half for Mikva.' I won the election with about 40 percent of the vote, Kennelly had about 35 percent, and

Sandy Banks was left at the gate. He told me years later that it was the best thing that ever happened to him because he went out and started a business and made a lot of money."

In the days of paper ballots, voting fraud was relatively easy. But when I was teaching at the University of Illinois in Chicago in the early 1970s it was still going on, even though voting machines had replaced paper ballots. One of my students, who had just been discharged from the army, had obtained a second-shift job at a recreation center on the Northwest Side through a political connection. On Election Day, his boss informed him that he was expected to vote using somebody else's name. Afterward, he came into my office, shut the door, and told me about the experience—sort of a confessional. He had been terrified to cast an illegal vote, but his job depended on it. So he went to the polling place, got his ballot in the name of someone else who was probably dead, and walked into the voting booth. But he didn't vote for anybody. That's how he handled his moral quandary. A good precinct captain, of course, would have gone into the booth with him.

Ab and I are still in the car driving around Hyde Park when Ab tells me another story that, I sense almost immediately, he thinks about often, even though it happened almost sixty years ago. He was barely thirty years old, on a train heading to his first legislative session in Springfield. He was with a number of other legislators—Tony Scariano, a rookie legislator like Ab, and several more experienced pols, including Republican Noble Lee from Hyde Park, another Republican from Lake County, and a few others. "We're riding on the train," Ab says, "and Tony said, 'OK, guys, what does it take to be a really good legislator?' And the answer they gave in unison was, 'Guts.'"

"Really?" I say, somehow not expecting that answer.

"Yup. I've never forgotten it. And I still think the first criterion for public officials is guts."

Guts, as Ab uses the word, means courage; he uses the two words interchangeably as we continue to talk. He thinks of guts in the moral sense, such as when one has the guts to do what is right, fair, or just. As he's talking, I have an unexpected flashback to an incident that happened in high school when I was running for senior class president. My opponent was my good friend Allen Toy, the lone Chinese American in the school. Shortly before the election, a classmate came up to me and said he was voting for me rather than Allen because Allen was Chinese. I was surprised, but I didn't say a word—no guts. It bothered me then, and it bothers me now. It bothered me not because I had learned about the Golden Rule in the Old Testament. I didn't. But as a Jew, I was keenly aware of the possibility of being slighted or rejected, even though it rarely happened. I didn't do the right thing at Washington High School because I wanted to be class president—a small matter, one might say, but I remember it.

Many months after Ab told me the story about his train trip to Springfield, he related a childhood incident that helped explain, to me at least, why having guts and doing the right thing resonated with him. We were talking about Obama and race relations, which we frequently did in our conversations. Maybe it was free association, but Ab suddenly remembered an event from his boyhood involving his grandfather, Max. His grandfather lived in Omro, a rural town about 100 miles northwest of Milwaukee, where he had a one-man scrap business. Ab adored his grandfather, who came to Milwaukee for the Jewish holidays. On one occasion, Ab says, "After High Holy services, we were someplace, either for tea or lunch. We were sitting with some Jewish slumlords and storekeepers in Milwaukee. They were talking in Yiddish, which I used to understand, and they were talking about their experiences with the schvartzes, the black people. They were telling stories about how the schvartzes didn't pay the rent and you had to throw them out. This one guy actually beat up a little black kid who was stealing from him. There would be a little bit of self-abnegation, but then they would say, the Yiddish phrase is *nu me darf machn a lebn*—'well, you've got to make a living.' My grandfather used to deal with farmers and prided himself that he never cheated them. As we came out from wherever we were, he said to me, referring to the conversation we had just heard, and I still remember, he had his hand on my head, and he said: '*es past nisht*.' That's not right."

It's lunchtime at the bustling Valois Cafeteria on Fifty-Third Street. Ab and I make our way through the line. He gets a chicken salad sandwich and asks for a glass of milk. "Have you always been a milk drinker?" I ask.

"Pretty much," he says. "Cows and I get along."

"Must be your Wisconsin genes," I say.

The place is noisy and crowded. Ab asks me to find a table because he can't see across the room, where there might be an open one. I dig into my baked chicken, and after the first bite, I conclude that the food is probably not the main reason to be here. The price is right, but for folks like Ab, it's all about nostalgia. The Valois is where he and young Barack Obama exchanged political gossip in the late 1990s and early 2000s. "The room used to work him," Ab jokes, referring to the trail of people who would stop by their table to pay their respects to Barack. "He loved it." Decades earlier, it was where the young Abner Mikva conspired with his friends and political peers.

"Bob Mann and I used to plan strategy here," he says. Ab and Mann, who was also Jewish and from Hyde Park, became half of a distinctive quartet in Springfield: the "Kosher Nostra." The moniker was invented by the irrepressible Tony Scariano. Its fourth member was a young legislator from downstate, Paul Simon, who later became a US senator and presidential candidate. Scariano had been inspired by newspaper headlines of an FBI raid on a mob family in New York. "We should call ourselves the Kosher Nostra," he announced to Ab. "You, Bob Mann, and Paul Simon will be the Kosher and I'll be the Nostra." To which Ab replied, "But Tony, Paul isn't Jewish." And Tony said, "Yeah, but he votes Jewish."

The four of them became close friends and roommates, sharing a Springfield apartment during the legislative session. In the infamous but colorful cesspool that was the Illinois legislature in the 1950s and beyond, my educated guess would have been that the four young, independent-minded, honest politicians were destined to be a tiny island of well-meaning irrelevance. But that's not Ab's evaluation after decades of reflection. "In thinking back over the years, I realized that the four of us often had a lot of influence. Partly it was that the legislature was open to ideas at the time, but also, the party division in the legislature was frequently close enough that the four of us could make a difference. On some issues, we could influence the votes of half a dozen others." And that included Republicans.

Ab and I both see ourselves as yellow-dog Democrats. In his case, he says he's voted for only two Republicans, both of them mayoral candidates running against Richard J. Daley in the 1950s. Of course, there were other machine Democrats on the ballot he wouldn't vote for, but he abstained very carefully. "I used to vote with my feet spread wide apart in the voting booth," Ab says. "I would pull the straight party lever, but then I would push up levers for certain Democrats I didn't want to vote for. I kept my feet still and didn't move around so that the precinct captains who were watching me couldn't tell what I was doing."

I've voted for a Republican only once, and that was in a recent special election in Arlington County, Virginia, where I've lived for forty years. The local Democrats had become so inept and untrustworthy that I voted for a Republican who ran as an independent. But he turned out to be more of the same. Good, competent people are less interested in running for public office these days, including for Congress. It's a troubling topic that Ab and I talk about in later conversations.

In Springfield, Ab won the respect of good-government groups, the press, and some of his colleagues because of his outspoken criticism of patronage politics, which was practiced by both Chicago Democrats and downstate Republicans, and his capacity to work with, among others, independent-minded Republicans on a range of reform issues: civil service, pensions, election laws, transparency in government. He developed friendly relationships with Republicans Don Hackmeister, Ed Derwinski, Noble Lee, and John Parkhurst, an able lawyer from Peoria who was known as the singing carhop from his days working at the Johnson and Zimmerman drugstore. The capable Jack Touhy, a machine Democrat who became speaker of the General Assembly, liked Ab and valued his ability. In Ab's last term, Touhy made him chair of the Judiciary Committee, despite Mayor Daley's disapproval.

But as a novice, Ab had to learn the legislative ropes, which included how to build coalitions, how to use the press, and how to navigate the social and moral culture of Springfield. He committed an early faux pas by displaying his Phi Beta Kappa key. Even though Ab did not have an undergraduate degree, Ed Levi had discovered that he was eligible for the Phi Beta Kappa honor and obtained it for him. "I was very proud of my Phi Beta Kappa key," Ab says, and in Hyde Park, he wore it dangling on his vest. But when he wore it in Springfield, Noble Lee, his Hyde Park neighbor and an experienced Republican legislator from the district, spotted it and said, "I have one of those, too, Ab, but down here it's not the coin of the realm."

Ab's first bill that made it to the floor of the Illinois house, he tells me, was an open-occupancy bill that prohibited racial and other forms of housing discrimination. By the 1950s, city blocks and entire neighborhoods on Chicago's South Side were flipping from white to black with lightning speed. Whites' fear of blacks moving into their neighborhoods was often fanned by unscrupulous, "panic-peddling" real estate agents. Ab was also sympathetic to legislation introduced in the Chicago City Council by Hyde Park alderman Leon Despres. Under that proposal, Ab recalls, "if a neighborhood had less than 50 percent minorities—the tipping line—they were subject to this law which required landlords to rent or sell to minorities. But if they were at 50 percent, they weren't affected by the law. It allowed Hyde Park and Kenwood to do what they were already doing." This reminded me of another controversial proposal by another Chicagoan, community organizer and author Saul Alinsky. In the late 1950s he proposed a quota system that would open up white Chicago neighborhoods to blacks but would still allow discriminatory practices—there is no other term for it—to limit the number of blacks as a means of "stabilizing" neighborhoods and promoting racial integration. On the white, working-class South Side of Chicago, and in similar neighborhoods in other northern cities, racial integration was apt to be a fleeting phenomenon. "A racially integrated community," Alinsky said provocatively but truthfully, "is a chronological term timed from the entrance of the first black family to the exit of the last white family." These kinds of proposals were well intentioned but ultimately unworkable.

Ab describes the tradition in Springfield that allowed a new member to pass his first bill. "So I get my open-occupancy bill out of committee and it comes to the floor, and I start to explain it. And one of the Republicans gets up and says, 'Will the gentleman yield.' He says, 'Is this your first bill?' I said yes. He shouts, 'Vote!' Which is the equivalent of moving to close all debate. 'The motion is to proceed on the vote; all those in favor say aye.' And then the scoreboard lights up, all red lights, all no's. I had heard about the tradition, but I didn't know what it was exactly. And then when the speaker of the house said, 'Have all voted who wished,' all the lights switched to green, and I had passed the first open-occupancy law through the house unanimously." But then it went to the other chamber, where, Ab recalls, among those lobbying to kill his bill was Joe Meegan, head of the Back of the Yards Neighborhood Council in Chicago. Meegan had helped Saul Alinsky organize the council in the late 1930s, and, for many years, it was a model of grassroots democracy. But by the 1950s, it was dedicated to keeping blacks out of the old packinghouse workers' neighborhood. Ab's bill died peacefully in the Illinois senate.

If you were a liberal from Hyde Park in the 1950s, pushing an open-occupancy bill was not an act of high courage, even though in Hyde Park low-income blacks as well as low-income whites were considered undesirables by the upper classes. Julian Levi, Edward's cunning brother, was the mastermind behind a massive Hyde Park urban renewal project in the late 1950s that, among other "achievements," removed the riffraff. When the young satirical team of Mike Nichols and Elaine May returned to Hyde Park, where their careers had started, Nichols needled that he had heard about a new community slogan: "Black and whites together, shoulder to shoulder, against the lower classes."

One day I ask Ab, "What do you know now that you're approaching ninety that you didn't know when you were seventy?"

And he says, "I know a lot of things now that I didn't know when I was thirty." I ask him to elaborate, and he immediately recalls his earliest years in the state legislature. "I really thought then that if you had a good idea, and the people who seemed to be the reasonable people thought it was a good idea, all it took was some initiative and you can make that into law. Remember, we were living in Hyde Park, which is kind of an isolated community. I didn't realize until much later how isolated it was. But I thought if I talked to people in Hyde Park and they agreed that it was a good idea, and you sounded it out in a couple of other places," that was all it took. "I literally started on all of this gun control stuff with that naïve notion."

When Ab introduced his first gun control bill in 1957, he didn't think it was an act of unusual courage until he received a call from a friend who was a criminal law professor at the University of Illinois. Ab had been incredulous when he discovered that it was legal to carry a loaded gun in Chicago. He thought there must be some inadvertent loophole in the law that he could remedy. But the law professor warned him not to get involved in gun control legislation. Even in the 1950s, the gun lobby was a feared foe in some quarters. "It will end your political career," the professor warned. "I thought he was crazy," Ab says. He ignored the warning, but he soon learned that facts and reason had a lower value in the legislature than they did in law school. "I had to learn that logic alone was not going to carry the day in Springfield." When Ab first told me that, I kind of shrugged it off as a banal truism. But he came back to it in a later conversation, insisting that it was one of his most important early insights. My conclusion: teaching young people critical thinking skills may be important, but so is the cultivation of political and organizing skills.

Navigating the corruption in Springfield was often more complicated than, say, pushing an open-occupancy bill. "Guts can mean that you tilt at some windmills," Ab says, which brings to mind the line by socialist Norman Thomas, who said he was the champion not of lost causes but of causes not yet won. "But you don't tilt at every windmill that comes along." When I ask Ab for an example, he tells me about a magazine article his friend Paul Simon wrote about corruption in the Illinois legislature. "Paul said that one out of three legislators was a crook, which is one of those statements that was probably true but since you can't prove it, don't say it." Simon's General Assembly colleagues, especially house speaker Paul Powell, were furious. Never mind that when Powell died in 1970, some $750,000 in cash was discovered hidden in shoe boxes in his suite at the St. Nicholas Hotel. Ab remembers Powell's venomous rejoinder to Simon's accusation: "'Well, two of you guys are sitting on each side of me. One of you is a crook. Which one of you do you think he means?'" Nobody would talk to Simon, Ab says. "He was treated to this cold isolation. I remember how it jarred him."

In Ab's case, he felt the sharp knife of disapproval when he broke with his party on a close vote. "I forget what the issue was, but the party leader was very, very angry. He demanded a standing vote where they call your name and you have to remain standing. Everybody on my side voted yes, and I voted no, so there I was standing up all by myself. There was cat-calling and hissing. There was a woman legislator who sat near me by the name of Lillian Piotrowski. She was a large Polish woman from the West Side of Chicago. She liked me, and I heard her say to some of the party guys, 'He has to vote crazy like that, he's from Hyde Park.'"

If you wanted to get things done in the Illinois legislature, you couldn't be a Boy Scout who wrote magazine articles about how corrupt the place was. And yet it was. But it was sometimes amusingly, inconsistently corrupt. I ask Ab how he dealt with it. "Well," he says, "Tony, Bob, Paul, and I were not the only honest people in Springfield. There were a lot more, probably a majority. Then there was a group that was only corrupt on some issues."

"Oh," I say, "Boy Scouts who were a few merit badges short of Eagle Scout?"

"Seriously," Ab says. "And they were great; even Paul Powell on certain issues. He was really into helping the aged. At that time in Illinois, they put liens on their property if the elderly went on old-age assistance and so forth. And Powell wanted to get rid of that in the worst way. You could not have bribed him to stop legislation like that. And I remember there was one guy, Bob McCarthy, a state senator from Lincoln, I think. He was a nice guy. We went drinking together. And one night he told us about a bill that went for $100. He said, 'You know, I took the hundred bucks. I was going to vote that way anyhow. But you've got to take the hundred dollars, or sometimes you just lose your effectiveness with the other guys.' He was serious. And on most issues, he was completely straight. The hundred bucks was the going price for that bill."

Even Ab, who quickly developed a reputation for guts and scruples, was not immune to the occasional offer of a sweet deal. He says, "I've been offered bribes twice in my life that I know of." The first time was an offer from the small-loan lobby. Ab had introduced pro-consumer legislation that would have made these loans considerably less profitable. One day Ab got a call from a lobbyist who said his ideas were "interesting," and the business group wanted him to write an article for its in-house magazine. Ab said he'd be happy to. "We'll pay you $5,000," the lobbyist said. "Sandy," Ab says to me, "I think I'm a pretty good writer, but not that good." Then, in the early 1960s, Ab was tossed an out-of-the-blue offer to do a little well-paying legal work. "The big pressure I felt being a legislator and a lawyer is that the more prominent I became in legislative affairs, the less time I was putting in billable hours," Ab says. One day he got a call from a lawyer he knew in Chicago. A trucking company out east needed a law firm to represent it in Illinois, the lawyer said, and the retainer was $1,000 a month, which at the time was a lot of money. The lawyer told Ab he wouldn't have to do any state licensing work; all the work would be on the federal level, with the Interstate Commerce Commission. It's good-paying stuff, the lawyer told Ab. And Ab said, "That sounds great." But then the lawyer told Ab that the trucking company work was coming to him through Marge Everett, and the trucking guy would like Ab and Marge to have lunch and talk about it. Marjorie Everett was the politically well-connected manager of Washington Park and Arlington Park racetracks. Ab and his reform pals Tony Scariano and Paul Simon had taken on the issue of racetracks. "It bothered us that they were not paying any real taxes to the state," he says. "So we were putting in bills to raise their taxes." As soon as he heard that lunch with Marge was a prerequisite for landing the new client, Ab informed the lawyer that Marge was unlikely to throw him any business. To which the lawyer said, "You know, we'd like you to soften up a little bit on her." Ab replied, "I think I'll take a pass."

But that wasn't quite the end of it. Having the guts to stand up to powerful interests did not go unchallenged. One day, former US attorney and now Illinois governor Otto Kerner called Ab into his office. Ab liked Governor Kerner because he was fairly progressive and seemed like a straight shooter. Later, he would become nationally known as chair of the Kerner Commission, which investigated the urban riots that swept the country in the 1960s and issued a 1968 report denouncing racial discrimination and warning, "Our nation is moving toward two societies, one black, one white— separate and unequal." Ab and Kerner sat down to talk. "There was no agenda," Ab says. "It was just the two of us. And he said, 'Ab, Marge Everett is one of the best friends the Democratic Party has. She's one of the best friends I have. And she would be one of the best friends you have if you let her.' And that's when I began to know that Otto was getting a little bit off the straight and narrow." Indeed, after he left office and became a federal judge, Kerner was charged with bribery and other crimes; at his trial, it was revealed that while he was governor he had purchased steeply discounted racetrack stock from Everett in exchange for giving her tracks favorable racing dates. Everett had deducted the payoff to the governor on her federal income tax returns as a cost of doing business in Illinois, which it often was. Kerner went to prison in 1974.

And then there was the charming, roguish Marshall Korshak, brother of Sydney, the Chicago mob's famous fixer-lawyer. Korshak became Ab's incongruous political friend and sometime mentor. I remember the "Marshall stories" told by my friend, journalist and author Nick von Hoffman, from Nick's youthful days as Saul Alinsky's top community organizer on the South Side in the 1950s and 1960s. Back then, I had no idea that Marshall Korshak and Ab were political pals of sorts.

"Marshall was the ultimate character," Ab says, and the Valois Cafeteria was one of the places they got together. The son of Jewish immigrants, Marshall Korshak was a generation older than Ab; he owned a liquor store, was a state senator, and later became the machine's 5th Ward Democratic committeeman. Street smart, tall, and good looking, with dark wavy hair, "he had this way of dominating the room," Ab says. "Dressed very, very well, drove around in his fancy 'Cadgellac,' as he called it, and always had this big roll of bills in his pocket." Some of those bills were probably put to good use in the legislature. "The way you bought the legislature," Ab says, is that "you'd give money to a Paul Powell in the assembly or to a Marshall Korshak in the senate, and they would distribute it to the boys. The votes were very cheap—fifty bucks, a hundred bucks."

Ab got some of Marshall Korshak's money, too. "When I would run for office, and I was running against the machine, he would call and say, 'I gotta see ya, Mifka.' That's how he'd sometimes say my name. So I'd come to see him. He says, 'You know, you could turn it back if you want, but I really want to help.' And he'd pull out his wad of bills and peel off five hundred-dollar bills and say, 'If you say it came from me, I'll deny it.'" At first, Ab was uncomfortable accepting such a large cash campaign contribution, although there was nothing illegal about it at the time. But Marshall and Ab were already friendly Hyde Parkers, and Ab insists that Korshak never asked for a political favor in return. "He never once called me to put pressure on me. Never. Not once. Not when I was in the legislature, not when I got to Congress. And I think about that. As far as I was concerned, that was the highest praise from anyone because he just assumed he couldn't buy me and never tried."

As I listen to all this, I'm beginning to understand how both Ab and Marshall benefited from their political friendship. Some of it was not political at all; they just liked each other. Ab appreciated, even admired, Korshak's style, a kind of *Guys and Dolls* pizzazz. Ab did not like dull. He also appreciated Korshak's zesty native intelligence. Ab did not like dumb. As for Korshak, he would have admired Ab's lawyerly intellect and credentials, his sense of humor, and his complete lack of pretense and self-righteousness.

The political part of the friendship was rooted in Hyde Park and in their shared liberalism, up to a point. A machine guy like Marshall Korshak benefited from a friendship with a popular young independent like Ab in the anti-machine part of his ward. And Ab, who wanted to get things done in Springfield, valued Korshak's connections and savvy. "I thought of him as a mentor," Ab tells me. "He would give me advice. He would tell me, you ought to go here or you ought to go there, or you ought to be nice to Claude Holman," a black machine alderman in the 4th Ward. And if you were a lawyer who had a client with a court case pending, Marshall Korshak could arrange to have the case assigned to a friendly judge.

On race, however, there was an ugly gap between Korshak's pro–civil rights assertions and his behavior. In that respect, he was more like the racist political machine that ran Chicago. "He always talked about the schvartzes," Ab says. One time, as they were leaving the Valois, Marshall grumbled about wasting their time at a joint where the food was so shitty. When Ab said, "This is where our folks are," Marshall replied icily, "They're not my folks."

"Traditionally, the white machine committeemen controlled the black wards well into the 1960s, except for Bill Dawson's turf on the South Side," Ab says. (Dawson was a congressman whose organization delivered a big black vote for the Democratic machine.) "The committeemen used mainly white supervisors who had the good patronage jobs, while the blacks who had low-level jobs were treated as the plantation hands who rang the doorbells. Many of these wards were 90 percent black or more, but the committeemen, who controlled the patronage jobs, were white." When Korshak became committeeman of the 5th Ward, with its sizable black population, he ran it in the traditional way. He wasn't promoting equal opportunity or affirmative action in his own backyard. On one occasion, Ab attended a political dinner in honor of another white committeeman. With the committeeman's black workers in attendance, Korshak got up, Ab recalls, and said, "'I want you to know that Brian has a heart that is as black as any of yours.' Afterwards, I said, 'Marshall, do you know what you were saying?' 'What? What did I say?'"

Michelle Obama's father, Fraser Robinson, may have gotten his first city job in the water department through Marshall Korshak, or at least with his blessing. In the 1950s the Robinsons lived in Woodlawn, part of which was in Korshak's ward and Ab's legislative district. When I ask whether Fraser Robinson was expected to do political work, Ab replies, "Oh, yeah. He worked a precinct in Woodlawn. I didn't know him, but one of his precincts was between Sixty-First and Sixty-Second Streets. In the 1950s and 1960s the machine had dual precinct workers in all the Woodlawn precincts. They had the white precinct captains who ran the precincts. And they in turn had the black precinct workers who had patronage jobs. They usually had three or four to a precinct because those were big votes. In Chicago, the black vote became heavy and important quite early." By the time Dick Daley was running for mayor in the 1950s, Ab says, it was a key cog in the machine's big Election Day victories.

Izzy Kiefus was a fabled precinct captain, and Ab remembers him from the 1956 Democratic primary. Izzy, like some of the white precinct captains in Woodlawn, had been trained on the old Jewish West Side. "They treated the blacks in Woodlawn the same way they had treated the Jewish immigrant population—that is, everybody votes." Well, on Election Day, Ab was making the rounds, and he stopped at the Jewish retirement home in Izzy's precinct. "I spoke a better Yiddish then," Ab says, "and I'd go in and talk with the residents in Yiddish. They seemed like my dear friends." Ab bumped into Izzy, who congratulated him. Ab asked him why. "You're going to win big," Izzy said. A little surprised, Ab said: "I am? I'm going to win this precinct?" Izzy replied, "No, you're going to get killed in this precinct, but you're going to win big in the district."

3

A Rookie Lawyer and Obamacare

It's a late summer morning in 2013, and I'm driving from Milwaukee to see Ab for the second time in less than twenty-four hours. Yesterday I drove his old Milwaukee friends Leonard and Ruth Zubrensky down to Chicago to have dinner with Ab and Zoe and then back to Milwaukee, a few hours to the north. Len, Ab's college roommate, is ninety-one, and he and Ruth no longer do much highway driving.

Shortly before 5:00 p.m., Len, Ruth and I take the elevator to the Mikvas' apartment. When we enter, I see half a dozen little missile-shaped oxygen canisters lined up on the floor, resting against the living room wall. A few feet away, rolled into a small pile, is some sea-green plastic tubing near Ab's "oxygen machine," as he later calls it. Breathing is his biggest daily health concern. After a brief round of greetings, I drive us all to Deleece, a contemporary bistro about ten minutes from the Hallmark. Zoe looks pretty; she had her hair done for our night out. If you didn't know Zoe before her stroke, you wouldn't have found her long stretches of silence unusual. We order drinks. Ab gets his usual, Meyers rum and tonic, no fruit. Len, the wine connoisseur, has a California Cabernet.

The conversation, led by the rambunctious Len, turns to the self-published book he has written, *How to Live for (Almost) Ever*. Len emphatically declares that he wants to live until at least 100. Ab says he has no interest in getting to 100—and what disturbs me is that he says it like he has thought about it. He's not that far away, I think. I want to be inspired. I don't want to hear that, at some point in the not-too-distant future, his—or my—life won't be worth living, even if we still have all our marbles. So the next day when I see Ab, I wait until we are almost ready to say goodbye before I ask him about last night. "You have no aspiration to live to 100?" I ask timidly.

"No, I don't," he says softly. There's a pause.

"Why?" I ask.

"I don't find these last years that invigorating. I don't feel as healthy, I'm not able to do many things. I think that I may have given up golf, I don't know. These years are not as much fun. What I always enjoyed about being in politics and government was waking up in the morning, jumping out of bed, and thinking about something I was going to do that day that was really going to be exhilarating. These days, first of all, I don't jump out of bed anymore. If I did, I'd be in bad shape. Secondly, there's nothing that I look forward to with that much anticipation on a daily basis. I'll look forward to participating in the graduation of one of our grandchildren or seeing them on the weekend. But it's not like today I'm really going to get involved in a battle that's going to change the world, make things better, or see that justice is done. Len obviously thinks about getting to 100 as a physical challenge, but I don't feel challenged. As far as I'm concerned," he says with a small smile, "I've already lived too old to die young."

Maybe, I think, Ab is exaggerating, or maybe next week he'll feel differently. I remind him that when we started our conversations, he was his typically passionate self about the gun control debate in the US Senate and wrote letters to Senator Pryor. "It revved me up for a little while," he explains, "but I didn't get up that morning thinking that today I'm going to write a letter to Mark Pryor telling him what I think about his idiotic vote. It isn't the same kind of stimulus." In fact, an hour earlier Ab told me about a letter he had just written to his old friend President Obama, furious about the rumors that Obama was going to nominate Larry Summers to head the Federal Reserve.

"So," I say, "your interest in having a voice and influence is still there, but, as you said, it's only here and there. But if someone came along, like [former congressman] Mike Barnes did recently, and asked you to join a lawyers' committee on gun violence—if it were a project that required two, three days a week—what about that?"

"Yes, that's what's missing," Ab says. "Up until two or three years ago, I was getting called on. I did things like the mediation of the Chicago Symphony strike, I chaired the investigation of the University of Illinois' admissions scandal and the commission investigating the fire in the Loop at 69 West Washington. Those were the kind of projects that stimulated me and got me excited. I'm not doing those anymore. But I'm not in any kind of depression, and I'm not a pessimist. As far as I'm concerned, I'll take every day that comes, but I don't expect them to be until I'm 100."

In the 1950s and early 1960s, when Ab wasn't in Springfield he was in Chicago practicing law, sometimes for pay, but often for nothing. Nick von Hoffman, who was trying to organize a small group of Puerto Ricans in

Woodlawn in the 1950s, remembers calling Ab late one night when some of his guys got into a little legal trouble. According to a grateful von Hoffman, Ab promptly rode to the rescue at the police station.

Many of Ab's billable hours were of the mundane variety, but there were exceptions. And when I ask Ab about his noteworthy legal cases, I'm surprised that the first case he mentions is one I discussed in Frank Haiman's Freedom of Speech class at Northwestern University only a few years after Ab argued it before the US Supreme Court. My friend Frank died before I could ask him whether he knew Ab considered that case one of his most notable. Ab's client in *Times Film v. The City of Chicago* was the distributor of a so-called dirty movie, but the case was not only about obscenity, censorship, and prior restraint. It was also a wonderful window into the peculiar intersection of morals and politics in Chicago. For decades, the city had an entity called the Film Review Board, and a film distributor could not show a film in Chicago without the board's approval. Other cities and states had licensing schemes, but Chicago's was distinctive. Board members were appointed by the mayor and the police commissioner, and they were typically women—mothers and widows of politicians and police. If the ladies on the board thought a movie was obscene, it didn't receive a permit.

The Film Review Board's moral sensitivity about sex—its exquisite prudishness—reflected the values and priorities of Chicago's Irish Catholic mayor, Dick Daley. When Daley was a young man in the state legislature, he was considered untouched by the graft and bribery that swirled around him. He was a little bit like Ab, I think, although Ab would cringe at the comparison. Ab and I are talking about Daley's brand of morality one day in February in Fort Myers Beach, Florida, where he and Zoe spend several months each winter. Over breakfast, Ab starts by saying, "One of the reasons that Chicago worked as well as it did under Daley"—for white Chicagoans and business interests—"was because of Daley's noncorruption. I didn't say integrity. His noncorruption was able to keep the others under control to some degree. It wasn't that there wasn't any corruption, but if it got too bad, Daley would kick them out. And he could do that because he wasn't part of the ring."

Even Daley's low bar of tolerance for corruption came crashing down when James Thompson—a young, crusading US attorney—started sending some of Daley's top lieutenants to the slammer in the early 1970s. Before the Thompson era, Ab says, there was an unwritten understanding that the US attorney would not meddle in the Daley machine's arrangements. In fact, for decades the US attorney's office was merely an extension of patronage politics practiced by the Democratic machine. That's why Otto

Kerner wouldn't hire Ab without the OK of a ward committeeman. "Big Jim" Thompson changed the rules virtually overnight. "One of the stories that went around City Hall," Ab says with a knowing twinkle, "was about a precinct captain who said, 'Jesus, if they're going to start enforcing the law, they could have given us six months' notice.'"

But when it came to sexual escapades, Daley was less likely to look the other way. Ab then tells me about the demise of poor Morgan Finley. "Finley was a state senator from the 11th Ward. He was Daley's state senator. One of the lobbyists for birth control in Springfield was a woman. She was a doctor. She deliberately seduced Finley. She got him drunk and seduced him, and then she went around the capitol telling everybody that she had seduced him. It got back to Daley. No more Finley. He was not slated again."

Ab's memorable encounter with Daley's Film Review Board started with the first case he handled for the Times Film Corporation, a small New York distributor of art movies. It involved the French movie *Le Blé en herbe*, or *The Game of Love* in English. "The movie was based on a book and pretty faithfully followed the story," he says. There was brief nudity—Ab recalls that an opening scene with a shot of a teenaged boy's bare behind as he comes out of the ocean is the only nudity in the film. "The plot is somewhat erotic," Ab says, "because it's about this young boy who has sex with an older woman and learns how much fun it is—and then he has sex with his young girlfriend. It's very sensitively done. It's the kind of thing that you would want young adults to see." Chicago's board banned the film because of the nudity, although the women on the board—Ab says they were all in their seventies—no doubt found the story line just as disgusting.

The test for obscenity at the time was that a movie was obscene if it aroused the sexual passions of an average person, Ab says. I remember one of the early cases in which the Supreme Court began to clarify its definition of obscenity. "Obscene material is material which deals with sex in a manner appealing to prurient interests," Justice William Brennan wrote in a 1957 case. Decades later, Brennan would become one of Ab's good friends, and his daughter Mary would clerk for Brennan. (A precocious little girl who sometimes displayed her mother's sense of humor, Mary informed her parents that she thought spinach was obscene.) Ab tells me that when he deposed the ladies of the Film Review Board, "I asked all of them if the movie aroused their sexual passions. 'Of course not,' they all said," and Ab mimics their indignation. "I got their admission. Then I get the police commissioner, who was then Timothy O'Connor." I recall that not many years later, Daley's top cop was forced out of office when the Summerdale police scandal erupted, revealing that O'Connor's cops were crooks. Even for

Chicago, the stench was so bad that Daley was forced to hire an outsider—a reformer, of all things—O. W. Wilson. "Commissioner O'Connor," Ab continues, was "a good six foot two, a strapping Irishman. He's up there in his uniform, and I said, 'Commissioner, do you know the definition of obscenity?' And he said, 'Of course I do. I went to law school before I went to the police academy.' I said, 'Good. Would you tell me what it is?' He said, 'Precisely. It's the prurient interest which arouses sexual passions in the average person.' I said, 'Did it arouse your sexual passions?' And he said, 'Yes!' And I said, 'Oh, so it aroused your desire to go out and commit an immoral act?' And he said, 'Of course not. I'm the police commissioner.' So I said, 'Well, what did it arouse you to do?' He said, 'Well, I had this desire to be with my wife.' At which point one of the newsmen leaned over and said, 'You should see his wife.'"

That was Ab's first Times Film case. It was won on appeal. The next time he represented Times Film, thirty-five-year-old Ab argued his one and only case before the US Supreme Court. It was not a triumphant experience.

Ab and I started talking about the Times Film case accidentally in late May 2013, when the big news was the recent Supreme Court decision upholding much of the Affordable Care Act, or Obamacare as it is popularly known. We were having lunch in the dining room of Ab's apartment building. He looked tired, as if he hadn't gotten a good night's sleep. At first, he spoke uncharacteristically softly, his voice weak and raspy, and I had a little trouble hearing him. But he perked up when we started talking about the Court's Obamacare decision and Chief Justice John Roberts's decisive vote.

Before Roberts joined the Court, Ab had heard from colleagues who knew Roberts that he was conservative but reasonable. These colleagues included Ab's good friend Judge Merrick Garland, who had served with Roberts on the US Court of Appeals for the DC Circuit. So Ab was disappointed, even angry, when Roberts turned out be as Far Right and rigid as the Court's hard-line conservatives—Clarence Thomas, Samuel Alito, and Antonin Scalia. When the Obamacare decision came down, Ab says, "I was shocked when Roberts at the last minute switched over and wrote the majority decision. Because the opinion clearly was written late in the process; Roberts just attached on to what had been the minority decision. There were a couple of changes, but it was not written from the beginning. He wasn't writing as the majority judge in the beginning."

"So the 5-to-4 decision really shocked you," I say, a little surprised at what I just heard.

Ab explains: "I thought that maybe [Anthony] Kennedy would come around, and I would not have been surprised if Roberts had gone along with Kennedy for institutional reasons—on the idea that such an important case would be better 6-to-3 than 5-to-4. That Roberts would be the switch, the fifth vote, surprised me completely. And I don't know what happened to Kennedy, but he's gotten worse, of course. He used to be much more, I think, thoughtful about the process and not quite so rigid. And I thought that when Sandra Day O'Connor left the Court, he would take that role. She had the prize role, being the deciding justice. You really do make the laws as if you're the only judge in the world. The other four have to go along with you if they want their position to prevail."

In the months leading up to the Obamacare decision, there had been endless speculation about whether the five Republican-appointed justices would hang tough, faithfully reflecting the Republican Party's virulent opposition to Obamacare and to the country's first black president. I tell Ab about a monthly lunch discussion I cohost in Washington. A few months before the Supreme Court heard oral arguments in the Obamacare case, our guest was lawyer Tom Goldstein, one of the country's leading handicappers of how the Supremes are likely to vote. He predicted that they would go 5-to-4 or 6-to-3 in favor of Obamacare, the main reason being that the Supreme Court usually avoids bucking Congress on something as momentous as the Affordable Care Act. He added that oral arguments didn't change justices' minds. Well, the next month, when the Court heard oral arguments, the solicitor general's performance in support of Obamacare was universally panned as a disaster. Even Goldstein started to hedge on his prediction. On *The Daily Show*, he told Jon Stewart the prospects did not look promising for the Obama administration.

"What about the oral arguments in Obamacare?" I ask Ab, who was an appeals court judge for fifteen years and served with Antonin Scalia and Ruth Bader Ginsburg.

"Well, if there's anything left of the old Kennedy, the old non-lockstep Kennedy, maybe a good argument would have influenced him. I don't know. But you didn't hear one. The interesting thing about arguments is that part of it turns on how the bench allows them to proceed—and that was such a hot bench. They hardly allowed anybody to really answer a question. They were fighting with each other in oral arguments." Goldstein made the same observation at lunch, I tell Ab—that oral arguments are often less about the apparent interaction between the justices and the lawyers arguing the case and more about the justices posturing among themselves. "If it's a big enough case," Ab says, "and they all had time to think about it and know where they are, that's what happens."

It's at this point in our conversation that Ab tells the story about his oral argument before the Supreme Court. That case was not about obscenity; it was about the constitutionality of the licensing system in Chicago. As Frank Haiman concisely framed it, the Times Film Corporation "decided the time had come to force a head-on decision on the question of the licensing of motion pictures per se. The test was accomplished when the corporation asked the city of Chicago for a permit to exhibit the Italian film version of the opera *Don Giovanni* (Don Juan) and refused to submit the film to the censor board for inspection. The license was denied, and the case was taken to court."

From his days as a Supreme Court clerk a decade earlier, Ab knew several of the justices who would be voting on the Times Film case: Hugo Black, Bill Douglas, and Felix Frankfurter. Ab and his law-firm partner Davy Feller agreed that Frankfurter was likely to be the decisive vote. According to Ab, their thinking was that Frankfurter might feel he should be on the side of freedom of expression, but his vote was not a sure thing. The plan was to make arguments that Frankfurter would want to embrace. "But Earl Warren just badgered the hell out of me," Ab says of the chief justice, an otherwise staunch civil libertarian. "And I ended up pitching my whole oral argument to try to persuade Earl Warren to be with me," virtually ignoring Frankfurter. It was a dumb, rookie mistake that Ab fully appreciated decades later, after sitting on the bench himself and listening to hundreds of oral arguments: lawyers should not waste time on either a vote they already have or one they can't get. When Ab finished his argument and walked past his partner, Feller said to him, "You blew it."

Stunned, Ab said, "What do you mean?"

"Come on," Feller told him, "you had Warren from the get-go. He doesn't read briefs. He didn't know anything about the case, but his natural impulse is to be against dirty movies so he gave you a hard time."

What he should have done quickly and deftly, Ab says, is "make Warren realize that there's a basic First Amendment right here" and, Ab laughs knowingly, let "his clerks bring him around. Then focus on Frankfurter. Davy was right. I didn't have to worry about Warren. Frankfurter was the guy." Ab lost Frankfurter and the case, 5 to 4. His not-so-satisfying consolation prize was a vigorous dissent that set the stage for pro–First Amendment rulings in the years ahead. The dissent was written by Chief Justice Earl Warren.

The Times Film case was decided just as I was graduating from Washington High School, class of January 1961. When Ab and I were talking about First

Amendment issues and my Freedom of Speech class with Frank Haiman, he asked how I happened to go to Northwestern University. The one-word answer: baseball.

Like Ab, I had done pretty well at Washington High and could have been admitted to almost any university. As an only child in a modestly affluent family, money was not an issue. I had a vague notion—something much less substantial than a clear idea—that I should go to an Ivy League school. I'm not sure I even knew which schools were in the Ivy League. My parents didn't know anything about colleges, and I don't recall getting any help from the high school guidance counselors. But one day, a month or two before my midyear graduation, there was divine intervention, or the secular equivalent. The freshman baseball coach at Northwestern, Tom Meyer, called his old Washington High School baseball coach—and my coach, too—Charlie Bilek. The Northwestern team had something of an emergency, Tom told Charlie. One of its scholarship players had just signed a contract with the Chicago White Sox. The team now had an extra scholarship—but only if it could find a high school kid somewhere in the Western World who could enter Northwestern almost immediately (me) and who could throw and catch a ball without hurting anybody, including himself (me). My coach said he knew a kid like that, and that's how I became a Wildcat and met my future wife and, eventually, Abner Mikva.

I was a better baseball player than I was a student when I entered Northwestern. Baseball was my passion, nurtured and fanned by my dad. As Ab correctly surmised, my dad played a lot of catch with me when I was growing up, usually after dinner, from spring to fall, on the sidewalk in front of our house. My dad had season tickets to the Milwaukee Braves games: box 33, tier 1, seats 7 and 8. From 1953, when the Braves moved to Milwaukee from Boston, until I started high school, I went to fifty or more home games every year with my dad; he went to virtually all seventy-seven. Those were exciting years, rooting for a new, winning major league team with future Hall of Famers Hank Aaron, Warren Spahn, and Eddie Mathews. But one of the most memorable nights was in 1953 when the Brooklyn Dodgers came to town with my first hero, Jackie Robinson. I was startled to see how big and bulky Robinson was. I had imagined him as a lithe base stealer. I didn't know he had also been a swift, muscular All-American running back at UCLA.

Oh, how proud my dad was of his only child—his son—going to Northwestern on a baseball scholarship. Freshmen were not eligible for varsity sports back then, so he had not yet seen me play when I called home one night after dinner early in my sophomore year. My mother answered. She was concerned, she said, because my dad was not home yet. The front door-bell rang. She put the phone down. The next grotesque sound I heard was wild, horrific screaming that seemed to go on forever. The police told my mother about my dad's fatal car crash on his way home—a game-ending heart attack, we learned later.

Ab and I have talked about our fathers, but neither of us is very comfortable with the subject. From the start, I had the sense that maybe Ab was unduly hard on Henry Mikva. So, one day after lunch, I say to Ab: "This Sunday is Father's Day. Do you think about your father? The way that you've talked about him, it sounds like he was not a person you wanted to emulate. But he seems to me to be a little more complicated, perhaps."

To which Ab replies: "He was more complicated, as I thought about it over the years. I dream about him a lot, which puzzles me. There isn't any particular role he plays. I wake up wondering why. He was very ill at ease in this country. I think he was smarter than I realized at the time."

That's about as far as Ab is willing to go about his father. When I ask Ab if he ever thinks about how he's like his father, he changes the subject.

I have my own hunches about how Ab and I tried to escape the shadows of our fathers, with varying degrees of success and regret. Henry Mikva was an angry man, and with good reason, it seems to me: bad marriage, bad luck as a breadwinner, contentious social and political views. He was the Rodney Dangerfield of his uncomfortable world, and like Dangerfield's old sad-sack comic character, Henry got no respect. Ab's first thoughts about his father that he shared with me, tempered only later by his pre–Father's Day reflections, were that Henry's losing ways were mostly self-inflicted. And that seems to be the source of much of Ab's anger at his father, which I can hear in his voice. Achieving respect would be of enduring importance to Ab, and I think that is why he still recalls so vividly Miss Hardgrove's admonition to his junior high classmates: "Abner is the best writer in this class, how can you not nominate him?" Yes, I think Ab has been angry *at* his father for much of his life, but he's also been angry *like* his father. Henry Mikva was angry about inequality and injustice. His Far Left proclivities, especially in the 1930s and 1940s, were shared by Ab's older sister. Ab's formative political years came later, in a far different, post-Depression environment. Ab's liberal Democratic politics were not his father's, but his abiding concern about social justice has his father's fingerprints on it, I think.

My father, Morton, was a much more conventional character than Henry Mikva. He was a meat-and-potatoes, black-and-white kind of guy—autocratic, loyal to his blood relatives, quick to anger. He voted for Democrats because Democrats were for the little guys, period, end of discussion.

Except for my father's instinctive political preferences, I don't know when I first felt that I wanted to be different—maybe it came from being a scared witness to my father's frequent blowups at my mother over forgettable transgressions. As a young adult, the two men I wanted to emulate were my favorite professor, the patient and tolerant Frank Haiman, and later, Ab Mikva. But as Mort's son, I could not escape his influence. Although I've never fully internalized what Frank and Ab represented to me, maybe I've become a generally, if not completely, satisfied amalgam of all three.

4

The "Dumb Kid" Learns Some Hard Lessons

We've planned a driving tour of the old East Side steel-mill neighborhoods, and I arrive at the Hallmark on this June day in 2013 to pick up Ab. He's late coming down from his apartment, and I'm worried that he's sick, maybe having trouble breathing, maybe on the way to the hospital. To calm my fears, I scan the lobby and notice a black man sitting in a wheelchair near the front door. He is in his eighties, I guess, subdued and maybe not feeling well, although as I watch him, I can imagine that as a young man he was athletic and strong. He is still handsome in a dignified way. On this warm morning he is wearing a wool, navy blue team jacket with cream-colored leather sleeves. Over his heart, a round patch is stitched on the jacket with an inscription: "Barack Obama, President of the United States." The same proud message is embroidered on the back of the jacket. I walk over and tell him I like his jacket and ask him where he got it. "At a shop at Eighty-Third and Cottage Grove," he replies. That's in Ab's old congressional district, I realize. I'm guessing the man got the jacket soon after the Obama miracle in November 2008. But before we have a chance for more conversation, I'm relieved to see Ab walking slowly from the elevator. He can't see me until we're a few feet apart. He's alive and ready to go. We're off to the East Side.

Like my dad, Ab can be an impatient man—with a fork and spoon, sometimes with words that come tumbling out, speed-reading books when he could still see the words, and, in the old days, behind the wheel, where the accelerator was his preferred pedal. By the mid-1960s, he was ambitious and impatient to get out of the state legislature and into the US Congress. He was forty years old when he ran against an incumbent Democrat; thirty-five years later, an ambitious and impatient thirty-nine-year-old Barack Obama bucked the political establishment on the South Side and ran for the US House of Representatives. At least in Ab's case, his loss was not humiliating.

Ab's opponent in the 1966 Democratic primary was eighty-four-year-old Barratt O'Hara, the lone member of Congress who had fought in the Spanish-American War. O'Hara was a good liberal, especially strong on civil liberties during the McCarthy years. But he was old. To emphasize Ab's comparative youthful vigor, albeit subtly, his campaign team put an exclamation point after his name on bumper stickers and campaign literature: Mikva!

O'Hara had the backing of the Daley machine. Ab knew he'd lose in the farther south and east 9th and 10th Wards, which were machine strongholds, but he had his own political base: Jewish South Shore, Hyde Park, and, if he ran a strong grassroots campaign, maybe he'd get enough votes across the Midway in black Woodlawn. He convinced himself that he could win. Not everybody agreed. His cagey political friend Marshall Korshak, the Daley machine's 5th Ward committeeman, asked to see him. "He told me not to run," Ab tells me. "He says, 'Next time it's a sure thing.' I said, 'I can't wait.' 'You dumb kid,' he said. I started to say something, and he said, 'Wait a minute.' And he peels off five $100 bills and says, 'Good luck.'" And then Korshak and his precinct captains went out to elect Barratt O'Hara by turning out the black vote in Woodlawn. Nothing personal. Korshak, Ab says, really wanted to see him win, but not at the expense of making Marshall look bad in his own ward.

When Ab lost Woodlawn and the primary by a small margin, perhaps nobody, with the exception of Ab himself, was more disappointed than Saul Alinsky. I wrote about it in my biography of Alinsky. In the early 1960s Alinsky had gained national prominence when he and his small band of crafty organizers and indigenous leaders created The Woodlawn Organization (TWO). TWO engaged in high-profile battles with a variety of villains—dishonest merchants, slumlords, officials of the segregated public school district. To send a political message to Korshak and Daley, Alinsky's people organized a dramatic caravan of forty-six buses that took some 2,500 black Woodlawn residents to City Hall to register to vote. The national media began to depict TWO as a new, important civil rights model for low-income black communities in the North. The Chicago-born Alinsky loved the national attention, but he was also excited about the possibility of breaking the Daley machine's hold on City Hall. If Mikva beat the machine with TWO's critical help in Woodlawn, that might create an opening for a black mayoral candidate—namely, TWO's charismatic leader, the Reverend Arthur Brazier. Seventeen years later, a black insurgent, Harold Washington, pulled it off. Maybe it could have happened sooner.

Alinsky and TWO went all out for Mikva. TWO staffers were put on the Mikva campaign payroll. For added muscle, they recruited the Blackstone Rangers, an increasingly notorious street gang. To blunt any vote buying by Korshak's precinct captains, the Blackstone Rangers were given an assignment: in the wee hours before the polls opened on Election Day, the Rangers plastered the inside doors of Woodlawn apartment buildings with signs warning residents that it was a violation of federal law to take money in exchange for one's vote. Hours later, when Korshak's precinct workers saw the signs, they were enraged, partly because they couldn't remove them. The Blackstone Rangers had used the same superglue the Chicago police used to affix irremovable signs to abandoned cars. Korshak called Ab: "Mifka," he began, bungling Ab's name again, "that's the dirtiest trick I've ever seen." But it didn't work, or at least it didn't help enough. Alinsky was angry because he thought TWO had allowed Korshak's precinct captains to steal the election. But in Ab's opinion, TWO simply wasn't strong enough to get out the vote for him. In any event, Korshak was right about one thing: next time, it would be Ab's turn.

I didn't know Ab when he was gearing up for his 1968 rematch with O'Hara, but I spent the summer of 1967 in the heart of what would become his congressional district. I saw firsthand some of the racial dynamics Ab would encounter over the next few years. My summer job was to help black Chicagoans find housing in the city's segregated white neighborhoods. It was linked to Dr. Martin Luther King Jr.'s tumultuous Chicago Freedom Movement campaign of the previous year. I had been in my first year of graduate school at San Francisco State College and missed the daily open-housing marches King held in Chicago in the summer of 1966. But I suspect that if I had been there, I might have been among the interracial protesters who were vilified and assaulted with rocks and bottles when they marched into white neighborhoods on the Southwest Side. King said the hatred he saw in Chicago was worse than what he had experienced in Mississippi. Hundreds of mainly white Chicago police were deployed to protect the marchers' First Amendment rights—not that they enjoyed the assignment. But as much as Mayor Daley loathed King's invasion of his fiefdom, he was not about to let King portray his police as no different from Bull Connor's storm troopers in Birmingham, Alabama. As the chaos continued, Daley hosted a City Hall meeting of local civil rights leaders led by Bill Berry, executive director of the Chicago Urban League. Berry invited Ab Mikva to be part of the delegation. Ab remembers a stone-faced and belligerent Daley demanding, "What does King want?" Regardless of what King wanted, what he got in his first civil rights venture in the North was almost nothing. A new mouthful of an organization was formed, the Leadership Council for Open Metropolitan Communities, which was headquartered in the Loop. The "leaders" of this purely voluntary undertaking included representatives of large real estate management companies that had quietly contributed to Chicago's reputation as one of America's most residentially segregated northern cities. They pledged their support for fair housing.

I went to work for the Leadership Council at its lone neighborhood outpost in South Shore, located at the corner of Seventy-First and Jeffrey. There were two of us. My boss was a delightful, dedicated African American woman, Helen Fannings. Our task was twofold: with the theoretical support of large real estate management companies, we were supposed to compile listings for rental apartments in white neighborhoods throughout the city and then help blacks rent those apartments. But with King back in the South, the real estate companies largely ignored us. We had to comb the classified ads in the Sunday newspapers for rentals. Only a modest number of blacks strayed into our office, and they often left confused. Understandably, they thought that a housing office in South Shore might help them find housing in, well, South Shore. But the old white, Jewish South Shore neighborhood was already rapidly becoming the new black South Shore. A case in point: two years earlier, little Michelle Robinson (future First Lady Michelle Obama) and her family had moved from Woodlawn into South Shore on Euclid Avenue, four blocks from our office. If anybody who looked like the Robinsons came into our office, we tried to persuade them that they could get a better deal on an apartment on the North Side—and in any event, we had no apartments to show them in South Shore. In effect, we were practicing the kind of quota system that both Ab Mikva and Saul Alinsky had embraced a decade earlier.

As the summer dragged on, humidity and futility filled our little ground-floor office. But then, one day, in walked Mr. and Mrs. James Turner, a soft-spoken, childless black couple in their early thirties who worked at the post office. They were looking for an apartment in South Shore. After I explained what our office was about, to my surprise and delight, they agreed to look at apartments on the North Side. The next day I met them at a multistory brick building in the vicinity of 6100 North Wolcott in the West Rogers Park neighborhood. There were no black faces in sight, except for the Turners. The building manager showed us a one-bedroom unit with a little alcove that Mr. Turner said would be ideal for his study, as he was attending college at night.

The Turners submitted an application to the Wirtz management company, one of the most prominent real estate firms in Chicago. The Wirtz family also owned the Chicago Blackhawks hockey team. Helen and I decided that it might be prudent if we had a white person submit an application for the same apartment. We got the approval from our superiors, and I asked my former Northwestern baseball teammate, Jim Bland, to apply. He had just started a teaching job, and his financials weren't nearly as solid as the Turners'. We waited. The Turners called to say they had received a letter informing them that the apartment had been rented to somebody else. I called my friend Jim at work and asked him to rush home and see whether he had received a letter from the Wirtz company. He had. The apartment was his. Helen and I were ecstatic. We had caught a major Chicago real estate company in the act of housing discrimination, plus we were certain that Wirtz would now be forced to rent the apartment to the Turners. At first, the company screamed about entrapment and denied it had discriminated intentionally. I phoned the Turners, explained what had happened, and told them, no doubt with a triumphant tone, that they were going to get the apartment, to which Mr. Turner replied: "We don't want to live where we aren't wanted."

Blacks certainly were not wanted in the white, working-class neighborhoods on Chicago's East Side, which was part of Abner Mikva's 2nd Congressional District after he defeated a frail Barratt O'Hara in 1968. The Democratic machine did not support O'Hara this time, and Ab heard it stayed neutral because Mayor Daley thought Ab was going to win. Being elected to Congress the first time, Ab tells me, was one of the greatest moments in his life, more satisfying and more important than becoming chief judge of the US Court of Appeals for the DC Circuit, considered the country's second most important court. More than forty years after his election to Congress, Ab proudly displays his feelings on his car's license plate: "It's 'AM2,' and then it has 'Retired Congressman' on the side in small letters," he says. Although the 2nd Congressional District was solidly Democratic, it was not always a comfortable fit for Ab. Race and class were a big part of his discomfort, as civil rights issues, especially housing discrimination and school segregation, became increasingly contentious in the North.

For more than a century, the East Side was dominated by steel mills, especially the massive US Steel South Works, which stretched for more than a mile along Lake Michigan. Starting in 1880, thousands of European immigrants and later Mexican immigrants came to Chicago for jobs at South Works and lived nearby in modest houses. When Ab was elected to Congress, South Works was still booming, with a workforce of some 9,000, according to what I read. Ab says it was at least 15,000. Although blacks worked in the mills, they did not live in the East Side neighborhoods. "The 10th Ward remained lily white until the 1970s," Ab recalls. "I take that back. There were some Latinos, but they were treated as whites." Overwhelmingly, the steelworkers had been reliable Democratic voters, but cracks in the political tradition began to appear as the civil rights movement spread to the North and to cities like Chicago. George Wallace, the segregationist Alabama governor, tapped into white racial animosities in the North when he campaigned for president in 1964 and 1968, and his racial appeals were successfully reformulated by Richard Nixon, Ronald Reagan, and Donald Trump. Or, as Saul Alinsky said succinctly if not eloquently: "New flies, same shit."

During a Labor Day parade after Ab was elected to Congress in 1968, he was booed by some white steelworkers, he tells me as we drive east on Ninety-Fifth Street toward the old South Works mill. "I represented the steelworkers for many years. Every Tuesday night I used to go to the union hall, I think it was around Ninety-Fifth and Commercial. I'd be the free lawyer for the steelworkers. They'd come there with spite fence problems, or their kids had gotten in trouble with the law. I was doing last wills and testaments and picking up workers' compensation cases. That was how we paid, in effect, for the cost of my being there. The fees on workers' compensation were set by law, but if you had enough of them, a law firm could do very well. That is what made the booing and the 'Commie go back where you came from' so hard to handle, because I knew so many of those people, they were my clients."

"Was it mainly your stance on civil rights or the Vietnam War?" I ask Ab.

"It was probably mainly civil rights. The war was a lot of it, too," says Ab, who was an early opponent of the Vietnam War. "But it was civil rights that struck home."

Ab was prominently identified with the civil rights movement. He attended the March on Washington in 1963 and had traveled with a support group of like-minded elected officials to Selma, Alabama, before the famous march across the Edmund Pettis Bridge. But when he was running for Congress, Ab says, his reputation as a fair housing advocate in the state legislature made it difficult for him to get house meetings in the steel-mill neighborhoods. "But this one minister got me a meeting in Hegewisch," he says. "He invited about fifteen of his parishioners to meet me. They really let me have it. And then the minister said, 'Well, you know, as I think about it, I could be in favor of your bill, Mr. Mikva,'" referring to Ab's open-occupancy bill that, in theory, would open up neighborhoods like Hegewisch to blacks. "The parishioners started to gasp and hiss," Ab remembers. "The minister said, 'Let me finish. Because, you know, I have just a modest house here like most of us. And if blacks could live all over the city, I don't think they'd want my little house.' Unfortunately," Ab laughs, "I never found a lot of people who agreed with him." And yet, Ab came to understand that the clash between "community" and racial justice was a classic Gordian knot. "I realized, by the time I ran for Congress, how people on the East Side felt about their neighborhoods," he says. "Their kids grew up and worked in the mills. Ed Sadlowski, a steelworkers' leader, used to say that he was educated to work in the mill. That's what he was taught how to do. And the expectations were a kid would buy a house right on the same block and raise a family. 'Those people' were a threat to break up those expectations."

Somehow, we've gotten off Ninety-Fifth Street, and we're lost. We can't find Lake Michigan and South Works, which Ab wants to show me. I've never been to the East Side, and it's been maybe forty years since Ab has traveled these streets. I'm calling out the street signs, which Ab can't see. "We're on 100th Street," I say.

"Turn right," he says. "What is this?"

"Paxton," I say.

"We're well west," he says. "Go right. This is not the East Side. So we must have been going west. So we're going south now. West is that way, east is the other way. No wonder we don't see the lake."

Finally, we get to Lake Michigan, but there is no South Works. Nothing. Ab is dumbfounded. He knew, of course, that South Works had shut down decades ago amid the general decline of the steel industry. It was called deindustrialization in the Rust Belt. But he can't believe that something so massive has virtually vanished.

And then he tells me a story about how he contributed to the demise of the steel mills on the East Side. It sounds apocryphal to me, but he insists it's true. "The worst thing that I ever did in the state legislature," he begins, "is that I blocked US Steel from building a new, modern plant on the lake. And I only got involved because Laura Fermi was living in Hyde Park, and she made an environmentalist out of me."

I knew Laura Fermi, I tell Ab. I met her in the 1970s when we were both working to stop the proliferation of handguns. At first, I was amused that the widow of Enrico Fermi, a father of the atomic bomb, was putting her energy into banning mere handguns. But those concealable weapons of mass destruction, as we have learned, can exact a deadly toll. Since the 1970s, far more Americans have been killed by handguns than the number of Japanese who were killed in Hiroshima and Nagasaki by our atomic bombs.

Laura Fermi was a soft-spoken, petite political dynamo in Hyde Park. In the mid-1950s she wore a button that said "Clean Air," Ab recalls. "I didn't know what it was. She started educating me." Ab then relates the details of his meeting with a US Steel lobbyist: "He said we'd really like to build a new mill on the lake. I told him I'd be opposed to it and I'm sure that most people in the city would be opposed to it. It was the tradition in the state legislature that if it's in your district, you could block legislation. Even though I wasn't one of the boys, it was in my district, and therefore I could block it. I kept the state from authorizing it." Perhaps US Steel was not too serious about building the plant, or it would have found a way around the objection of a junior member of the legislature. Nevertheless, Ab still feels guilty about his role. "I took credit for saving the lake and the environment, but as time went on, my credit became more and more tarnished as I realized that I said no to 15,000 jobs, because they probably built a plant in Ohio or some other place. I have thought about that many, many times. I began to realize that issues like the environment and free trade are not freebies."

As we leave the East Side and the old 10th Ward, we head north for lunch at another one of Ab's old favorites: Manny's Deli, off Roosevelt Road. Along the way, Ab tells me his too-good-to-forget story about Ed Vrdolyak, or "Fast Eddie," as the newspapers and his detractors called him over the years. A smart, tough son of Croatian immigrants, he was a quintessential Chicago wheeler-dealer who managed to stay out of jail—until late in his career. In 1968, when Ab was elected to Congress, Vrdolyak was elected Democratic 10th Ward committeeman. They were on the ballot together, Ab says, but "I don't think I carried the 10th Ward. Anyway, I'm trying to get along with him, and in 1969 or maybe it was 1970, I came back from Washington for the weekend and my staff tells me there's a 10th Ward precinct workers' party that night at a restaurant on Indianapolis Boulevard, a famous Polish restaurant. It was the Manny's of the 10th Ward. And I said to my staffer, 'I didn't get an invitation?' She said no. I thought that was crazy. I want to get along with these precinct captains. I need them for the election. The tickets were 25 or 50 bucks. So I called Vrdolyak and I said, 'Eddie, I don't care if you don't give me a freebie, I'm happy to pay the 50 bucks. I'll come by and pay my respects to the captains.' And he said, 'Ab, I don't think you want to come to this party.' 'Why not?' I asked. And he said, 'Well, we're going to auction off a prostitute.' That was the first and only time Vrdolyak did me a good turn."

5

Watergate, Congress, and a Liberal's Laments

It's a cold, rainy Chicago morning a handful of days before Christmas 2013. I'm driving on North Broadway, about five minutes away from picking up Ab at the Hallmark, when I spot an exuberant jogger with a full white beard dressed in a Santa Claus suit and wearing Day-Glo yellow running shoes. I call Ab to tell him that I'll be there shortly. But a young woman who helps Ab and Zoe during the day answers the phone and informs me that the Judge—which is how most people address him—is downstairs at physical therapy. I didn't know anything about his "physical therapy," so I ask him about it when he gets in the car.

"Mostly I row on a machine a couple times a week for about fifteen minutes," he says in a way that makes it sound boring. "I do stretching exercises. She gives me balancing exercises. I told her that I wanted to be able to swing a golf club next month when we're in Florida. So she gives me balancing exercises. Today—this is a good one. I'm standing on a soft foam rubber mat. It's very unsteady. She has me putting golf balls toward a hole. It's hard standing on that mat."

"So you're going to give it a try in Florida," I say.

"I'm going to give it a try," he says. "Today I felt pretty stable, but I worry—I remember," and he begins to laugh, "that a couple of years ago I didn't realize how much my balance had changed. I was in a sand trap with one foot up and one foot down, and I took a swing and fell right over. It was a funny feeling and embarrassing."

For most of their adult lives, Ab and Zoe have been avid golfers, often playing on the public Jackson Park course in Hyde Park. Perhaps the high point of their golfing careers was playing a round with Bill Clinton when Ab was the president's White House counsel. I ask if Zoe can still swing a club. "I don't know if she'll be able to do it again this year," he says. Last year, or maybe it was the year before when they were in Florida, Zoe would ride the course in a golf cart until they got close to the green. "She would come to about eighty yards in front of the green," Ab says, "and would take out a pitching wedge or nine iron and get the ball up to the green, and then she would putt. So she'd walk eighty yards or so at each hole. It was good exercise for her, better than just sitting in the cart watching me." He's optimistic now because Zoe has been feeling better in recent weeks. "She's much better than last year," Ab says.

Last year Zoe was recovering from the aftereffects of stomach surgery. "Actually," Ab says, "the surgery was not bad. She had a flipped stomach. She came out of that pretty well, but the anesthetic took her weeks to overcome. She's remembering things better. She had been doing, not foolish things, but her basic memory was gone. She would eat with the wrong utensils. She'd try combing her hair with a toothbrush. None of that anymore. She remembers the places she's supposed to go. She's walking much better, much better."

"That's great," I say.

"We're very optimistic," Ab says.

I assume that they will fly to Florida—to their condo in Fort Myers Beach—and Ab confirms this but says he's also shipping his car down on a truck. "I can drive in the immediate community," he tells me. "I drive to the golf course."

"And your kids aren't screaming at you?" I ask.

"Well, they're screaming at me. But they mainly scream when I say that I'm thinking about buying a new car, which would be much safer."

"You really tell them that you're going to buy a new car?" I ask, not quite believing that he really plans to.

"Just to aggravate them," he says mischievously.

It was in the winter of 1974 that Frank Haiman introduced me to Jack Marco, Ab Mikva's talented campaign manager. When I first volunteered to stuff envelopes in the Mikva campaign office on Thursday afternoons, I had not met Ab, nor did I know much about him. But Frank must have told me that Mikva was a terrific guy, and that was good enough for me.

In 1971 Ab lost his politically safe seat on the South Side of Chicago after a court decision created new boundaries for congressional districts. Ab's district was carved up and parceled out to other Democratic incumbents. Mayor Daley was not going to do Ab any favors, of course. Independence and integrity were not without costs. Had he been one of the boys, I ask Ab, what would the machine have given him as a consolation prize? "Maybe a judgeship," he says. So Ab moved to a northern suburb, Evanston, where I lived, and ran in a newly created, Republican-leaning, suburban congressional district in 1972. I didn't know him then, and until our recent conversations, I hadn't known about the personal costs of the move or the political betrayal by an old friend.

When Ab, his wife, and three young children first moved to Washington after he was elected to Congress, they gave up a vibrant, urban social scene in Hyde Park, as well as the comfortable, spacious house with a big side yard at 5545 Kenwood Avenue, which they had rented for fourteen years. They were paying only $65 a month for the Hyde Park house when they left for their new life in McLean, Virginia. "The problem was the kids never did like living in suburban Virginia," Ab says to me. And soon the storm clouds gathered over Ab's political career. "In the second term there was unrest about reapportionment, and by the second year of the second term, I was spending every weekend back in Illinois figuring out where I was going to run. Zoey was unhappy about moving to Evanston and starting all over again." In fact, Zoe had to restart her professional career more than once, teaching in elementary schools in Chicago, Washington, and Evanston. But as I've come to understand, Zoe was ultimately supportive of Ab's political career because she felt that her husband could really make a difference as a legislator. And Ab was lucky in another respect: just as he had found his calling in the study of law, he discovered that he had an affinity for politics and the legislative process.

Ab's first political hurdle when he and the family moved to Evanston was the 1972 Democratic primary. Ab's opponent was Nick Blase, a Regular Democratic committeeman from Cook County and the mayor of Niles, one of the suburbs in the new 10th Congressional District. He portrayed Ab as an ambitious carpetbagger, which was only partially true, because there were familiar faces in Ab's new surroundings. Many of his former constituents on the South Side, Jews in particular, had leapfrogged to the northern suburbs of Evanston and Skokie when blacks started moving into South Shore and other Chicago neighborhoods. Still, Ab felt he needed all the political help and endorsements he could get. He never imagined that a holdout would be one of his Kosher Nostra buddies, his dear friend and Springfield roommate Paul Simon.

By 1972, Simon had made peace with Mayor Daley and was running in the Democratic primary for governor against the insurgent Dan Walker. To avoid offending Daley and the Democratic Regulars, Simon would not endorse Ab. "It was not only that I was mad at him," Ab tells me, "but my supporters were furious, too. He asked to see me in my apartment that I was renting in Evanston. Paul said, 'Ab you don't need my help in the primary, and you know I'll be with you in the fall.' And I said, 'Paul, there may not be any fall. And I just want you to know that either there's personal loyalty or there isn't. You do what you want, but I'm telling you that I won't forget it.'" Perhaps in a case of just rewards, Ab won his primary race, while Simon lost his.

I ask Ab, "How do you get over something like that? What was John F. Kennedy's line about forgive but don't forget?"

"Well," Ab begins, "obviously I didn't forget." Ab thought he knew Simon better but admits, "I forgot how ambitious he was. After the primary, he was at my beck and call for anything I wanted, but I remembered that he didn't support me, and I never forgot it." Even Simon's belated help was not enough, though. In November, Ab lost a close election, while Democrat George McGovern lost in a landslide to Richard Nixon. When our paths finally crossed in 1974, Ab was set to give it one more try.

It is almost impossible to exaggerate how exciting and momentous the summer of 1974 was if you were involved in Democratic politics. Richard Nixon, the personification of political evil for Democrats, was on the ropes as evidence mounted that he had been deeply involved in various "dirty tricks," including a break-in by Republican operatives of the Democratic National Committee's office in the Watergate complex in Washington and the criminal cover-up that followed. Nicholas von Hoffman, the community organizer turned journalist, was a regular commentator on the CBS-TV program *60 Minutes* at the time, and he caused a furor when he proclaimed on air that Nixon was already a political goner, likening him to "a dead mouse on the American family kitchen floor. The question is: Who is going to pick it up by the tail and drop it in the trash?" For throwing this slightly premature stink bomb on national television, von Hoffman was fired by CBS. Toward the end of July, the House Judiciary Committee approved articles of impeachment, charging Nixon with obstruction of justice, abuse of power, and contempt of Congress. Although the bipartisan committee votes essentially signaled the end of the Nixon presidency, it was a riveting, unprecedented historic event when Richard Milhous Nixon addressed the nation from the Oval Office on the night of August 8 and announced that he was resigning. Vice President Gerald R. Ford was sworn in as the country's thirty-eighth president at noon the next day.

At our little Mikva campaign office in Skokie, we must have been thrilled with Nixon's resignation. I don't recall, and neither does Ab. But exactly one month after Nixon's resignation, another political shoe—and gift—dropped that was completely unexpected: President Ford announced on a sleepy Sunday morning that he was granting Nixon a "full, free, and absolute pardon," short-circuiting a possible indictment, trial, and jail time for the former president. Ford explained that he was doing it for the good of the country. "Although I respected the tenet that no man should be above the law, public policy demanded that I put Nixon—and Watergate—behind us as quickly as possible," Ford wrote in his 1978 autobiography. At the time, Ford's unexpected, controversial pardon had the aroma of a backroom deal. It added to the political cynicism, distrust, and division spawned by the Vietnam War and the Watergate saga. The pardon probably cost Ford the presidential election two years later. And it was a significant factor in the Democrats' big congressional victories in 1974, when seventy-five Democratic "Watergate babies" were elected to the House of Representatives, including, by less than 3,000 votes, Ab Mikva.

But only a generation after Watergate, Ford was transformed from political pariah to hero for pardoning Nixon. The political establishment had come to accept Ford's rationale, and it didn't hurt that Jerry was a genial fellow. In 2001 Senator Edward Kennedy, who had been a leading critic of the pardon, presented Ford with the John F. Kennedy Profile in Courage Award. *Washington Post* reporters Bob Woodward and Carl Bernstein, who had been instrumental in exposing the illegalities of the Nixon White House, also came to believe that Ford's pardon was an act of political courage.

I've never been persuaded by the revisionism. One day, Ab and I are talking about current episodes of political corruption, and I ask him about the Nixon pardon—what he thought then and what he thinks now. "I sort of felt then, not that I would have done it or recommended it, but I understood the rationale for doing it," he begins. He imagines that Jerry Ford's former House friends, Republicans like Ed Derwinski and Bob Michel, may have told Nixon that if he resigned, he would be pardoned. Nothing of the sort has been documented, but Ab knew the players—"creatures of the House," he calls them. Ford trusted these men and would have listened to them if they had said, "Jerry, you've got to pardon Nixon." Ab says, "I understand that it was a legitimate, pragmatic decision, even though I would not have done it."

I'm a little surprised when Ab starts to talk about political corruption as a form of white-collar crime that deserves more punishment, not less. "I have a stronger feeling about white-collar crime," he says. "I really think that if we're going to have jails it makes much more sense to use them for white-collar crime. That's where the punishment angle, the humbling angle—I just don't think that you should treat white-collar crime as not really a crime." He says that he and his daughter Mary, who is an Illinois appellate court judge, have had spirited arguments about these issues. "She thinks

Blagojevich should not have gone to jail," Ab says, referring to former Illinois governor Rod Blagojevich, who is serving a fourteen-year prison term for, among other transgressions, attempting to barter Barack Obama's former Senate seat for a suitable payoff. "How can you say that?" Ab asks his daughter. Her response is that Blagojevich tried to do some bad things, but he wasn't successful. He was impeached, and that's as it should be. Mary thinks impeachment was sufficient punishment. "But to my mind," Ab says, "if Blagojevich hadn't gone to jail, it would have been a mockery."

Ab feels the same way about former Virginia governor Robert F. McDonnell, who was found guilty by a federal jury in September 2014 of eleven counts of public corruption. McDonnell's wife, Maureen, was also found guilty on eight counts of corruption-related charges. The McDonnells received $177,000 in lavish gifts and sweetheart loans from Richmond businessman Johnnie Williams, in exchange for the governor's help. That help, as summarized by good-government advocate Fred Wertheimer, included "asking Virginia's secretary of Health and Human Resources to send an aide to meet with Williams. He hosted a lunch event to feature Williams's company, at which free samples of a nutritional supplement [produced by Williams's company] were distributed. He asked state university researchers at the event whether there was reason to explore the supplement further. He touted the benefits of the nutritional supplement in a meeting with top state advisers to discuss the state's health plan and asked those advisers to meet with company representatives."

Part of McDonnell's defense was that these were routine courtesies he would extend to any constituent. "But," I say to Ab, "if I, Sandy Horwitt, a Virginia constituent, asked Governor McDonnell to help my nutritional supplement company, I'm pretty sure I wouldn't have gotten the same treatment."

"Take the watch," Ab says to me, referring to the $6,000 Rolex McDonnell received from Williams. "Even if McDonnell just introduced Williams to the head of a state department, that's bribery as far as I'm concerned."

"How much jail time should McDonnell get?" I ask Ab.

"He should get at least five years, and as far as I'm concerned, ten would be a good number."

When McDonnell was sentenced to only two years, Ab was annoyed. Then, in early 2016, the Supreme Court agreed to hear McDonnell's appeal, and I read Ab an excerpt from a *Washington Post* story: "The McDonnell case strikes at the core issue of when, and to what extent, money should be allowed to influence politics. The high court is essentially being asked to clarify the line between a public official legally performing a routine courtesy for a benefactor and a politician corruptly using government power in exchange for a bribe." I ask Ab to share his thoughts about that. He begins by saying, "We should expect more from politicians. A good, honest politician should always be looking in the mirror and saying, 'Am I doing this for legitimate reasons that I can defend to my kids, or am I really caving in?' The first experience I had with this dilemma was when I was in the legislature. Some of these great reformers, some who were active in the IVI in Hyde Park, would come up to me, they would see me on the street, and they'd say, 'Ab, I got a parking ticket. Can you help me?' I finally figured out the solution was to say, 'Yeah, I'll pay it.' Then they'd say, 'Oh, I don't want you to pay it. Can't you do something?' And I'd say, 'I pay mine.' I lost a friend, but I salved my conscience. It gets harder and harder as you get up to different levels of decision-making. Obviously, somebody who makes a big contribution to your campaign—and 'big' is in the eye of the beholder, a thousand dollars could be a big contribution—they were going to get through to me. They had bought access. Sometimes access is all they need if they've got a good case, if it's meritorious." And then Ab asks me whether I remember, when he was in Congress, the language he inserted in letters he sent to government agencies whenever he asked them to help a constituent with a problem or issue. I do remember. The sentence was, "Please consider this request consistent with your normal rules and procedures." "Yes," Ab says. "Mostly it was to salve my conscience."

In listening to Ab, I'm reminded of Edmund Wilson's observation about the inevitable challenge of where to draw moral lines. It may be impossible to draw a line precisely at the point where night ends and day begins, Wilson said, but we must try. "That's true," Ab responds. "And life is full of line drawing. Every time we put an age limit on people's behavior, like when they can start to drive or drink, we're drawing lines." I observe that, when it comes to political corruption, some people want to draw lines that distinguish between the appearance of impropriety and a quid pro quo. "That's right," Ab says. "And that is the fight in the McDonnell case. And where I come down is that appearances ought to be very important, both in the law and in the behavior. Because government doesn't work unless people have confidence in it. But also there ought to be a line that people draw on their own—they ought to be concerned about how they want to appear. When I was teaching ethics at various law schools, I used to say that lawyers should look in the mirror a lot and try to see whether they are still the law students who started law school with high aspirations about what they would do with their law school education, rather than just becoming money machines who grind it out just to make rich people richer. And I still feel that way, and I feel that way about politics, too. Politicians ought to look in the mirror a lot. Very few people start out in politics to make money. They start out in politics because they think they can do good. When you lose that, you start drawing bad lines." That's at least part of what the McDonnell jury concluded, I tell Ab. They saw a governor taking big gifts—and not just a few big gifts, but many—and then doing things to help the gift giver. "That's why McDonnell did it," Ab says. "Why would you accept a watch—not just any watch, but a $6,000 watch—when the guy is doing business with the government?"

In February 2016 I ask Ab how he thinks the Supreme Court will decide the McDonnell appeal. He says he doesn't know. He seems to have doubts about where the Court, including its more liberal members, will draw the line when it comes to the appearance of impropriety. He hopes Justice Elena Kagan, his former law clerk and deputy when Ab was Clinton's White House counsel, doesn't have any doubts about the case. "This is something we used to talk about a lot in chambers. We talked about it in the White House. We talked about Whitewater and so forth. I said we had to worry about appearances as much as the actual matter because whether Bill Clinton would win or lose a court case is not the measure by which we were supposed to operate." Still, Ab was uncertain that a majority of the Court would embrace the argument that "doing favors for a wealthy benefactor is the same as corruption."

In late June, seven days before Ab died in hospice care, and unbeknownst to him, the Supreme Court unanimously vacated McDonnell's conviction. "There is no doubt that this case is distasteful; it may be worse than that," wrote Chief Justice John G. Roberts Jr. "But our concern is not with tawdry tales of Ferraris, Rolexes, and ball gowns. It is instead with the broader legal implications of the government's boundless interpretation of the federal bribery statute." The decision was widely criticized by good-government advocates. "The Court may be right that the kinds of actions McDonnell took are something that government officials do routinely, and noncorruptly," Fred Wertheimer wrote. "As the Court said, 'conscientious public officials arrange meetings for constituents, contact other officials on their behalf, and include them in events all the time.' The facts in this case, however, do not portray a 'conscientious public official' engaging in the routine activities of the job. They portray a brazen exchange of very substantial financial benefits given in return for help from an officeholder to promote his benefactor's business product within the government headed by the officeholder. . . . It is behavior that increases the public view that the system is rigged to allow those who pay the piper to call the tune."

Ab's sense of justice has much to do with social class and public trust. As we talk, I say that he seems comfortable applying higher standards of behavior to people of a higher social status. "Yes, we expect more of those people," he says. "And that's even true of white-collar crime in the private sector. We should be able to expect more of the head of a huge utility company, for example, that rapes the company's pension fund. There should be a greater expectation. We aren't entitled to any expectation of a kid who's been a victim of child abuse, started using drugs at fourteen, and has never been able to get a real job. There shouldn't be any expectations. That doesn't mean, of course, that I want to turn him loose and let him be a predator. But on the other hand, he didn't disappoint us. What did we expect?"

Moreover, Ab has come to believe that jail time is much more likely to deter white-collar crime. "The problem with most of our criminal justice system is that jail time is not much of a deterrent except for white-collar crime. For white-collar crime, you can't make the fines big enough; they'll just steal more. But you put someone in jail, or you take away their license to do something, it makes all the difference in the world. The best part of the Taft-Hartley Act—I can't say this around union audiences—but it was the piece that said a union officer who was convicted under Taft-Hartley could not hold union office for five years. These junior officers would say, screw 'em, I'm not going to lose my ability to make a living just to cover up for some jerk at the top. So if they had just used some token punishment that included slammer time, it would have made a big difference."

Ab and I periodically revisit the topic of crime and punishment during our conversations. On one occasion, we are driving though a working-class Milwaukee neighborhood pockmarked with foreclosed and abandoned houses, telltale forest-green plywood covering the windows and doors— sad, silent testimony to the subprime mortgage scandal and financial crisis in 2008 and beyond. We're going to see the effects of the Wall Street– generated foreclosure disaster for at least a generation, I say, and those bankers should be flogged in public. Part of the scandal is that virtually no senior executive from Wall Street or any of the big banks was put on trial, much less convicted of the deceptive practices that led to the financial meltdown in 2008. Although Attorney General Eric Holder's Justice Department negotiated billions of dollars in settlements with the big banks, these sums were well within the range of the cost of doing business—hardly big enough to cause serious financial pain, and certainly not costly enough to end the careers of senior executives.

When I'm finished with my tirade, Ab says, "This is where people are a victim of their own background," and he's suddenly referring to his old acquaintance from Washington legal circles, Eric Holder. When Ab was a judge on the US Court of Appeals for the DC Circuit in the 1980s and 1990s, Holder was a rising young lawyer. Ab recalls that Holder was a good local judge and US attorney and a well-regarded number three at the Justice Department. But before becoming Obama's attorney general, Holder worked at Covington & Burling, "a very white shoe law firm," Ab calls it. And that had an effect on Holder, Ab says, when he became attorney general. "He's been pretty good on the justice system generally," is Ab's appraisal, "but when it came to civil justice, as far as he was concerned, you don't send white-collar criminals to jail. That's not nice."

"You think that's part of his mind-set?" I ask.

"Absolutely," Ab responds with no hesitation. "They don't do things like that at Covington & Burling, representing criminals. Not criminal criminals," Ab says sarcastically, "just crooked criminals."

Maybe it was only a coincidence, but less than a year after Holder left office in early 2015, the Justice Department announced with great fanfare that it was adopting a new, aggressive policy on Wall Street prosecutions. The *New York Times* reported on its front page: "Stung by years of criticism that it has coddled Wall Street criminals, the Justice Department issued new policies on Wednesday that prioritize the prosecution of individual employees—not just their companies—and put pressure on corporations to turn over evidence against their executives. The new rules, issued in a memo to federal prosecutors nationwide, are the first major policy announcement by Attorney General Loretta E. Lynch since she took office in April. The memo is a tacit acknowledgment of criticism that despite securing record fines from major corporations, the Justice Department under President Obama has punished few executives involved in the housing crisis, the financial meltdown and corporate scandals." What catches my eye are the words "the Justice Department under President Obama," not the Justice Department under Eric Holder. On another occasion, Ab and I will have to talk about his friend Barack's role in all this and how it squares with his appraisal of the Obama presidency.

The year 1975 was only several hours old when my wife Joan, our two-and-a-half-year-old son Dusty, and I pulled into Arlington, Virginia, across the Potomac River from Washington. We had driven all night from my mother's house in Milwaukee to beat the moving van, which, we had belatedly been informed, was scheduled to arrive at our rental house early on New Year's Day. We were lucky to have made it. En route, we were speeding along the midnight black Pennsylvania Turnpike in our Plymouth Valiant when Dusty, sitting between us, suddenly yanked the gearshift into reverse. As I write this, I can almost feel my heart pounding again as the engine shut down and we coasted helplessly to the side of the road. In that pre–cell phone era, we were stranded and doomed to who knows what. I assumed that the legendarily indestructible Slant-Six engine was also doomed. After we sat there for a while trying to comprehend what had happened and assess our options, I summoned a combination of courage and desperation and turned the key in the ignition. Expecting either dead silence or an explosion, I was in deep disbelief when the engine started right up. Slowly, carefully, we inched forward, then tried going a little faster; soon we were cruising toward the nation's capital. My budding career as Ab Mikva's speechwriter and press secretary had not ended pathetically in the middle of nowhere.

I may have been an unprepared rookie in our small, fast-paced congressional office, but Ab was ready for action. He had made important friendships during his previous stint in Congress. But as we reflect on those early years, I realize how different the House was when Ab first arrived in 1969— and not just because of the entrenched seniority system dominated by southern conservative men, many of them racist.

One of the institutional barnacles in the late 1960s was an insidious anti-Semitism. "The first time that I ran into anti-Semitism in a meaningful way was when I came to Congress," Ab tells me. "Every time I got up to seek recognition in my first term, when John McCormack was Speaker, he'd say, 'The gentleman from New Yawk.' Because to him the idea that there were two Jews from Illinois was impossible. Illinois already had a Jew, Sid Yates." And then there was the House chaplain. "I think this was in my second term. The chaplain would end his prayer with, 'In the name of the Father, the Son, and the Holy Spirit.' I used to go to the prayer almost every morning when the session opened. I went up to him after one of those prayers and said, 'You know, I'm Jewish and the prayer in the name of the Father, Son, and Holy Spirit makes me uncomfortable. Can't you use a more ecumenical prayer?' And he looked at me and said, 'Well, if you don't believe in the Father, Son, and Holy Spirit, why are you here?' I tried to get him fired. John McCormack said that's not a fight you want to take on. So I guess I kind of dropped it and stopped going to prayers until we got a new chaplain."

The provincial, pre–Vatican II Catholicism of John McCormack wasn't the only troublesome part of the House culture in the late 1960s and early 1970s. Emanuel (Manny) Celler, a Brooklyn-born Jew and longtime chairman of the Judiciary Committee, was an uncompromising anti-feminist. Ab served on Celler's committee and remembers when his new liberal friends, Don Edwards and Bob Kastenmeier, engineered a committee vote approving the Equal Rights Amendment, over the outspoken objections of Celler. "It was coming to a final vote," Ab recalls. "Manny gave his peroration to the committee. 'You men'—there were no women on the committee—'will be sorry about the mischief you will be spreading to the country today. Women are inherently unequal. In my religion women aren't allowed to sit on the same floor as men. Men get up every morning and say a prayer thanking God that they weren't born a woman.' And then to give something to the non-Jews who were on the committee, he said, 'There weren't any women at the Last Supper.'" Well, somebody told the colorful, take-no-prisoners Congresswoman Bella Abzug what Celler had said about the Last Supper. And, Ab says to me with a sly smile, "Bella came up to Don Edwards and said, 'Tell Manny that there will be plenty of us at the next one.'" In 1972 Manny Celler, the longest-serving member of the House, was defeated in a Democratic primary by Elizabeth Holtzman.

In his first two terms, as a junior member of Congress, Ab had few opportunities to make a big splash. But it's fitting, I think, that two of the exceptions had to do with young people. Ab's congressional campaigns, as I saw firsthand, attracted high school and college student volunteers by the boatload—which is to say, Ab attracted them. One day in 2014, I was supposed to meet Ab at Northwestern Memorial Hospital in Chicago, where Zoe was a patient. When I didn't see Ab in the lobby, I went to the information desk and described the man I was looking for. The woman asked his name. "Abner Mikva," I said. She smiled and said, "I know who he is." I thought she was going to say something about Judge Mikva or Congressman Mikva, but instead she told me that she had recently Googled information about the Mikva Challenge and sent it to a friend. The Mikva Challenge is a nonprofit that some of Ab's former congressional staffers established to honor his and Zoe's public-service contributions; it has become one of the country's leading civic education organizations for high school students. Ab and Zoe were intimately involved from the beginning, reshaping the focus and programs beyond our original sketchy but well-intentioned ideas. From its inception in 1997, the emphasis has been on providing high school students, especially young people of color from low-income neighborhoods, with opportunities to get involved in political campaigns, elections, and voting and learn how to become effective citizens by tackling issues that are important to them.

Back in 1971, Senator Edward Kennedy asked Ab and his Illinois Republican colleague Tom Railsback to be House floor managers for what became the Twenty-Sixth Amendment to the US Constitution, lowering the voting age to eighteen. With the Vietnam War still raging, the old slogan "Old enough to die, old enough to vote" finally got some traction. Ab says, "Kennedy caught it at the right time. The amendment sailed through Congress, totally bipartisan." And the amendment was ratified by the states in record time: three months and eight days.

But perhaps Ab's most significant legislative achievement during his first stint in Congress came after a visit to Hyde Park High School. As the two of us were talking one day about the Mikva Challenge and how to engage young people in the political process, I mentioned that by the time I met Ab, he had already recognized the value of speaking at high schools—but at least partly, I assumed, for self-serving reasons. It was a way to reach not only students but also their voting parents. Still, it was a little unusual, I thought, for Ab to spend so much time with teenagers. "I tried to visit every high school in the district at least once a year when I was in Congress, and I started it when I was in the state legislature," he says. "I found it informative and fun." And then he tells me about Hyde Park High on the South Side.

"By this time, Hyde Park High School was overwhelmingly black," Ab recalls. "This one student got up and said, 'Congressman, what are you going to do about all those camps where they're going to put all us black folks?' And I said, 'I don't know anything about camps. I don't think they exist.' He said, 'No, they exist.' Afterward he came up and showed me a photo in *Muhammad Speaks*, the Black Muslim newspaper. And there's a photo of a piece of ground with a sign that said, 'No Trespassing, Property of the United States Government.' And there was a story about it. I remember sending Leon Davis, who was on my staff, down there. He took pictures and he said, 'Yes, there's a camp down there. It's empty, but it's there.'"

In Washington, Ab and his staff started asking questions and discovered that the student's concerns were not far-fetched. "It turns out," Ab tells me, "that during the McCarthy era, one of the Internal Security Acts had a provision that said during a time of an insurrection or other disorder, the attorney general can open up these camps and hold dissidents until order is restored. And funds were authorized to provide for these camps. To their shame, liberals like Hubert Humphrey and Paul Douglas had voted for it."

It also turned out that Japanese members of Congress, especially Congressman Spark Matsunaga, were concerned about the camps, which were reminiscent of the internment camps for Japanese Americans during World War II. "They had been putting in a bill every year to repeal that section," Ab says, "and every year the bill would go to the Internal Security Committee, which was the renamed Un-American Activities Committee, and the bill would not even receive a proper burial." As an independent outsider in the Illinois state legislature, Ab had learned how to be creative, and he wondered whether there might be another way. Instead of trying to repeal that section of the law, he thought it might be possible "to insert a new section into the criminal code that said 'no one shall be detained in any federal institution without specific authorization of the Congress.' The wording was a little stricter than that, but it would have clearly trumped the section in the Internal Security Act. So I took the idea to the parliamentarian. He was a pretty good guy. This was during McCormack's time, but he was still a pretty good guy. I asked him what would happen if I put in a bill like the one I was thinking of. Which committee would it go to? He grinned broadly and said, 'Well, amending the criminal code, that would go to Judiciary.'"

So Ab and his legislative aide, Ken Adams, drafted a bill, and it was sent to the Judiciary Committee. Except for his anti-feminism, committee chairman Manny Celler was a good liberal on civil liberties, as were other committee Democrats and Republicans such as Tom Railsback and Hamilton Fish. "We passed it in a walk," Ab says. "It came to the floor and Dick Ichord, the chairman of the Internal Security Committee, made a complaint that we were stealing his jurisdiction. But jurisdictional arguments usually didn't sit well once a bill got to the floor. And by then, his committee had started to wane. It passed the House overwhelmingly, and it passed the Senate by a voice vote. President Nixon signed it, and we had a big party about ending the camps. And it all came from a kid at Hyde Park High School."

When Ab returned to Congress after the 1974 election, his Chicago friends assumed he would return to the Judiciary Committee. I remember how disappointed Frank Haiman was when he heard that instead of Judiciary, where Ab would have been a leader on civil liberties and civil rights, he was going to be a member of the powerful tax-writing Ways and Means Committee. This was the handiwork of Ab's friend Phil Burton, the sharp-elbowed, politically creative, reform-minded congressman from California. Burton, who had also attended Washington High School in Milwaukee, was elected chair of the Democratic Caucus after the 1974 election. I ask Ab if Burton got him a coveted seat on Ways and Means so that he could raise more campaign money. "No, no," he says quickly. "I think Phil sort of knew that I wasn't going to be a big hitter among the money players." Burton's political calculus, according to Ab, was that the prominence and prestige of Ways and Means would help Ab in the next election. "Phil got me and Andy Jacobs [from Indiana] on the committee; we were both retreads [former members]. He didn't like Andy particularly. But Andy was the other one to whom Phil applied his rationale. Traditionally, they'd put people on Ways and Means who were party loyalists and had safe seats. Well, mine was the least safe seat. I won in '74 by only a couple thousand votes. Phil's argument was that Andy and I were both retreads and we deserved a good committee so we could make our seats safe."

Burton's friendly maneuver was not universally appreciated. When word got out about Ab's committee assignment, Chicago mayor Richard J. Daley was quickly on the phone complaining to Speaker of the House Carl Albert. Albert had been the chairman of the tumultuous 1968 Democratic National Convention in Chicago, during which Daley's club-wielding police had brutally attacked young anti–Vietnam War protesters in Grant Park and elsewhere in the city, much of it captured on national television. It was later called a "police riot" in a postmortem on the chaos in Chicago. Ab says, "Albert was disgusted by the way Daley handled the situation. And Daley in turn thought Albert hadn't controlled the convention. So they developed an intense dislike for each other." Daley's man in Congress, Dan Rostenkowski, was already on the Ways and Means Committee and was unhappy about Mikva's appointment. He delivered the news to Daley. "Daley calls Albert, who told me the story later," Ab tells me. "'Carl, what the hell is this guy Mikva going on Ways and Means for? He isn't the caucus's choice. Why are you putting him on?' And Carl said, 'Dick, that's the way things go in a democracy.' Albert told me that story with great glee."

In the House, Ab was a leader in the important reform organization known as the Democratic Study Group (DSG). And within the DSG, he was part of a small subgroup of friends and like-minded reformers who called themselves simply The Group—Don Edwards of California, Bob Kastenmeier of Wisconsin, Benjamin Rosenthal of New York, Don Fraser of Minnesota, and several others. They hung out in the House gym or plotted strategy in the DSG offices. Ab also became the reform leader on Ways and Means. In my first weeks on his staff, I reached out to Ralph Nader's Tax Research Group, led by Bob Brandon. From then on, Ab was the point man on the committee for Brandon and his tax reform organization.

Later, when Tip O'Neill became Speaker of the House in 1977, he used Ab for political intelligence. "I became sort of Tip's adviser on Ways and Means," Ab says. "Although he liked Rostenkowski, he also knew Rosty was taking orders from Daley, and he trusted me. So, when a bill came up that was controversial, he'd corner me, or I'd go see him and he'd ask, 'This is really bad?' And I'd say, 'Yeah, this is really bad, Mr. Speaker.' Once I was grousing about something and he said, 'You shouldn't grouse because you have a lot of influence here.' And just then one of the Democrats came up and said to me, 'Is this bill OK?' We were voting on a tax bill. And I said, 'Yeah, it's OK.' And Tip said, 'See, you have more influence with these guys than I do.' That wasn't true, of course, but I was an influential member when I came back to the House after the '74 election."

Tip and Ab were not always on the same side of an issue. When O'Neill was the majority leader, Ab recalls, he tried to slip in a tax break for the New England Patriots football team. "At the end of a legislative session, traditionally the dark special interests would slide things through on unanimous consent because it was too late to get them in any other way," Ab says. "It was understood that if you had something that was really dark, you got the Speaker's agreement and the minority leader's agreement, and after that, it was unanimous consent." Ab and a small band of reformers had set up a "watch committee" on the House floor to block these end runs. One day, Ab says, "I was on watch duty. Somebody from Massachusetts asked for unanimous consent"—and here, Ab starts to mimic the person, who was talking so fast, intentionally, that it was impossible to understand anything except for the word "Patriots." "I stood up," Ab tells me, "and said 'I object.'" A few seconds later, the ample, white-haired Tip O'Neill slid into the chair next to Ab. He recounts Tip's opening pass: "'You know, the Patriots are very good for Boston, and they've got a real problem. This bill would give them a little tax relief. Don't you think that you can withdraw your objection?' I said, 'Tip, we have all agreed that we're not going to let anything go through on a tax matter on unanimous consent. If it's such a good idea'—and Tip cut in and said, 'Ab, you know those things are hard to get through committee.' I said, 'Tip, what can I tell you?' He sighed and walked away. They didn't get a tax break that day."

With Phil Burton and other Mikva allies playing key roles, major reforms bordering on revolution came to the House of Representatives immediately after the 1974 election. The reform process had started some years before, but with the influx of relatively young, liberal Democrats in 1974, the power in the House was redistributed in ways that hadn't been seen in decades. The entrenched seniority system was fundamentally altered, if not quite abolished. The Democratic Caucus voted to oust three long-serving committee chairmen, an unprecedented act. Democratic committee assignments were taken away from the old, conservative-dominated Ways and Means Committee, led for years by Wilbur Mills of Arkansas, and transferred to a committee controlled by the Democratic leadership. Ab Mikva never would had landed on Ways and Means before democratization came to the House. That's probably what Carl Albert meant by his pithily sarcastic remark to Dick Daley about democracy. The Internal Security Committee was abolished. In addition, there were a variety of new sunshine rules—more recorded votes and committee meetings that had to be open to the public. In 1975 smoke-filled-room decision-making was largely banned, well before smoking itself was finally prohibited in the House in 2007.

Ab became chairman of the House reformers' Democratic Study Group in 1977, which warranted a congratulatory phone call from President Jimmy Carter. But now, forty years later, I am startled to hear that Ab has misgivings about some of the reforms, including the sunshine provisions. I thought about those sunshine reforms when Obama was running for president in 2008. Although I had to look up the quote, I remembered the essence of what Obama said about his approach to health care reform, which would be different from the Clinton administration's failed attempt and, specifically, First Lady Hillary Clinton's penchant for secrecy. Candidate Obama said: "You know, I respect what the Clintons tried to do in 1993 in moving health reform forward. But they made one really big mistake, and that is they took all their people and all their experts into a room and then they closed the door. We will work on this process publicly. It'll be on C-SPAN. It will be streaming over the net." That reform-minded statement was no doubt dismissed as mere campaign rhetoric by cynical Washington lobbyists, but I suspect that ordinary Americans, even sophisticated ones, took it literally and approvingly. That was the reaction of my friend John McKnight, a Northwestern University professor and an old friend of Obama's (Barack asked John to write a letter of recommendation when he applied to Harvard Law School).

After Obama became president, however, many of the crucial negotiations on health care legislation were held behind closed doors. But back in 1975, I say to Ab, one of the big House reforms was that the markup of bills in committee had to be done in full public view, and Ab had been an enthusiastic supporter. To which he replies, "But I wasn't all right. I may not have been all wrong, but I wasn't all right because we paid a high price for that. You lose the ability to horse-trade and compromise. It would be nice to be able to restore the confidence of the people in their government, letting them see how it works. But when you take away the opportunity of horse trading"—and here I interrupt and say, "So the old adage is true that making legislation is like making sausage. You'll never eat sausage again if you see how it was made, and you'll never vote again, either." And Ab says,

"Right. When you have fifty separate 'republics' or states, it's very hard to get anything done nationally. The pork barrel and the perks are the glue that holds us together. But when you watch health care legislation being made in Obama's first term, like the 'Cornhusker Kickback,' when they attempted to win the vote of a Nebraska senator by giving Nebraska an extra $100 million, people think it's all corrupt."

And then Ab tells one of his favorite stories, with a generous dash of poetic license, to illustrate that the legislative process is often less about facts and truth than it is about telling people what they want to hear. In 1977 Ab's House colleague and friend, the witty Arizonan Morris Udall, was managing a strip-mining bill that had come to the floor for a vote. President Carter had indicated that he would sign the bill if it got to his desk—an uncertain proposition, since the landscape had been littered with almost as many failed attempts to regulate strip mining as the tons of coal stripped away. Ab says, "Somebody from West Virginia gets up and says to Udall, 'Will the gentleman from Arizona assure us that this bill absolutely protects state sovereignty and that states won't lose control over their land?' And Udall says, 'The gentleman is absolutely correct. This bill protects state sovereignty.' And later, one of the pro-environmental members gets up and says, 'Will the gentleman from Arizona absolutely assure us that once and for all the legislation creates federal standards and makes sure that the federal government will do something about this terrible problem of strip mining?' And Udall says, 'The gentleman is absolutely correct. The bill once and for all sets up federal standards for strip mining.' Then Udall goes into the cloakroom for a drink of water, and one of the wise guys says, 'Hey, Mo, they both can't be right.' And Udall looks at him and says, 'The gentleman is absolutely correct.' Well, when Carter signed the bill and it came before the courts, it had more holes in it than Swiss cheese. But that's the way compromise works. And in a way, that's how Obamacare was passed, except they made it so complicated that no one could understand it or talk about it."

6

When the Nazis Came Marching In

Two years into our conversations, I mention to Ab a *Chicago Magazine* story from the 1970s that included a snotty, unattributed assertion that his kids were unhappy about him being away from home so much. "It was snotty," he says. "It made it sound like my kids were being neglected." But for driven, ambitious men like Ab Mikva and Barack Obama, politics is not a family-friendly occupation. Michelle Obama was often unhappy about her missing husband when he was in Springfield and forgoing lucrative possibilities as a full-time lawyer or the head of a foundation. Ab tells me about Springfield: "By the time I was there for a while and became chairman of the Judiciary Committee, I was spending four to five days a week down there when the house was in session. I wasn't spending much time at home or at the law firm, and I think the highest pay I got from the legislature was $5,000." And then there were the all-consuming years in Congress and the move to Washington, followed by the reapportionment disruption and the family's move from Washington to Evanston. "I really feel that during those critical teenage years, I was not much of a father," Ab says. Then Ab recalls a day some years ago, watching his grandchildren play on the beach at the Mikvas' place in the Indiana Dunes. "Zoey and I were there watching the grandkids. It was very nostalgic for me. They were doing the same things their mothers had done, taking the sand from the beach to the lake and then the water from the lake to the beach. I said to Zoey that my only regret is that I wasn't around more to watch our kids do those things. And she said, 'How dare you. They grew up so well. What makes you think that they would have grown up that well if you had been around?'"

I ask Ab whether his kids ever say anything about those years when he was away so often. "Not really," he says, but then he mentions that none of them have shown any interest in elective office. "Mary went through a campaign that she really didn't like, but she wanted to be a judge. I think the part they took away from it is that politics is contra-family. That continues to bother me. And I'm sure it's gotten much worse, because as much time as I spent on politics and fund-raising, members of Congress today have to spend much more time on it, especially raising money."

Because I never had an urge to run for public office, I mostly avoided the kind of family trade-offs Ab recalls. As a writer, and in my work for public-interest organizations, I controlled my own schedule. I was not an absentee father; I missed exactly one baseball game out of more than a hundred that our sons Dusty and Jeff played in from Little League through high school. My priority as a father was family first. But I have some guilty regrets as a son. As my mother's only child, I was the most important person in her life, especially after my father died in 1962. And like Ab received from his mother, I had my mother's unconditional love from beginning to end. But when I had the exciting opportunity to move to Washington and work for Ab, I took it. I was uncomfortable telling her about the decision, and I know she didn't feel good about it, although she never said so. My rationalization was that we'd stay in Washington for only a couple years and then move back to Chicago or Evanston, less than a two-hour drive from my mother's house in Milwaukee. But two years quickly turned into four years, and Joan and I liked living in the Washington area. We never left. For the next twenty-five years, my mother visited us several times a year, and our sons had great fun in Milwaukee when we spent time with her and stayed at Grandma's house. Oh, how she loved her grandsons Dusty and Jeff. She lived with us for the last year of her life, as she was dying of pancreatic cancer.

At Ab's suggestion, we're having breakfast at a local institution, Walker Bros., in well-to-do Wilmette, one of the North Shore's Gold Coast suburbs in Ab's old 10th Congressional District. Ab's campaigns were remarkable because they relied not on media but on old-fashioned door-to-door canvassing by thousands of volunteers. His campaigns emulated the Chicago Democratic machine's fabled precinct operation, the difference being that in Chicago, the canvassing was done by patronage workers. Because of his dedicated volunteers, and because he was an inspiring candidate, Ab managed to win three consecutive elections in that district, albeit each time his victory margin was less than 1 percent. That may be a modern-day record for congressional cliffhangers. In 1976, when Jimmy Carter was elected president but lost in the 10th District by about 30,000 votes, Ab won by a mere 201 votes. Actually, on election night, Ab and his campaign staff thought he had lost. It wasn't until three days later that the official count showed otherwise. He might have won by at least a few thousand votes if all the absentee ballots had been counted. We had organized college students on scores of campuses around the country to vote absentee for Mikva, and thousands of them did. And in that close election, Ab's campaign manager, Jack Marco, believed the student vote made the critical difference, even though many of the ballots were not delivered to the polling places in time to be counted. As required by Illinois law, the absentee ballots were mailed to the office of the clerk of Cook County, Stanley Kusper, a staunch machine Democrat. Stanley, we came to believe, was in no hurry to have the ballots from split-ticket Mikva voters counted, as they were not likely to vote for the machine candidates on the ballot.

So as Ab and I reminisce about his always-in-doubt elections on the North Shore over his ham and cheddar cheese omelet and my apple cinnamon pancake, I'm surprised to hear Ab describe those days as "absolutely the best period of my life. Even with all the ups and downs and crises, it was so exciting, and the people were great." At first, I'm a little puzzled about his rosy recollection. I had always thought that running in his old, heavily Democratic district on the South Side was much easier for him. (Later, in another conversation, we talk about the importance of having competitive legislative districts and the currently hot topic of gerrymandering.) But being as competitive as he is, I think part of the appeal was that he achieved what many people thought was impossible. When he informed his friend Paul Douglas, the intellectual senator from Illinois, that he was planning to move to Evanston to run in the new congressional district, Douglas advised him not to do it. Ab says, "I still remember him telling me, sounding very sonorous and professorial, 'Oh, my dear boy, don't go to Evanston. They'll kill you in Evanston.' And he started to recite how much he had lost Evanston by." Ab got a similar reaction when he made a courtesy call on the patrician New Trier Democratic committeeman Lynn Williams. Ab told a skeptical Williams that he thought he could win because Democrat Adlai Stevenson III, running for the US Senate in 1970, had done pretty well on the wealthy North Shore. Unconvinced, Williams replied dryly, "Are you going to change your name to Abner Mikva III?"

Unlike his old South Side turf, the northern suburbs had few blacks, relatively few union households, little poverty, and lots of Republicans. Yes, there was a liberal base, mainly in Evanston and Skokie, the two largest suburbs, but not quite large enough to ensure victory. I ask Ab if he felt uncomfortable about his new terrain, if he had to become a different kind of representative. "Not really," he begins. "I actually felt that I was under less pressure up north than I was on the South Side. Not because of winning or losing but that the Democrats on the North Shore were my kind of Democrats, whereas on the South Side many of them were Reagan Democrats. They didn't agree with me on the environment, on civil rights, on the war, on guns, or on welfare. I mean, the black population did, but many of the whites didn't. So for me, it was a very liberating kind of move. I felt that I could be as vigorous as I wanted to on any of the issues that were important to me and not be fighting my district."

Well, the key qualifying phrase was that Ab could be as vigorous as he wanted to be "on any of the issues that were important" to him. He wouldn't pander or buckle on something he truly believed was important; that was the line he would not cross, a matter of personal integrity as well as his philosophy of representative government. He remained a committed liberal, his voting record little changed from his days representing the South Side, according to liberal and conservative groups that tracked congressional votes. A small but useful example: Not long before the 1976 election, there was going to be a politically unpopular vote on a congressional pay raise. Jack Marco suggested to Ab that maybe he could "be somewhere else" during the vote. Ab's immediate response: "I did not run so I could dodge tough votes. I came here to make a difference, Jack. If I can't win, I can't win." Ab equated a pay raise with a vote for good government. He remembers the ostentatiously corrupt Paul Powell in the Illinois state legislature opposing pay raises and warning his colleagues, "If you raise the pay, somebody good will run against you." Because Ab almost always stuck to his principles, and because he was exceptionally smart, all of us working for him were inspired and devoted.

But from the moment I started working for Ab in 1974, it seemed like we were constantly running steeply uphill toward the next tough election. In our Republican-leaning district, it wasn't only because Ab's Republican opponents incessantly caricaturized him as an out-of-step big-labor, big-government, tax-and-spend liberal. The 1970s, specifically the post-Watergate and post–Vietnam War part of the decade, heralded the beginning of the end of Democratic liberalism as a reliably winning political formula for the next two generations. To many Americans, by the close of the 1970s, government seemed incapable of addressing intractable problems such as the energy crisis, inflation, and unemployment. Jimmy Carter, an appealing candidate but an awkward and unlucky president, became the face of government ineptitude. Still, I don't think many of us realized at the time that the era of Ronald Reagan was just over the horizon.

Ab tried to make gestures, if not concessions, to win over at least some of the more moderate Republicans in the 10th Congressional District. Pitching it as a good-government reform, Ab introduced sunset legislation that would force federal regulatory agencies to go out of business after a fixed period unless they could demonstrate their worth and Congress reauthorized them. At a news conference where Ab explained the legislation, some reporters were skeptical and questioned why a liberal was introducing a bill to curb government regulation.

Ab was particularly annoyed with his Republican opponents' canard that he was a lockstep liberal big spender. In the real world, when the discussion moved away from the abstraction of "government spending," most voters, including Republicans, favored spending on education, health, housing, and so forth. Only foreign aid and welfare were predictably unpopular. The benefits of social programs were widely popular, which was the main reason Ronald Reagan, the conservative hero, did little to change the size and shape of government. As for the label of big-spending liberal, one day Ab announced to his staff that he wanted us to document who the big spenders really were in Illinois' twenty-four-member congressional delegation. We designed a chart and meticulously recorded every authorization, appropriation, and budget vote for eighteen months. Ab meticulously began to vote against as many of those spending bills as he could justify: agriculture (corporate subsidies), defense (bloated, wasteful), transportation (too much for highways, too little for mass transit), and so forth. When we totaled up the results for each Illinois member of Congress, the two leading anti-spenders were the very conservative Phil Crane and Abner Mikva. I took our chart and methodology to a reporter at the *Chicago Daily News*, my friend Bob Signer. He wrote a banner headline story, "How the 'Illinois 24' Spend," and included our chart showing that Crane and Mikva were the stingiest. It appeared just weeks before the 1976 election. Maybe that's how Ab eked out his 201-vote victory.

"I've thought about this often," Ab says somberly. "I feel worse about the way I carried out my job in that instance than anything else that happened in fifty years of public life." Ab is referring to what he did, and didn't do, when a small band of Nazis planned to hold a demonstration in heavily Jewish Skokie, the largest, most pro-Mikva suburb in his congressional district. And he isn't the only one with guilty regrets. I was an all-too-compliant accomplice. In retrospect, one might say that neither of us had the guts to do the right thing.

Back in the 1970s, Skokie, which proclaimed itself the world's largest village, was home to about 30,000 Jews out of a population of 70,000 or so. Unbeknownst to many of us until the Nazi furor unfolded, as many as 6,000 or 7,000 were Holocaust survivors and their families. It was said that Skokie had more concentration camp survivors per capita than any other American city.

The prospect of Nazis "marching" in Skokie, and whether they had a constitutional right to do so, eventually became a hot national topic. The contentious issue was debated in Illinois and federal courts, in newspaper and TV reports, and later in books and a TV movie. But in early 1977, when the Nazis, led by Hitler wannabe Frank Collin, sought a permit to demonstrate in front of Skokie's village hall, there appeared to be no looming legal or political battle. Recognizing that Collin's Nazis had a First Amendment right to demonstrate, Skokie officials, some local rabbis, and the Anti-Defamation League reached a consensus: thirty to fifty Nazis would be allowed to demonstrate for thirty minutes, but they would be ignored when they did. Depriving the Nazis of publicity was a strategy other municipalities had employed, a so-called quarantine strategy.

But soon thereafter, Skokie Holocaust survivors objected vociferously and began to organize. They were terrified at the prospect of seeing Nazis in brown shirts, jackboots, and swastikas marching into Skokie. It was all too reminiscent of the horrors they had experienced in Nazi Germany— and some of the survivors shared graphic details of their trauma with reporters and at community meetings. Collin and his Nazis, skilled in the low art of vile anti-Semitism, were adept at provocation. Collin told a Chicago newspaper columnist: "I hope they're terrified. I hope they're shocked. Because we're coming to get them again. I don't care if someone's mother or father or brother died in the gas chambers. The unfortunate thing is not that there were six million Jews who died. The unfortunate thing is that there were so many Jewish survivors." Say what you will about Collin, he was not a Holocaust denier.

Although the Nazis never intended to "march" through Skokie neighborhoods, the difference between a march and a demonstration in front of the village hall became a meaningless distinction in the minds of most people. The Nazis were coming to Skokie—that was the terrifying message. The battle lines were drawn: either you were on the side of the Nazis who claimed a First Amendment right to demonstrate in their Nazi uniforms or you were on the side of the Holocaust survivors. In Skokie, it was obviously not a close call. By the spring of 1977, Skokie officials made a U-turn and quickly enacted three ordinances designed to prevent the Nazis from holding their demonstration. One of the ordinances prohibited demonstrators from wearing military-style uniforms. To anybody familiar with First Amendment precedents, as Ab and I were, the ordinances were almost certainly unconstitutional. The Illinois chapter of the American Civil Liberties Union (ACLU) represented the Nazis. The ACLU leaders, including board member Frank Haiman, had every reason to believe that this would not be a difficult case to win in a court of law. The court of public opinion was another matter.

When Congress was in session, Ab was on a Monday-through-Friday schedule. His weekends back in the district were typically crammed with speeches to local groups. Maybe once a month he spoke at a synagogue— there were seven or eight in the district, as I recall. His note cards for those speeches, which I wrote, included remarks about the prospects for peace in the Middle East and his views on various domestic issues. Skokie and the Nazis never made it onto those note cards. I don't know how often he was asked about it because he never told me, and I didn't ask. I think we had an unspoken understanding that the best course of action was to say as little as possible about the issue. Even when the debate heated up later in 1977, surprisingly, no Chicago reporter asked Ab to share his thoughts on the Skokie-Nazi controversy. No news was good news.

Then, one Monday morning, Ab walked into our congressional office and came straight to my desk. He looked like he always did on Mondays— haggard and years older after getting out of bed in Evanston at four in the morning and taking a Best taxi to O'Hare to catch a United Air Lines flight to DC. The first words out of his mouth were: "I've agreed to write an article about why the Nazis should not march in Skokie." I remember feeling somewhere between stunned and horrified. In one of our recent conversations I told Ab how shocked I had been by what he said to me that morning, and he replied: "I bet you were." Back then, his tidy explanation was that the Jews back in the district still loved him, everything was fine, but they wanted him to be their champion on this issue.

In one of our conversations, I tell Ab that I can see a connection between his decision to speak out about the Nazis coming to Skokie and President Obama's delayed public response to a controversial murder case: a Florida jury's acquittal of George Zimmerman, a white man, for killing Trayvon Martin, a young African American. Obama's words, which Ab heard too, are why we started talking about Skokie a few weeks after the president suddenly held a news conference in the summer of 2013 and said: "You know, when Trayvon Martin was first shot, I said that this could have been my son. Another way of saying that is Trayvon Martin could have been me thirty-five years ago. And when you think about why, in the African American community at least, there's a lot of pain around what happened here, I think it's important to recognize that the African American community is looking at this issue through a set of experiences and a history that—that doesn't go away." When I heard Obama make this statement a full week after the jury verdict, I was a little cynical. Why was he talking now, I wondered. I brainstormed and came up with two possibilities: either his daughters Malia and Sasha had asked him why he wasn't saying anything about it, or it had something to do with opinion polls. The next day, the NBC–*Wall Street Journal* poll reported that Obama's approval rating was down to 44 percent, and it was down among blacks. They wanted their champion to speak up.

In Ab's case, the pressure was building to speak out about the Nazis, although I didn't know it then. He tells me now about the phone calls he was getting, and one in particular from a Holocaust survivor who left a message on his answering machine. Ab continues the story, with a perfect impersonation of the heavily accented message: "'Mikwa,' he said—eastern Europeans pronounce my name Mikwa—'the last time you ran I got you more votes in Skokie than anybody else. And this time I'm going to get you as few votes in my precinct than anybody else unless you immediately resign from the A-C-L-U. You don't have to call me or anything, because if you resign, I'll read about it in the newspaper. Good-bye.'"

"That was some lobbying call," I say to Ab.

"That was one kind of call, and those I think I could have withstood," he says. "But there were these survivors who said if the Nazis march they would hide in their basements. They were so frightened of the brown shirts and swastikas, not legally, but emotionally. Why should citizens be put in that kind of torment? And then I would look for little things to try to equivocate my way through. I remember one time the Nazis decided they wanted to march on the Fourth of July. And David Goldberger, the counsel for the ACLU, went into court and tried to get the date for them. I remember calling him up and saying, 'Where the hell is it in the Constitution that says they can march on the Fourth of July?' There was silence and then he said, 'Et tu, Abner?'"

Ab was no ordinary congressman. He was a prominent defender of the First Amendment when he was chairman of the Judiciary Committee in the state legislature and when he served on the Judiciary Committee in Congress. As a lawyer in the 1950s and 1960s, he represented Times Film Corporation and its controversial sexy movies as well as *Playboy* magazine and one of its occasional writers, comedian Lenny Bruce, whose allegedly obscene material periodically got him in legal hot water. Even if Ab was not a card-carrying ACLU member in 1977, the organization embodied his intellectual values and was led in Illinois by like-minded friends.

The ACLU lost tens of thousands of members, probably many who were Jewish, in Illinois and throughout the nation over the Skokie-Nazi issue. It made little difference that Goldberger, the Nazis' lead ACLU counsel, was Jewish or that Aryeh Neier, executive director of the national ACLU, had lost three grandparents in the Holocaust. As an ACLU board member in Illinois, Frank Haiman spoke to community groups and tried to explain the organization's position. It was a tough sell. During one appearance near Skokie, a survivor told Frank that he didn't deserve to live. And when Frank spoke in Cleveland, Ohio, where he had grown up, an incensed rabbi threw a punch at him that barely missed.

The ACLU's explanation at these forums was, essentially, what Ab now believes should have been his position. "The right position," he tells me, "should have been, given all that I had done and said before that, should have been, look, it's going to be painful but we should let them march because you can't have a right that's good for most days but not when it's really something you don't like. And I knew that. But the political pressure was so heavy, not just political pressure in the sense of votes, but feeling like I wasn't representing my constituency."

As Ab's loyal staffer, I never challenged him about writing the article arguing that the Nazis shouldn't march in Skokie. I might have, but I didn't. And to make matters worse, I soon discovered that it wasn't going to be a freestanding article. Ab was writing one half of a pro-con debate in the liberal Jewish magazine *Moment*; the other article, defending the Nazis' right to demonstrate, was being written by well-known constitutional scholar Monroe Friedman, the former dean of Hofstra University Law School. Professor Friedman had truth, justice, and the Constitution on his side. Ab and I were left with sophistry. My draft of the article, to which Ab added several sentences, drew on what I had learned in Haiman's classes on the freedom of speech—that the Supreme Court had carved out constitutional exceptions for "fighting words," group libel, and restrictions on the time and place of demonstrations. But the Court had either moved away from these earlier decisions or, in the case of time and place restrictions, now tended to come down on the side of the demonstrators' right to public protest, even when it inconvenienced a community or might provoke a violent reaction. As Ab's law school professor Harry Kalven had written, the First Amendment should not be sacrificed to the heckler's veto. "I do not want the Nazis to march in Skokie," Ab wrote in his—and my—*Moment* magazine piece. "I continue to hope that the courts will eventually rule that the Constitution does not require that the Nazis be issued a permit to march in Skokie."

The key federal court decision came down firmly on the side of the Nazis' First Amendment rights. It was written by district court judge Bernard Decker, a Republican appointed by President John F. Kennedy in 1962. Regarding hate speech, Decker wrote: "It may very well be that hatred tends to spawn violence . . . and serves no useful function in itself. Nevertheless, the incitement of hatred is often a by-product of vigorous debate on highly emotional subjects, and the basic message in [the Supreme Court decision of] *Cohen* is that a great deal of useless, offensive and even potentially harmful language must be tolerated as part of the 'verbal cacophony' that accompanies uninhibited debate, not for its own sake, but because any attempt to excise it from the public discourse with the blunt instrument of criminal sanctions must inevitably have a dampening effect on the vigor of that discourse." Judge Decker acknowledged that the anti-Semitic, racist beliefs of Frank Collin's National Socialist Party of America "were completely unacceptable to a civilized society." As despicable and false as those beliefs were, however, they should not be silenced. In her book on the Skokie-Nazi affair, Professor Philippa Strum writes: Judge Decker "asserted that the correct interpretation of the theory behind the First Amendment was that false ideas did exist but that they had to be condemned by the market-place and not by government." Decker's twenty-five-page opinion in the Skokie case, Strum says, "is one of the definitive statements about the theory and practice of speech under the American Constitution."

Despite winning in court, Collin and his small band of Nazis never demonstrated in front of the Skokie village hall. Perhaps fearing that they would be embarrassed by the far larger interfaith counterdemonstration that was planned, Collin accepted a deal to demonstrate in Federal Plaza at the federal building in downtown Chicago. Even there, he was vastly outnumbered by civil rights protesters. (In the early 1980s Collin was arrested, convicted, and sentenced to seven years in the Pontiac Correctional Center for taking indecent liberties with children.)

Like Ab, I feel worse today about the self-serving evasions we told. Back then, the end seemed to justify the means. In November 1978, five months after the Nazis' planned demonstration in Skokie, Ab was reelected, again by less than 1 percent. He won Skokie with 71 percent of the vote.

In the Skokie-Nazi episode, the ACLU performed its traditional role by defending the Nazis' First Amendment rights. But in the aftermath of the violence that occurred during a protest march by white supremacists in Charlottesville, Virginia, in the summer of 2017, the ACLU is now reconsidering its longtime policy. In Charlottesville, the ACLU of Virginia represented the white supremacists, who sought a permit for a march to protest the removal of a statue of Confederate general Robert E. Lee. "The events of Charlottesville require any judge, any police chief and any legal group to look at the facts of any white-supremacy protests with a much finer comb," ACLU executive director Anthony Romero said. "If a protest group insists, 'No, we want to be able to carry loaded firearms,' well, we don't have to represent them. They can find someone else."

But the esteemed Ira Glasser, retired ACLU executive director, is troubled by the ACLU's apparent new policy, and so am I. I think Ab would be, too. As Glasser argues, "Violence can obviously be curbed. No-brainer. So can imminent violence under the Supreme Court's *Brandenburg* decision. But just brandishing weapons, without more, is not violence any more than hanging someone in effigy is a real hanging. I believe open carry can and should be legally restrained, and not only in the context of First Amendment activity. But once courts allow the *fear* of violence, without more, to curb expression, it is a very slippery slope." The violence that erupted in Charlottesville was mainly attributable to the failure of local and state police to keep the white supremacists and the counterprotesters a safe distance apart. That is the traditional, necessary role of law enforcement when unpopular or even hate-filled speech is likely to produce a reaction that jeopardizes public safety. This is the price we pay for freedom of speech. "I do not recall," Glasser says, "the ACLU, back in the '60s, taking the position that the mere brandishing of guns by Black Panthers, without more, disqualified them from being represented by the ACLU in otherwise legitimate free speech cases. So why now, other than different political sympathies? What's the content-neutral legal principle here?"

Frank Haiman was his usual magnanimous self throughout the Skokie ordeal. He understood Ab's predicament, and his fondness and respect for Ab, the Skokie episode notwithstanding, never wavered. Fifteen years later, Frank wrote a brilliant book on hate speech and the First Amendment. The book begins with a foreword: "Professor Haiman has a devastating capacity to disrobe the emperor. In the field of First Amendment literature, where lawyers and judges . . . weave complicated and gossamer webs to explain often irreconcilable laws and cases, Professor Haiman has frequently punctured the balloons we use to obscure our confusion. . . .Whether it is the

Nazis marching in Skokie or graffiti artists painting racial and religious epithets . . . Professor Haiman acknowledges society's urge to 'do something' . . . but he points out the futility of pretending that something other than speech is involved or that we can avoid the price we pay whenever freedom of speech is relegated to lip service. . . . Frank Haiman will be pleased to know that he has once again afflicted the comfortable." The foreword was written by the chief judge of the US Court of Appeals for the District of Columbia Circuit, Abner J. Mikva.

7

Scalia's Big Lie and Beating the NRA

It's the last week in February 2014, and my wife Joan and I are flying to Florida to visit Ab and Zoe at Fort Myers Beach. Our plane from Washington is delayed, and by the time we land and fight the bumper-to-bumper traffic on the bridge to Fort Myers Beach, we arrive just in time to pick up Ab and Zoe for dinner at a waterfront restaurant overlooking the Gulf of Mexico. The Mikvas have been at their condo for a couple of months. They both look good, but at breakfast the next day Ab tells me about their nagging health issues since they've been in Florida. Zoe's left foot hurts, and she doesn't have much energy, so no golf for her and not much for Ab. They've been coming to Fort Myers Beach for years, but now the relative isolation of the place has become a problem. I ask Ab whether he's driving his car. "I drive from our condo to the shopping center and occasionally to the Publix," he says. "But I don't drive off the island anymore." Their doctors are on the mainland, so the Mikvas have to call a cab or make other arrangements when they have medical appointments. "We're debating whether we need to do something else next year," Ab says, "maybe a cruise." That sounds more like an acknowledgment of the inevitable narrowing of possibilities, to put it euphemistically, and Ab delivers it with all the enthusiasm of an election-night concession speech.

But by now, I have learned that Ab will not be easily defeated by the unrelenting, unpredictable foe of old age. I hope I will be able to emulate him if I live long enough. Several weeks later, my phone rings in Arlington. It's Ab calling from Florida. He's fired up and ready to go, to plagiarize an Obama campaign slogan. Actually, he's livid. His old friend Newt Minow has just written an op-ed in the *Chicago Tribune*, Ab says, endorsing the conservative Republican candidate for governor, Bruce Rauner. "It's a terrible piece," Ab says. "I've been steaming about it all afternoon, thinking about what I want to say." I'm incredulous. Minow, like Ab, was an early supporter of Barack Obama and a prominent Democrat all the way back to the Kennedy administration. Ab says to me, "Would you help me put together a piece? I know pretty much what I want to say." Wonderful, I think to myself. Just like old times. For the next twenty minutes, Ab dictates the main themes he wants to develop, and I take the rest of the day to flesh them out. Meanwhile, he alerted the *Tribune*'s editorial page editor that he was writing a response to Minow's piece. A few days later, it appeared. "Newt Minow and I have known each other since our high school days in Milwaukee more than 70 years ago," Ab's 700-word response began. "In all those years, I can't recall a single important election or candidate that the two of us, good Democrats both, disagreed on—until now, I am sorry to say. I find my friend's abandonment of Governor Pat Quinn unfair and mystifying, and his embrace of a wealthy, conservative, first-time Republican candidate, Bruce Rauner, unwarranted and troubling. I think that Newt's usual good political judgment has been compromised by his social friendship with the Rauner family." After highlighting Governor Quinn's successes in difficult economic circumstances, Ab accused Rauner of relying "on shopworn, conservative Republican bromides: cut spending, taxes and regulation. When I ran for Congress some 40 years ago, my conservative Republican opponents used the same mantra—and they lost." What he found "especially disturbing about Mr. Rauner's candidacy," he wrote, "is that it's inspired by the electoral model of regressive Republican governors in the Midwest such as Scott Walker in Wisconsin. That model features voter suppression, cuts in education and safety-net programs and all-out war on public employee unions resulting in a poisonous political landscape that makes bipartisan cooperation virtually impossible."

After Ab's piece ran in the *Tribune*, I ask him whether he's talked to Minow. "Not since I called him the day before it was published and told him it was coming," he says. "It's funny. My daughter Laurie serves on the Legal Services Board with Martha Minow, Newt's daughter. They just had a meeting in Washington last weekend. And Laurie was a little trepidatious about how Martha would react. Martha came up to Laurie and said, 'Let's just hope that we have as much enthusiasm when we're their age.'"

Yes, winning three straight photo-finish elections in the 1970s was exciting for Ab and me and many others, but the odds of landing in the winner's circle one more time were not getting any better. It wasn't only the voters; it was the never-ending machinations of the Daley machine, too.

Until Ab reminded me, I had forgotten that in 1975, Richard J. Daley had almost pulled off the epitome of an arrogant, naked power grab: a mid-decade redistricting scheme designed in part, Ab heard, to give one of Daley's sons a seat in Congress at the expense of Abner Mikva. After the 1974 election, Ab says, when the Democrats controlled the Illinois state legislature, "Daley thought he could pick up another seat in the city, and he carved out a district for Richie," referring to Richard M. Daley, the future six-term Chicago mayor. The newly proposed congressional district, which appropriated Ab's Democratic base in Skokie and Evanston and then snaked miles to the west and south, was a classic gerrymander. Ab said it looked like a handgun. When Ab told reporters that he was a target of Daley's redistricting scheme because of his independence—he had not supported Daley's recent reelection—Daley raged that Ab was "a partisan, narrow-minded bigot who thinks he has a divine right to his congressional seat."

The Republicans in Springfield were against the remapping. One of the unknowns was whether the anti-Daley, independent-minded Democratic governor Dan Walker would veto the redistricting and then take credit for thwarting Daley. Ab, who spent weeks plotting strategy with his old Springfield pals, says, "The Republicans decided to try to kill the redistricting bill on a motion to strike the enacting clause. It took a constitutional majority, 89 votes, to pass it. The vote count was at 85. Clyde Choate, who had been [Democratic downstate leader] Paul Powell's number-two guy, and his downstate buddies were having dinner at a nearby restaurant." There was no love lost between Choate and Daley or between Choate and Walker or, for that matter, between Choate and Ab. Ab continues, "One of my allies saw that Choate and the others hadn't voted. So he rushed to the restaurant and told Clyde what was going on. Daley, of course, wanted it to pass; Walker wanted it passed so he could veto it. So Choate thinks for a moment and says, 'Well, there are three people in this state I really hate—Daley, Walker, and Mikva. So fuck two of them. Let's go.' So at the dramatic moment, Choate comes in with his buddies and they vote, the enacting clause was struck, and that's the end of the redistricting bill."

Since Ab had been living on the political razor's edge for years, I guess it shouldn't have been a big surprise when he convened the Washington congressional staff in March 1979 and told us that, the next day, President Carter was going to nominate Ab for a judgeship on the US Court of Appeals for the DC Circuit. But of course, it was a big, shocking surprise. Later that day, I was at the Brookings Institution for a tax reform seminar and bumped into Barber Conable, the cerebral, respected Republican congressman from upstate New York who served with Ab on the Ways and Means Committee. I told Conable that Ab was going to be a judge. I can still see the stricken look on his face, as if he had just been told that a good friend had died. I knew how he felt. Conable said it was terrible news, that it was much more important to have Ab in Congress. He was upset and saddened. Whether Ab might have won again in 1980, a bad year for Democrats, we will never know. I'd like to think he would have. But he would not have survived another congressional redistricting after that.

As a popular member of Congress, Ab's judicial confirmation by the US Senate should have been, well, as grandly routine as a coronation. But it wasn't. Incredibly, it was another Mikva cliffhanger, thanks to the National Rifle Association (NRA), his longtime nemesis.

Shortly after Ab was elected to Congress in 1968, he got a call, he tells me. The caller says, "'Senator Mansfield would like to see you.' It's not every day that a freshman member is being invited to see the Senate Majority Leader. I come. He's smoking his pipe. He said, 'I understand that you're against guns.' And I said, 'Well, I have been, but I haven't done anything here yet.' He said, 'If you're smart, you won't.' And then he said, 'You're probably not that smart.' He said, 'I'm from Montana. I never paid much attention to gun legislation. I'm not a hunter myself. . . . But after Bobby Kennedy was assassinated, President Johnson asked me to put through this bill [which prohibited the mail-order sale of rifles and shotguns, among other provisions]. I did it because I thought it was a good idea and besides which he's the president. He needed to do something.' And then Mansfield said, 'I can't believe how hateful those National Rifle Association people can be.' He reaches into a drawer and pulls out a chart that looks like a bull's-eye with his face on it. 'This is what they're passing out in Montana for their rifle practice.' I said, 'That's disgusting.' And he says, 'I'll show you something that's even more disgusting.' And he pulls out a piece of paper with a bull's-eye and my face on it. I had never seen it before. I was flabbergasted. He says, 'See, you're a national celebrity.'"

Mansfield was right: Ab wasn't politically smart enough—or, more precisely, he wasn't temperamentally cautious enough—to avoid combat with the National Rifle Association. True, even in his Republican-leaning suburban North Shore congressional district, polling showed that voters overwhelmingly favored strong laws to control handguns. The biggest political divide on guns in the United States has always been between urban and rural voters. But it's probably true that in his congressional district, like elsewhere in the country, the only voters who cast their ballots solely on the issue of gun control were opposed to it. In a closely divided district like Ab's, those single-issue voters might make a crucial difference. And the NRA tried to mobilize them. At the time, as I recall, Ab didn't seem to think it took extraordinary political courage to sponsor legislation calling for a ban on the manufacture, importation, and sale of handguns except for the police, the military, and licensed pistol clubs. It was the first bill he introduced in every Congress, and as his aide, I worked on that legislation when Ab returned to Capitol Hill in 1975.

"Hidden death" is what Ab and I called handguns like the easily concealable .22-caliber Iver Johnson Cadet revolver used to kill Senator Robert Kennedy at close range. We were both pretty good at inventing names for the handgun violence that started to rise in the 1960s and has remained at uncivilized levels ever since. I'm not sure which of the many well-deserved vilifications of the NRA were authored by Ab and which were my doing. In our rhetoric of ridicule, the NRA became the National Ripoff Association. We said that if the street-crime crowd had a lobby organization in Washington, it would be the National Rifle Association. When our coed softball team, the Mikva Marvels, defeated the NRA's squad by a score of 7 to 3, Ab inserted a statement in the *Congressional Record*, which I wrote, saying that the Marvels' margin of victory was similar to the margin by which the American people favored strong handgun control laws. "The weapons for this contest," we noted, "were restricted to baseball bats, gloves, and balls, no doubt putting the NRA at a disadvantage." (I was the captain of the Mikva Marvels, and beating the NRA team was one of the highlights of my athletic career.) Ab initiated congressional investigations of some of the NRA's favorite government-supported subsidies and boondoggles, such as the Civilian Marksmanship program and the Pittman-Robertson Act, which earmarked the excise tax on firearms and ammunition for target-shooting ranges. By the time Ab was nominated for his judgeship, it's fair to say that he was the NRA's least favorite member of Congress.

"I knew that I would be somewhat controversial, but I didn't figure it was going to be that kind of a fight," Ab says to me, referring to his DC Circuit nomination—one of the most unexpectedly politicized judicial appointments of the era. When the Senate Judiciary Committee started its confirmation hearings in July 1979, Ab had a roster of bipartisan heavyweights in his corner: Senator Ted Kennedy, the committee chairman; Joe Biden, who chaired the hearings; Speaker of the House Tip O'Neill; and several influential House Republicans, including minority leader John Rhodes and Illinoisans Bob Michel and Henry Hyde. Ab's old House colleague, former president Jerry Ford, sent a strong letter of support.

Then there was Guy Vander Jagt of Michigan, who told the committee: "I can well understand that people might think it . . . incongruous that a rather conservative Republican is here on behalf of a rather liberal Democrat. In my case it is even more incongruous when you realize I am chairman of the National Republican Congressional Committee charged with electing a Republican candidate in Ab Mikva's district in Illinois. . . . I have made two all-out efforts in 1976 and 1978 and came within a whisker both times." And then, causing some laughter in the committee room, Vander Jagt added what many were thinking: "One might suspect I am here on behalf of the promotion of Ab Mikva to the bench because that is the only way I am ever going to elect a GOP candidate in his seat. . . . I am not here for that reason," Vander Jagt insisted. "I am here because I have a deep and a high personal regard for Ab Mikva as a person, for his integrity, intelligence and for his fairness." I suspect that Vander Jagt was being truthful, mostly. But not many months later, a nice Republican won the special election in Illinois to replace Ab in Congress.

After the congressional lovefest at the Judiciary Committee hearings, a lineup of venom-spouting right-wingers testified that Ab was unfit to be a judge because he was pro-pornography, soft on crime because he opposed long mandatory sentences, and anti-life because he supported legalized abortion. A pro-life witness, a philosophy professor from Niagara University, solemnly suggested "provid[ing] a handgun for every fetus."

But the main attraction was the public face of the NRA: executive vice president Neal Knox. Ab and Knox had tangled some months earlier during an acrimonious debate at Johns Hopkins University. Now the petulant Knox told the committee, "The people I represent here today see Mr. Mikva's views toward them as an affront and his nomination to a federal judgeship as an insult. . . . He is a radical. In his attitude toward firearms owners, Mr. Mikva is a bigot."

Only once in Knox's prepared statement did he mention the Second Amendment, and then only briefly. Knox stated that the NRA did "not believe that government should determine who shall have a firearm . . . [or] censor our personal decision whether we should own any type of firearm, by imposing a prior restraint upon such a purchase." But Knox stayed away from resting his assertions on the Second Amendment—and for good reason. Until the Supreme Court's landmark *Heller* case in 2008, the Court had always concluded that the Second Amendment applied only to militias, not to the individual right to bear arms. That was also the view of the former dean of Harvard Law School, Erwin Griswold, a Republican, who wrote in 1990, "It is time for the NRA and its followers in Congress to stop trying to twist the Second Amendment from a reasoned (if antiquated) empowerment for a militia into a bulletproof personal right."

As Ab and I are talking about his confirmation hearing, we take a detour to the *Heller* case and his thoughts about Justice Antonin Scalia. (Scalia died suddenly in early 2016, after Ab and I had this conversation.) Ab is livid about the *Heller* case and furious with the opinion's author, Scalia, his old colleague on the Court of Appeals. I mention that Scalia recently granted an interview to journalist Marcia Coyle, whose article cites Scalia's belief that his majority opinion in *Heller,* striking down the Washington, DC, ban on handguns, is "the greatest vindication of his originalist approach to constitutional interpretation." To which Ab immediately replies: "I think he's gone mad, I really do. I'm saying this on the record. His cognitive functions are just starting to go down."

And then Ab says to me: "Scalia has pulled the biggest lie ever perpetrated on the judicial landscape and the body politic, the idea that the Second Amendment has anything to do with self-defense. It never was intended as such, it doesn't say that. He just reads out the first dangling participle at the beginning of the clause. He ignores totally the legislative history that exists. And I'm still so angry at John Paul Stevens"—Ab's friend, who wrote the dissent in the 5-to-4 decision—"for an equally long and boring opinion. The *Heller* decision is about this thick," Ab says, spreading his arms. "I used up all of my reading capacity reading it under my magnifying machine. I read both the majority and the dissent and they're both awful. Stevens took on Scalia on everything Scalia said, but he didn't get to the real history. For instance, there was a clause in the original draft protecting conscientious objectors because it was about the militia. They took that out. But it was so clear that the Second Amendment had nothing to do with self-defense. No one ever thought that there was even any chance that Congress or the state legislatures would take away your right to have a rifle. And pistols were mostly arms of the elite. But everybody had a rifle to protect themselves against the Indians and to go hunting and so on. It was not an issue. But the issue as to whether we should have a standing army was very important."

As I listen to Ab, I remember that when the NRA was headquartered in Washington, DC, it conveniently and tellingly displayed only part of the Second Amendment on the side of its building: "the right of the people to keep and bear Arms, shall not be infringed." Nowhere to be seen was the crucial beginning and context: "A well regulated Militia, being necessary to the security of a free State." But since *Heller,* the political discussion in the country has been altered, with nearly every politician piously parroting the opinion that everybody, except for the insane and two-year-old toddlers, has a Second Amendment right to own a gun. "The Second Amendment stuff is complete bullshit," Ab says. And then he adds that his friend Barack Obama, a former professor of constitutional law at the University of Chicago, also knows it's bullshit. "He knows that," Ab says without a trace of doubt.

But at Ab's confirmation hearing, the NRA had more dangerous legal ammunition than the Second Amendment. It argued that Ab was ineligible to become a federal judge because his appointment was prohibited by Article I, section 6, clause 2 of the US Constitution, the so-called emoluments clause. The clause reads in part: "No Senator or Representative shall, during the Time for which he was elected, be appointed to any civil Office under the Authority of the United States, which shall have been created, or the Emoluments whereof shall have been increased during such time." During Ab's current term in Congress, the NRA's Neal Knox told the Judiciary Committee, a cost-of-living pay raise was scheduled to go into effect for certain government employees, including federal judges. It didn't matter whether Ab had voted for it; the pay raise—the emolument—was due to go into effect on October 1, during Ab's congressional term. Therefore, Knox said, Ab was constitutionally prohibited from becoming a federal judge.

The NRA tried to marshal support from legal scholars to legitimize its constitutional argument. Ab found out the NRA offered Phil Kurland, a prominent conservative lawyer and professor at the University of Chicago Law School, $10,000 to testify, but he refused. But, Kurland told Ab, he thought the NRA was right about the emoluments clause. "Then the NRA went to a Northwestern professor," Ab says. "They offered him only $5,000 because he was only at Northwestern. He had been one of my daughter Mary's favorite professors. After he agreed to testify and was on the witness list, he came to Mary and told her he wasn't going to do it. He was getting heat from his colleagues. Then he told Mary, 'I hope you realize that I'm not going to testify even though I think the NRA may have been right because of my admiration for you. I didn't want to hurt your father. You understand, don't you?' And Mary, bless her, said, 'Sure I do. You're a son of a bitch.'"

With a Democratic majority on the Judiciary Committee, Ab had assumed his nomination would be approved and sent to the Senate for a vote before the August congressional recess. But it wasn't so simple. The NRA's emoluments argument had become credible, and it was inadvertently buttressed by a Justice Department advisory memo. Although Justice Department lawyers argued that there was nothing in the emoluments clause per se that would make Ab ineligible, the memo was ambiguous, at best, about the constitutionality of the nomination if Ab were confirmed after the pay raise went into effect on October 1. Because the pay raise was only *scheduled* to take effect on October 1, it did not become a fact until then, the Justice Department concluded. Or, in nonlawyerly language, Abner Mikva would turn into a pumpkin unless he were confirmed before October 1. Rather suddenly, the Mikva nomination was in trouble. Strom Thurmond, the ranking Republican on the Judiciary Committee, wanted the committee vote postponed until September. The old Dixiecrat from South Carolina suspected Ab may have been a Communist.

But Thurmond and the Republicans could not have sidetracked the process without help from the NRA-friendly Senate majority leader, Robert Byrd of West Virginia. According to what Ab heard, it seems that one of President Carter's aides went to see Byrd about scheduling floor time for the Mikva nomination. "You know, the president is really for this guy," the aide told Byrd. To which the courtly senator replied, "I don't give a shit. The president doesn't vote in my state, and my people don't like people who take their guns away." Ted Kennedy then delivered the bad news to Ab: the committee vote was going to be postponed until September. Maybe by then, Kennedy said unconvincingly, the heat generated by the NRA will have cooled down a bit.

Ab and his family spent most of the August recess at their vacation house in the Indiana Dunes. He called me one day, and I had never heard him sound so defeated. Maybe this was after he got a call from his old House Republican friend from Mississippi, Thad Cochran, who was now on the Senate Judiciary Committee. I didn't know about the call then, but Ab tells me now that Cochran tracked him down in the Dunes because he thought the nomination was in big trouble. "Thad said, 'Ab, right now the vote in committee would be 7 to 6, and I'm the seventh. If you think I'm comfortable being the only Republican voting for you and making the difference—you better get your ass back here and tell Kennedy to get working.'" Back then, I could hear how pessimistic he was, and I said something insipidly cheery, like, "I'm sure you'll get confirmed in September." To which Ab replied morosely, "If you believe that, I have a bridge I'll sell you."

Ab and some friends started working on several anti-Mikva Democrats on the Judiciary Committee. They managed to flip two of them, one of whom was a Jewish senator from Florida, Richard Stone. "They got the condo ladies on his ass," Ab says with a laugh. When Congress reconvened in September, the Judiciary Committee approved Ab's nomination by a vote of 9 to 6. But the critical question was whether the nomination would make it to the Senate floor before October 1. The Judiciary Committee had voted on September 11. If the NRA could stall the vote for nineteen days, it could claim a big victory. And NRA members, more than a million of them, were flooding Senate offices with anti-Mikva mail.

Ted Kennedy told Ab he had better talk to Strom Thurmond. "He's not going to vote for you," Kennedy said, "but he's raising a lot of hell about your nomination. Call him and calm him down." So one day, Thurmond's guy, Duke Short, came to see Ab. According to Ab, "Duke's opening line was, 'I want to let you know that the senator doesn't think you're a Communist, but he thinks you have a lot of Communist ties.'" When Ab asked why Thurmond would think that, Duke responded that there were some things in Ab's FBI file. "That can't be," Ab answered, "because I wrote to [J. Edgar] Hoover and asked him for a copy of my file. All it had were nasty letters I had written to him and his curt responses." Then Duke said maybe the files had come from the House Un-American Activities Committee. And Ab said, "We got rid of that committee and the files had to be destroyed." Duke replied that maybe the files had been copied. When Ab asked to see the photocopies, Duke said he couldn't show them to Ab, but he'd read the files to him. "Oh, before he read it to me," Ab remembers, "he asked me if I knew so-and-so. I said yeah, he was a professor at the University of Chicago and active in Hyde Park. According to Duke, he and others in the files were all members of a Communist cell. Several people had been on my campaign committee when I first ran for the state legislature. They were discussing my candidacy. At one point, someone said, 'Well, he's a Goddamn social democrat, but he's better than the machine thugs,' or something like that. So they agreed to support me. I never knew anything about that. I knew these people were for me and some of them were considered left-wingers. They were probably names that you ran across when you were writing your Alinsky biography because they were friends of Alinsky. I can't remember their names. Anyhow, that was the rap on me."

"That's some story," I say to Ab, trying to visualize the creepy scene of Strom Thurmond's guy sitting in Ab's congressional office and dishing dirt from the 1950s. "What happened after Short left?" I ask.

"Duke kind of went with the flow," Ab surmises. "He was no more interested in who was a Communist or who wasn't. But he sort of understood that I was Kennedy's friend and that Strom ought to pull back. So there was an understanding at some point that Strom just voted against me but didn't block me."

Ab made a personal lobbying visit to every senator who would agree to see him and whose vote was in doubt. One of those senators was S. I. Hayakawa, a conservative Republican from California. I knew Don Hayakawa, as his friends called him, from my graduate-student days at San Francisco State College. He was a renowned professor of general semantics and a political liberal when I knew him. He liked me because I introduced him to a couple of pretty girls who lived in my apartment building. Several years later, he became president of San Francisco State during the campus protests of the late 1960s. He squashed the student protests, became a hero to Reagan Republicans, and reinvented himself as a conservative. I thought Ab was wasting his time seeing Hayakawa. I was wrong, which taught me not to assume anything in politics. Don and Ab hit it off. Ab told me they talked about their days at the University of Chicago, where Hayakawa was a lecturer in the 1950s. Hayakawa found Ab to be a man of substance, and he voted to confirm him.

Ab also received an unexpected visit from Senator Orrin Hatch, the Utah Republican, who just showed up at his office one day. Why he came was a mystery. Maybe it had something to do with Hatch's friendship with Ted Kennedy. Hatch said that Ab was a good man, and Hatch's reason for voting against his confirmation was nothing personal; it was all about the NRA. And then, Ab tells me, Hatch assured him that if the Senate vote were close and Ab needed him, he'd be there for Ab. About Hatch's unctuous promise, Ab says, "If he couldn't be for me when it didn't matter, I somehow doubt that he'd be for me when it really made a difference."

The NRA came up short. In Washington, it's impossible to measure an organization's influence or power with precision, so it's unclear why the NRA had to settle for much less than the full monty. In any event, somebody worked out a face-saving deal so the NRA could claim it wasn't a big loser—which it was—when the Mikva nomination went to the Senate floor for a vote before October 1. To this day, Ab can only guess why he beat the clock. "Here's what happened, I think, on the time business," Ab says about the deal that was brokered. "The NRA got [Idaho Senator James] McClure to lead the Senate fight against me. He said that he was going to filibuster against the nomination. Kennedy went to McClure. He persuaded him that, ultimately, we'll get cloture, plus, it's silly to do cloture on a judicial nomination. Kennedy told McClure, we'll give you an amendment so you'll have an opportunity to sue in court on the emoluments issue." The amendment was short and to the point: it established standing for any member of Congress to bring suit against anybody appointed to the Court of Appeals for the District of Columbia who had been a member of Congress. It could apply to only one person. "Except for my middle initial," Ab says sarcastically, "it was a bill of attainder." He remembers when Kennedy called to tell him about the deal. "He told me to tell Tip that it's OK, that Kennedy put it on a rider to some bill. The rider, of course, would have to pass the House, too. I went to see Tip," Ab says, referring to House Speaker Tip O'Neill. "Tip said, 'Goddamn it. I'm not going to let my people vote for that kind of crap. The hell with them.' I said, 'Tip, I don't get a vote on my judgeship if we don't pass it.'" So the amendment was quickly passed by the Senate and the House, and on Tuesday, September 24, the Mikva nomination finally went to the Senate floor.

During the debate, Kennedy took the lead and spoke eloquently about Ab's exceptional "ability, sensitivity, and, perhaps most important, integrity." Several other Democrats also praised Ab's record, but a small, pleasant surprise was an apparently principled endorsement by Senator James Exon, a Nebraska Democrat. Some Democrats from the West and South, where the NRA was strongest, thought it would just be easier to vote against Mikva, as Exon himself acknowledged. In fact, Ed Zorinsky, his Democratic colleague from Nebraska, had taken the easy way out. But Exon told the Senate, "The easy vote is not necessarily the correct one." Stating that Ab was well qualified to be a judge, Exon said it troubled him that the "National Rifle Association has sounded the alarm across America on this nomination" based solely on one issue: gun control. He said, although "I find myself generally in sympathy with the goals and aims of the NRA . . . , to cast a negative vote on this nomination for that single reason would not . . . be prudent and would set up criteria for future judicial confirmation processes that would deal a devastating blow to the foundations of our judicial and constitutional guarantees. The right of dissent and thoughtful discussion remains fundamental to our system."

The floor debate ended with Senator McClure's laundry list of objections, ranging from the emoluments issue to Ab's intemperate views about the gun lobby. "So intense is Mikva's anti-NRA bias," McClure began his peroration, "that a purely recreational softball game between his staff and the NRA's became the subject of a *Congressional Record* insert." And then this otherwise obscure senator, hailing from a state best known for a potato, read from beginning to end what I had written for the *Congressional Record* about the Mikva Marvels' historic victory. The Marvels had been immortalized!

Ab was confirmed by a vote of 58 to 31. Without the NRA's campaign, a popular, respected member of Congress probably would have been confirmed unanimously. Ab recalls not only the 58-to-31 vote but also which Democrats voted with the NRA. One of the scaredy-cats who wouldn't risk the NRA's wrath was a Senate heavyweight, Democrat Frank Church of Idaho. It apparently didn't help him; he was defeated for reelection the next year. I say "apparently" because there is rarely solid evidence that the NRA can mobilize enough single-issue voters to elect or defeat candidates. For decades, the NRA has thrived on its bully-boy reputation. Too often, members of Congress are afraid to call the bully's bluff. In the case of Ab's nomination, southern and western Democrats and Republicans who voted for the Mikva nomination—Thad Cochran (R-MI), Sam Nunn (D-GA), Jack Danforth (R-MO), Dale Bumpers (D-AR), Nancy Kassebaum (R-KS), Fritz Hollings (D-SC), and others—were not defeated by the NRA when they ran for reelection.

Ab remembers that immediately after the Senate vote, "they literally hand-carried the confirmation to the White House. They wanted it signed because they were concerned that somebody might move to have the vote reconsidered." Ab was quickly sworn in, just ahead of the lawsuit McClure filed in Idaho. Ab, the lawyer and jurist, says, "They knew so little about what they were doing. They sent the lawsuit to a three-judge court. If it had gone in the regular way to a district judge, it's likely that it would have gone to a judge that McClure had appointed in Idaho."

"Why did it end up in a three-judge court?" I ask Ab.

"Because in the rider they said it should go to a special constitutional three-judge court, which consists of a circuit judge and two district court judges. The three-judge court is, in effect, a trial court and an appellate court. Since it was a three-judge court, it had to be three judges, including one from the circuit, who was a wonderful Ninth Circuit judge. One of the judges was one of McClure's boys. They ruled that McClure didn't have standing because the issue had already been decided by the Senate when it confirmed me, and therefore there was no standing. There was no way Congress could confer standing about a constitutional matter. The Constitution says that the president shall nominate, the Senate shall confirm, and once that's done, that's all she wrote."

As Ab and I near the end of our discussion about his Senate confirmation battle, I ask him, "If you were fifty-four years old again, and your friend Barack Obama nominated you for the DC Circuit, what would the result be?"

Ab's answer is short but not sweet: "He wouldn't nominate me," he says in a flat, joyless voice. "If there is one person who can claim a closeness to him and a responsibility for his election, I can. And I'd like to think that I had the credentials besides, but he wouldn't nominate me." I ask him why, struck as much by Ab's sad expression as by his words. "I was controversial. I was considered an outspoken liberal." And these days, Ab adds, "any senator can threaten a filibuster, and that blocks the nomination. Barack's administration does not feel that they should use up chits on controversial nominees. So what you get are nominees who have never lifted their heads above the trenches on anything."

Abner Mikva's graduation photo from Washington High School in Milwaukee, 1943.

Zoe and Ab's wedding, September 19, 1948.

University of Chicago graduates: Zoe receives an MA and Ab completes law school, 1951.

Supreme Court Justice Sherman Minton and his law clerk Abner Mikva, about 1951.

Zoe and Ab with, *in the foreground*, Ab's sister, Rose, her daughter Rhona, and parents Ida and Henry Mikva, early 1950s.

Zoe and Ab with their daughters Laurie, Rachel, and Mary in Hyde Park, late 1950s.

Campaigning on Chicago's South Side, mid-1960s.

Congressman Mikva at a
public hearing with aide
Jack Marco, about 1971.

Ab sitting between Senator Robert F. Kennedy and Chicago Mayor Richard J. Daley, Ab's political nemesis, early 1968.

Ab with his former law firm colleague, Arthur Goldberg, who later became a US Supreme Court Justice, late 1960s.

When Ab was serving his second term in Congress, he helped Senator Edward Kennedy, *left*, pass the Twenty-Sixth Amendment in 1971, which lowered the voting age to eighteen, late 1960s or early 1970s.

Thomas "Tip" O'Neill, Speaker of the US House of Representatives, relied on Ab for political advice, 1977.

The coed Mikva Marvels softball team, composed of Ab's congressional staff and their friends, defeated the National Rifle Association team, 7 to 3, a symbolic victory for gun control advocates like Congressman Mikva, 1977.

President Jimmy Carter at a rally to reelect Congressman Mikva, Skokie, Illinois, 1978.

Another defeat for the NRA when the gun lobby failed to block Ab's nomination to the US Court of Appeals for the DC Circuit. Ab and his former congressional aide Sandy Horwitt celebrate after Ab took the oath of office, 1979.

The Mikvas with US Senator Paul Simon, Ab's old friend and roommate in the 1950s and 1960s when they were in the Illinois state legislature in Springfield, 1990s.

Ab and Zoe with First Lady Hillary Clinton and President Clinton, at the White House when Ab was White House counsel, 1994.

Ab with Barack Obama and Ab's old friend Newton Minow in Newt's Chicago law office in December 2006, when Senator Obama was considering a presidential candidacy. According to Minow, Obama "wanted Ab and me to advise how could he be a good father and still campaign."

Zoe and Ab with some of the thousands of urban high school students in Chicago and, later, in other cities, who are inspired by the nonpartisan Mikva Challenge to participate in civic and political affairs and discover a voice about issues they care about.

Ab, Zoe, and Mikva Challenge students from Chicago campaigning for Barack Obama in the Iowa presidential caucus, late 2007 or early 2008.

Ab and Zoe in Washington with, *left to right*, Senator Amy Klobuchar, Representative Jan Schakowsky, Senator Dick Durbin, and his wife, Loretta, about 2008.

In Milwaukee to celebrate Washington High School's centennial in 2011, Ab meets friends Len and Ruth Zubrensky at Jake's Delicatessen, 2011.

Ab's family joins him at the White House where he received the Presidential Medal of Freedom. *From left to right*: Laurie Mikva, Jordan Cohen, Jake Mikva, Michelle Obama, Mary Mikva, Abner Mikva, Barack Obama, Steve Cohen, Rachel Mikva, Mark Rosenberg, Rebecca Cohen, 2014.

Ab with his protégé, Judge Merrick Garland, and his former law clerk, US Supreme Court Justice Elena Kagan, at a party celebrating the Presidential Medal of Freedom Ab received from President Obama, 2014.

Mikva grandchildren with Zoe and Ab, 2002.

8

Politicians in Black Robes and Judge Mikva's Proudest Decision

Ab is breathing heavily after walking about forty feet from the men's room back to our breakfast booth at The Bagel. When we return to his apartment later that April morning, two years into our conversations, I ask about his breathing. "My breathing is just short," he replies. "As you know, I have COPD and sometimes I get very short of breath doing nothing. And when I try to exercise in physical therapy downstairs, they put this thing on me. If my oxygen reading goes down, they make me stop." Ab takes me into his office and shows me a small plastic device he uses to measure his oxygen level. He clips the device onto his left index finger. "It measures the percentage of oxygen you're getting," he tells me. "What does it say?" I look and see that the top number is 92 over 64. "That's good," he says. "Anything above 90 is fine." His doctor wants him to consider using a portable oxygen tank, but he won't. I don't ask, but I suspect it's because of vanity and his refusal to give in to the indignities of old age.

The walls of his small office are adorned with framed photographs, including one of Ab and President Clinton in golfing attire. Then I notice his brightly lit computer screen. "Can you read the words on that screen?" I ask.

"Barely," he says. "And that's enlarged." I notice the magnification is set to 325 percent. "I can't see the whole screen at once," Ab answers. That's because he has macular degeneration. "You don't have peripheral vision," Ab explains. "I have a little bit of peripheral vision. I can see the screen better this way," and he turns his head to the right while rolling his eyes to the left and looking back at the computer screen. By memory as much as by his limited sight, he's able to find a link on the screen for today's *New York Times*. "I click on that and I drag it over to where it says Abner Mikva. I download and then it's on my iPod. I get about fifty minutes' worth of the *New York Times*. And I read my books the same way." He's cheerful about all this, noting that he's "reading" more books these days than he has in years. I find his cheerfulness about his near blindness reassuring. He says he's lucky that he can benefit from new technology like the iPod. But not everything he wants to read is available on audio. He points to the older technology near his computer. It's an enhanced-vision reader machine that magnifies a printed page. "It's a marvelous machine," Ab says, "but I can only see a few words at a time." Last week, he says, he used it to read an article in the *American Prospect* about his friend Supreme Court Justice Elena Kagan. "But then the bulb burned out, and I was blind for a week," he joked.

A few weeks after Ab's hurried, unceremonious swearing in to beat the McClure lawsuit, there was a reenactment and celebration at the US Courthouse. I have a lovely photo of Ab and me on that occasion, he in his brand-new judge's robe and both of us wearing triumphant smiles and the longish sideburns that were still fashionable at the end of the 1970s. Looking at the photo now, however, I'm reminded of Barber Conable's stricken face when he heard that Ab was leaving Congress for the bench. Becoming a judge, even on the second most important court in the country, was not Ab's preference. We didn't dwell on the topic in our conversations, but at one of our early breakfasts at The Bagel, Ab says, "I liked being on the court. I enjoyed it and thought it was interesting work. It was intellectually stimulating. But it didn't have the same excitement or creativity that I felt in Congress, where I really felt that I could help make things happen." I remember that when I occasionally visited Ab in his oh-so-quiet chambers, the only signs of electricity were the lightbulbs. This was not Abner Mikva's preferred habitat, I thought.

One December morning I pick up Ab at the Hallmark. Actually, it's been renamed the Brookdale by the national company of the same name, but everything else, including the crummy food, is unchanged. Wearing his winter down jacket, and not being as flexible as he used to be, Ab struggles to fasten the seat belt. I help and mumble something about car safety devices having their pluses and minuses. "Airbag Abner," he suddenly says. It was the title of a typically snarky *Wall Street Journal* editorial chastising Ab for one of his early decisions on the Court of Appeals after Reagan became president. Ab tells me about the decision. "When Reagan had come into office—remember that his big pitch was to get government off our backs? So he issued an executive order revoking all the rules that had not yet become final requiring the auto manufacturers to install airbags. The insurance company State Farm opposed the revocation and brought a case. It's interesting; the insurance companies are very much safety inclined."

"Because it reduces their costs," I say.

"Right. So they brought the case," Ab continues, "and I held that you can't get rid of a rule any differently than you can when you put it in in the first place." In other words, there's a reasonable public rule-making process that has to be followed, and a president can't arbitrarily short-circuit it. "The Supreme Court upheld me, and the *Wall Street Journal* was furious," Ab says. "'Airbag Abner' they called me," he says, laughing.

I begin to get a better sense of how Ab approached his role as a judge not only from the cases we discussed but also from how he selected his clerks and the qualities he valued. It wasn't merely a matter of high IQ—any serious applicant for a clerkship on Ab's court was likely to be smart. He begins by telling me about one of his clerks who had all the apparent credentials but wasn't, as it turned out, what Ab wanted.

Although Ab talks about him by name, I'll use a pseudonym: Frank. "Frank was president of the *Harvard Law Review*," Ab begins, "which I have to admit had a lot to do with my choosing him. If you didn't know anything else about law students in the country, the president of the *HLR* is more likely to be a bright, bright guy than anybody else you can pick. I was a good feeder at the time for Supreme Court clerkships. But a lot of the other feeders on my court turned him down. So I picked him, even though the personal interview didn't go too well. But sometimes they're shy, uncomfortable. I usually chose kids directly out of law school. Some of my colleagues wanted them to have a district clerkship first. I thought that two years of clerking was enough, one year with me and one year with the Supremes. Anyway, he was a so-so clerk."

"Why was that?" I ask.

Ab begins to explain the politics of judging, which, being an inveterate politician, he values highly. "Appellate court judging is in some ways the best example of how compromising and finding common ground should work. Because as a single judge [on a three-judge appeals court panel], you can't do a thing." He mentions his old friend William Brennan, the long-serving Supreme Court justice, who used to say, Ab paraphrases, "What's the first rule of the Supreme Court? You got to get five votes." As an appellate court judge, Ab says, "You have to know that you're going to have at least one more person with you. And you have to know if you want the opinion to be meaningful, to have an influence on the law. You have to reckon how it's going to sit with academia, with other judges that you think are your peers, whether it's going to be appealed to the Supremes and how they're going to handle it, and so on. A lot of those things you have to anticipate in advance, because if you wait until after you've written the decision to measure those things, you may not have a majority."

In listening to Ab, I begin to understand that, given the political chess match he's describing, he would have found being an appeals court judge in Washington more satisfying than I used to think. Political chess, however, was not the strong suit of Ab's otherwise brilliant *Harvard Law Review* clerk. Frank, Ab says, "was totally unaware, well, not unaware, but incapable of handling that. If he would write a memo for me, it would be pure law, without regard to any of the ebbing and flowing and backing and forthing that legal doctrine has. And when he wrote on a hot subject where maybe I didn't have a second judge with me, or if the rest of the court might en banc my decision and overturn it, Frank still wrote a pure decision. 'This *is* the law, this *is* the way it ought to be.' And sometimes, and I don't want to make him sound like a purist, but he frequently said, 'This is what the law should be,'" Ab says, laughing. In contrast, Ab mentions two of his other clerks. "Elena," he says with a smile, referring to future Supreme Court Justice Elena Kagan, "understood the ebbs and flows almost too well. And James Castello was perfect. He understood the ebbs and flows but also understood that for me, there were hard lines I wouldn't go beyond."

Ab received hundreds of applications for clerkships each year, in part because he became known as a feeder for the Supreme Court—that is, some of the justices chose their clerks from among Ab's. "I had Brennan and [Thurgood] Marshall and [Harry] Blackmun and [John] Stevens as justices who would look especially favorably at my clerks because they knew I chose carefully and because they knew I sought high competence." I'm not surprised that the justices he mentioned were among the Court's liberals. Did that mean he was looking for "liberal" answers from his clerks?

For some reason, I think about John Yoo, the conservative lawyer who became famous, or infamous, for writing his "torture memos" while working in the Justice Department's Office of Legal Counsel (OLC) during the Bush-Cheney administration. He conveniently provided legal rationales for the "enhanced interrogation techniques," including water boarding, employed by the CIA and embraced by Vice President Dick Cheney. I ask Ab if he remembers Yoo. "Oh yes, I remember him very well," he says. I tell Ab that my impression, as a lay citizen, was that Yoo wrote opinions that the White House and Cheney wanted to see. Ab responds by contrasting what the lawyer's role should be at the OLC with what it was during the Bush-Cheney years. "If the head of the OLC is tempering his or her opinions because they are worried about a subsequent subpoena, then the president isn't getting the best advice," Ab says. "If you want complete candor and honesty from your subordinates, then you don't want to have them worry about who is looking over their shoulder. But John Yoo was a crazy ideologue."

"An ideologue and a partisan," I say to Ab.

"He was a partisan," Ab says. "He was appointed to give legal dressing to these outrageous, illegal views of Dick Cheney. And he did. Cheney should have been impeached."

Recently I met one of Ab's former clerks, Jeffrey Bleich, who went on to clerk for the conservative chief justice William Rehnquist. How often did that happen? I wonder. "Not too often," Ab replies. Ab and Rehnquist knew each other when they were both law clerks at the Supreme Court. Ab tells me that when Bleich went to clerk for Rehnquist, Bleich said, "'Mr. Justice, Judge Mikva asked me to give you this.' And he hands him a copy of the Constitution. And Rehnquist, who has a pretty good sense of humor, smiled and says, 'Yeah, I bet he thinks I never read it.' Rehnquist flips through it and says, 'Well, as your former boss knows, he and I agree on one amendment to the Constitution, the Third.' The Third is you can't keep troops in private homes except in time of war."

Ab had a fatherly fondness for most of his clerks. To broaden their horizons, he took them on mini–field trips. One was a visit to the Lorton Reformatory, a prison used by the District of Columbia until it was closed in 2001. Located in nearby Lorton, Virginia, it was overcrowded and had an unsavory history. Ab told his clerks he wanted prison officials to know that a federal judge had his eye on Lorton. On other occasions, he took the clerks for lunch in the Members' Dining Room in Congress, followed by a short tour of the Capitol. And Sheryll Cashin remembers attending her first Passover Seder at the Mikvas' Capitol Hill townhouse.

A new experience for most of his clerks was drafting an opinion without using footnotes. "Do you know my reputation on footnotes?" Ab asks me one day.

"I had heard that you became an absolutist," I say, without knowing the details.

"Footnotes always bothered me," he says. "There is this famous story about footnote 4 in the *Caroline Products* case when the Supreme Court inserted a whole doctrine of law in the footnote that overwhelmed the decision. I don't like to read footnotes. They're distractions. Well, one day in the early 1980s, I think, Stephen Breyer and I were having lunch with Arthur Goldberg. This, of course, was after Goldberg had been on the Supreme Court. Arthur was expostulating on how judges' opinions had become too long because the law clerks were allowed to do too much, they kept putting more into footnotes, they were mischievous, and so on. After lunch, Breyer and I were walking back to my courthouse, and we agreed that we should stop using footnotes." Ab told his clerks: no more footnotes. They were skeptical, to put it mildly. "They said, 'Well, you're a new judge and you're going to be measured by the top law schools, and the footnotes are a sort of measure of the scholarship that goes into the opinion.' I said, 'That's ridiculous.' And later I wrote a law review article, 'Goodbye to Footnotes,' that was very well received."

"When you were picking clerks," I ask, "if someone you interviewed was as strong a conservative as Elena Kagan was a liberal, is that someone you would not gravitate to?"

"That depends," he begins. "I didn't have a real litmus test. So, if he or she was a member of the Federalist Society or argued against *Roe v. Wade* philosophically, that wouldn't necessarily have been a disqualifier. But no question, as we talked and they made it clear that they didn't like Roosevelt or Carter or Clinton, obviously it would influence me." But Ab did have something close to a litmus test when it came to the Constitution. "I don't know what I would have done about someone who was terrific in almost every other respect but who claimed to view the Constitution as strictly as Scalia claims to view it. The idea that you measure the words as they were measured in 1787 would bother me."

Although Ab selected clerks with whom he was philosophically comfortable, he insists that their legal competence and honesty were most important. "I was looking for integrity that would have them give me the best analysis they could come up with, independent of what the political consequences were or what they thought I wanted to hear," he tells me. "I had a couple of clerks who had a political outlook on many things that were different than mine. I wanted them to give me not their opinions but their best work based on what they knew about the arguments and legal issues. I would say that, with very few exceptions, I think my clerks lived up to that."

But when Ab was a young Supreme Court clerk in 1952, he learned a lasting lesson: judges sometimes, if not often, make decisions for political reasons. "I hope I haven't already told you this," Ab begins as we're having breakfast at The Bagel one day. "It's one of my favorite anecdotes." He starts to tell me about a school desegregation case that preceded the momentous *Brown v. Board of Education* decision in 1954 by two years. Civil rights lawyer Thurgood Marshall, Ab says, "was pushing that 'separate but equal' was inherently unconstitutional. We got the case late in the year." As the Court's term was winding down, the clerks hadn't heard anything about a decision. "Very few justices told their clerks what the state of negotiations was. We never knew. Well, we used to have a custom of inviting a different justice down to lunch once a month. We had our own dining room so we could talk about Court business without being overheard. This was May of 1952, and the equivalent of *Brown v. Board* had been argued, but nothing is coming out. We had Justice Frankfurter down for lunch, and one of the clerks said, 'Mr. Justice, why isn't the Court acting on the school desegregation case?' Frankfurter looked at us—all white males, of course—and said that it would be a mistake to decide the case in the middle of the presidential election. That if we come down with this momentous decision, the two candidates will choose up sides. Neither one will have read the opinion, and we'll be in a civil war. Well, all the clerks were aghast that the Court would hold up its decision because there was an election going on," Ab says, his emotional tone re-creating the clerks' incredulity and disapproval.

In retrospect, Ab came to appreciate Frankfurter's wisdom, enhanced perhaps by fortuitous events. In 1952 the Court almost certainly would have produced a divided opinion under Chief Justice Frederick Vinson, rather than the unanimous decision his successor, Earl Warren, orchestrated in 1954. With the force of that powerful decision, President Eisenhower, who had refrained from endorsing the *Brown* decision, nevertheless federalized the Arkansas National Guard in 1957 to ensure that nine black students could attend the all-white Central High School in Little Rock, despite opposition by the Arkansas governor. It was a pivotal event in the civil rights movement and for the country. Eisenhower did not favor court-mandated integration, but "it was the law of the land," Ab says, "and he obeyed it. Back when we had that lunch discussion with Frankfurter, all of us, including his own clerks, thought delaying the decision was a dreadful example of the Court being political. With the hindsight of sixty-some years, Frankfurter was right."

In some respects, Ab has a similar analysis of the politics involved in the Supreme Court's 1973 decision that legalized abortion. His first objection about *Roe v. Wade*, he tells me, is that "the country wasn't ready for it. We were starting to move in that direction slowly—I'd passed a bill out of the Illinois house that got rid of our anti-abortion law. And in the 1960s New York and California had passed laws. In fact, I have a picture somewhere in my files of Governor Ronald Reagan signing a pro-abortion bill with all the legislators around him and with a quote underneath the photo to the effect that 'this law will get abortions out of the back alleys and into hospitals where they belong.'" Yes, I remember that too. In 1967, shortly after Reagan was elected governor, he signed the Therapeutic Abortion Act. He later said, after the anti-abortion movement found a home in the Republican Party, that he had made a big mistake and regretted that decision more than any other.

But "that's the way the game is supposed to be played," Ab says, referring to how the political process has to move forward before the Supreme Court steps in with a ruling. Ruth Bader Ginsburg, Ab's colleague on the Court of Appeals and now a Supreme Court justice, had a similar view on the abortion issue. Ab says, "I think that if the Court had allowed it to continue in the political process, as we all assumed it would before *Roe v. Wade*, then we would have built the kind of national constituency for legalizing abortion that would have allowed it to become law in most northern states. We never would have gotten it through the South or some of the western states. But it would have been the law in enough of the country that either the Court could have taken it or maybe Congress would have passed a national law. The political consequences would not have been enormous, just the way same-sex marriage has become almost a nonissue as state legislatures have moved through it. Now when the Supreme Court comes out with a pro–same-sex-marriage law, the country is ready for it." Instead, Ab says, the Supreme Court's premature ruling in 1973 led to a "tremendous uproar." When Ab was in the Illinois legislature, he recalls, the mail he received was at least as likely to support his pro-choice position as oppose it. But "once the Court came out with *Roe v. Wade*, do you remember what the mail was like in Washington? There was this ton of mail because the antis had an issue. *Roe v. Wade* made a big political difference because we've lost a lot of good political horseflesh. Good people have lost House and Senate races on this issue."

Ab's second objection is about the argumentation in *Roe v. Wade*. He says, "With all due respect to my good friend Justice Blackmun," who wrote the decision, "it was a terrible decision technically. He tried to say it was science, that it was based on the science of when a baby is viable. But science has overwhelmed his argument. Babies are viable—I don't know about the first trimester, but they certainly are by the second trimester. Plus, it wasn't an evolutionary decision. He tried to evolve it out of *Griswold*," Ab says, referring to *Griswold v. Connecticut*, which found that the Constitution ensures a right to privacy. "But it just doesn't follow *Griswold*, it really doesn't. This is an altogether different issue. The right to privacy from government intrusion is altogether different than a fundamental religious concept that is at the heart of the debate about abortion. So the Court took this huge leap forward from very shaky ground."

But Ab has discovered that his legal and political critique of *Roe v. Wade* is often not appreciated, even in his own family. "I learned from my daughters, if not from political events, that if you don't defend it but agree with the result, then you're nitpicking about an issue that people feel very strongly about. Mary and Laurie just used to beat the hell out of me whenever it would come up. They'd say, 'You're going to let all these women die while you're messing around with the legislature, is that what you're arguing?'"

I say to Ab, "So, as two smart lawyers, your daughters just dismissed your position?"

"They were outraged," Ab says. "They think my position is crazy, that the Supreme Court did the right thing. So it wasn't the best crafted decision, they say. They consider that a technicality. They believe that *Roe v. Wade* was an important, fundamental good that was done by the Court."

"For Mary and Laurie," I say, "it's a moral question of means and ends."

"Yes," Ab says. "If you're a woman and a liberal woman, you feel very strongly about this."

"Well," I say, "I don't want to take sides in your family, but on another life-and-death issue, assisted suicide, I remember that you said some years ago it wasn't ripe for the Supreme Court to take it up. Isn't that justice delayed, and therefore the Supreme Court is not really concerned with justice?"

To which Ab replies: "It *is* about justice, but you're talking about *social justice*, not justice in an individual case. If you're talking about some broad principle for our whole society, then you've got to have the people behind you. You can't just deliver it from on high when judges are not on Mount Olympus but on Constitution Avenue—no, the Supremes are not even on Constitution Avenue, they're on First Street," and he laughs about the pedestrian-sounding address where the merely mortal justices do their work.

"It seems like you believe," I say to Ab, "that the Supreme Court should follow the election returns. You know who the author of that is?" I ask.

"Yes, Dunne," Ab says. "The Constitution may follow the flag, but the Supreme Court follows the election returns," he quotes Chicagoan Finley Peter Dunne almost verbatim.

"That's what you're advocating?" I ask.

"Yes, yes. But again, if you're talking about somebody having a bad trial who is about to be executed, then I'm for a minimal decision that saves the guy's life. But you don't expand on that to say therefore capital punishment is abolished unless the country is for it."

When Ab mentions capital punishment, which we both oppose, it reminds me of the execution of Ricky Lee Rector. Ab remembers it too. Rector was convicted of murder in Arkansas. By the time of his scheduled execution in January 1992, Rector was so mentally impaired that he said he was going to save the pecan pie from his last meal until after the execution. Arkansas governor Bill Clinton, who was campaigning for president at the time, could have stopped the execution. Ab cuts in and picks up the story: "Clinton went back to Arkansas from his campaign and signed the execution papers."

"Yes," I say, "and there are people like Rector who die because it's permitted. Are we talking about something other than justice in these situations?"

"No," Ab replies, "because that's an example of it coming out exactly the wrong way because Clinton did exactly the wrong thing. He should have kept that guy from being executed. He was for capital punishment, or so he said. The real Bill Clinton is not for capital punishment. He thought that was a political necessity in Arkansas. On the other hand, I don't think a governor on his own should refuse to execute people. If you're elected, that's part of the law. Persuade the legislature to change it, as they have in Illinois." Yes, since Barack Obama served in the state senate, Illinois has abolished capital punishment. It took more than a century after a young Clarence Darrow, one of Ab's early heroes, introduced a bill in 1903 to abolish it—and it took half a century to abolish it after Ab introduced his own Darrow-like bill.

When Ab became a judge, many of his fans, including me, hoped there would be a Supreme Court nomination in his future. And it might have happened had not Jimmy Carter been defeated for reelection, followed by twelve years of Republicans in the White House. Two of Ab's colleagues on the Court of Appeals were nominated by Ronald Reagan while Ab was on the bench: Antonin Scalia in 1986 and Robert Bork in 1987. Scalia and Bork shared a similar conservative philosophy, but Scalia was confirmed unanimously by the US Senate, while Bork encountered a ferocious liberal campaign to defeat him. And much to my surprise, Ab supported Bork's controversial nomination.

I hear the backstory one summer day when Ab and I are touring his old Hyde Park neighborhood. He points to an apartment where he and Zoe lived when Ab was in law school and mentions that Bork lived nearby, on Hyde Park Boulevard. "We were classmates and friends," Ab says. "He was as far to the left when he was in law school as he became far to the right. When he was called back to the Marine Corps during the Korean War, he was so mad that he talked about leaving for Canada. We talked him out of it. Reluctantly, he went back into the marines. According to his account, they straightened him out. And he came back totally the reverse of what he had been politically. Before the marines, he was the head of the student lawyers' guild, which was left wing."

After law school, when both Ab and Bork were practicing law in Chicago, they and their wives played bridge on Friday nights. "He had married this wonderful Jewish woman, Claire Davidson," Ab says. "She remained liberal. When we played bridge, he would think of the most provocative things to say to upset the three of us. He'd say, 'You know, if you cut off welfare all at once, the fittest would survive and the others would die off because they couldn't support themselves. And that's the way it should be, the survival of the fittest. We'd get rid of all the leeches. It would be good for society.' And Claire would say, 'What kind of monster did I marry?' But I always thought that much of his writing and speaking was as an agent provocateur. He didn't really mean it."

Years later in Washington, Bork and Ab stayed in touch. Bork remarried after Claire died, and Ab was an usher at the wedding. On the Court of Appeals, Ab says, "we were fairly friendly. He wasn't a moderate, but he was somewhat reasonable. You could persuade both him and Scalia on some issues, remind them that they were intermediate judges, not Supreme Court judges."

Curious, I ask Ab about his relationship with Scalia. "Very pleasant," he says. "He was a very good colleague, none of the nastiness that he has now." I ask him what made Scalia a good colleague. "On judicial administration, he was very cooperative. He didn't look to make trouble just for the sake of making trouble, which Silberman did," Ab says, referring to another Reagan appointee, Laurence Silberman. "Scalia was practical when there were some employee problems or some judge problems."

And then Ab tells me about a sensitive matter involving one of their colleagues, liberal icon Skelly Wright, who had been appointed to the Court of Appeals by President Kennedy in 1962. Judge Wright had begun to exhibit symptoms of Alzheimer's disease, Ab tells me. "It was getting bad enough that he would lose his way to the courthouse, and he'd get cases mixed up. He'd start asking questions about a different case than the one we were hearing." To protect him, his clerks told Judge Wright that whenever he was on a panel with Ab or Pat Wald or Harry Edwards, he should vote with them. "It became obvious after a while," Ab says. "I remember that Scalia and Bork went to see Pat Wald," who preceded Ab as chief judge. "They said, 'Look, we don't want to make a public problem out of this, but you shouldn't have two votes. If you don't get him to take senior status by the end of the year, we're going to file a complaint.' That was very civilized. He took senior status, and that solved the problem."

The opposition to Bork's Supreme Court nomination was anything but civil, and some contend that it changed the norms of political debate in the country for decades to come. Liberal groups and senators painted Bork as a dangerous ideologue. Fearing that Bork would tip the balance on issues such as abortion and affirmative action, liberals went after this Supreme Court nominee with a vengeance. The most prominent liberal spear-carrier, Senator Ted Kennedy, thundered, "Robert Bork's America is a land in which women would be forced into back-alley abortions, blacks would sit at segregated lunch counters, rogue police could break down citizens' doors in midnight raids, schoolchildren could not be taught about evolution, writers and artists could be censored at the whim of the government, and the doors of the federal courts would be shut on the fingers of millions of citizens for whom the judiciary is—and is often the only—protector of the individual rights that are the heart of our democracy." Bork's typically combative response to Kennedy was: "There is not a line in that speech that is accurate."

I ask Ab if he was surprised at the way the Bork hearings went. "Yeah. In fact, I supported him," Ab says. "Zoey was opposed, but I was supporting him because I thought he wasn't quite as crazy as he sounded and that once he got on the Court, he would be free to be rational." I'm thinking to myself that maybe Ab was being a little Pollyannaish about Bork. But then he tells me that Ruth Bader Ginsburg has become much more liberal on the Supreme Court than she was on the Court of Appeals. Ginsburg's husband, Marty, a well-known tax lawyer and friend of wealthy Texas businessman Ross Perot, "had an influence on her when she was on the Court of Appeals," Ab says. "She was very conservative on commercial cases, and we used to have a lot of those. I would be more likely to persuade Bork than I would to persuade her."

As a federal judge, Ab couldn't publicly take sides on Bork's nomination, but he told another old friend, Senator Paul Simon, that he liked Bork despite his conservative views. He was, after all, a Reagan nominee. But then Bork paid the senator a courtesy visit, and when Simon mentioned that Ab Mikva spoke well of him, Bork couldn't wait to set the record straight. "Well, you understand that Ab Mikva and I don't agree on anything," he said. It was an unnecessarily contentious response, the kind that helped doom Bork's nomination.

Supporting Bork wasn't the only quietly bipartisan political work Judge Mikva engaged in from time to time. One day during the George H. W. Bush administration, Ab got a call from Ken Starr, the solicitor general. Starr had previously served with Ab for six years on the Court of Appeals. He was a Reagan appointee, like Scalia and Bork, and the conservative Starr and Ab had a cordial relationship. One of Starr's deputies had been nominated for a seat on Ab's court, but his Senate hearing was being delayed.

Could Ab help? Ab recalls that Starr described his deputy as "a really good guy. He's not going to agree with you philosophically, but he cares about the institution, and he'll help you with your problems—he didn't say Silberman, but we knew what we were talking about." When Ab asked his name, Starr said, "John Roberts"—the future chief justice of the Supreme Court.

Ab had met Roberts at a legal function and thought he seemed like a nice guy. Ab eventually learned more about Roberts's background and discovered a casual connection to the Mikvas. Although Roberts was born in Buffalo, New York, he grew up in Long Beach, Indiana, on the Lake Michigan shore. The Indiana Dunes area was a popular summer vacation spot for Chicago families in the 1950s, including the Mikvas. In 1955 or 1956, nearly a decade before the Roberts family arrived, Ab and Zoe were looking to rent a house in the Dunes, and Long Beach was the first town they looked in. "The real estate broker was very enthusiastic," Ab remembers. "'Oh, yes, we'd love to have you and your little baby.' Then he started emphasizing that what we'd like about Long Beach is that they were very selective about whom they rented and sold to. By the third time he said that, I asked if it mattered that we were Jewish. He said, 'Oh, you don't want to rent here. You want to go up the lake.'" The Mikvas eventually found a place in Michiana, where the Jews lived, sandwiched between Long Beach and Grand Beach, an Irish Catholic enclave where Mayor Richard J. Daley had a vacation house and Jews were not welcome. "I remember," Ab says, "when we first moved into Michiana and I'd jog just inside Grand Beach, I'd sing Jewish songs in a loud voice."

"In Yiddish?" I ask.

"In Yiddish, absolutely," Ab says. "I'd sing, 'My Yiddishe Momme,'" and Ab begins belting out the refrain right there at The Bagel, mixing in the kind of schmaltz reminiscent of Sophie Tucker's old signature rendition. Ab and Sophie, who was billed as the last of the "red hot mamas," could have teamed up in the Catskills.

We return to the subject of John Roberts and Ken Starr's call for help. "If it was somebody I thought was worth helping, I would call a couple of senators," Ab says. "And so I called Joe Biden, who was the chair of the Judiciary Committee, and told him what Starr had said, that Roberts was the best you're going to get under the Bush administration." And at that point, Ab says, after the Gulf War and with Bush's popularity sky-high, it looked like Bush would be reelected. "I never would have done it if I thought there was a chance that a Democrat would be elected," Ab tells me. "Biden said that the Roberts nomination hadn't come to the committee, but he'd look for it." Then, about six months later, Starr called Ab again and said the Senate had still not moved on the Roberts nomination. Ab called Biden, who told him the problem wasn't in the Senate; the White House had not nominated Roberts. "I found out later," Ab tells me, "that this very ideologically conservative woman at the White House, I don't remember her name, had put a brick on the nomination. So time marches on, Bush is not reelected, Clinton is in, and as far as I know, that's the end of Roberts."

When Roberts became chief justice in 2005, Ab was optimistic about him. Ab's friend Merrick Garland, who had served with Roberts on the Court of Appeals—Roberts eventually made it onto Ab's old court, nominated by George W. Bush—described Roberts as "conservative but reasonable." Instead, Ab tells me with great dismay, "he's been very, very far right. Roberts and Scalia, Alito and Thomas are as rigid as rigid can be." That's why Ab was shocked when Roberts belatedly switched sides—which is what Ab thinks happened—and wrote the majority decision upholding the constitutionality of most of the Affordable Care Act. "Maybe that confirms what Starr said about him in the first place," Ab speculates, "that Roberts is institutionally minded. He realized that if he took the Supreme Court to another *Bush v. Gore* or *Citizens United* conclusion, the Court would lose a lot of chits."

For Ab, the rigidity and often nonsensical constitutional theories of the Supreme Court's majority are personified by Scalia. We start this discussion when I observe that it feels like the country has reverted to the Gilded Age of the late nineteenth century, when large fortunes were accumulated and used to manipulate and control the political process. The wealth-dominated politics of our new Gilded Age are being ratified and enabled by the Supreme Court through *Citizens United* and other cases. Ab initially responds with something of a theoretical preface: "On the basic principle of plain meaning, I agree with Scalia. If a law or the Constitution says something very specifically, such as thou shalt not kill, that does not mean thou shalt not kill everybody except his brother-in-law. That means thou shalt not kill. If you're a judge, don't look for legislative history. Don't look for what 'shalt' means in an ancient dictionary. The meaning is plain; read it as it's written and enforce it as it's written. On that, Scalia is absolutely right."

But the meaning of the law is often not so plain, and I can feel Ab's hackles rising as he sharpens his judge's tools and pivots to what he calls "the splendid ambiguity of the Constitution." "Due process, what is the meaning of due process?" Ab asks rhetorically. "What is the specific meaning of equal protection? If the poor have to sleep under a bridge, therefore the rich have to sleep under a bridge? That's crazy." And then Ab refers to the inspiring Hugo Black, a champion of the First Amendment and a Supreme Court justice when Ab was a clerk. Black, a former US senator from Alabama, always carried a pocket-size copy of the Constitution, a practice Ab adopted. Black portrayed himself as an absolutist when it came to the First Amendment and the Constitution. "The Constitution says what it means and means what it says," Ab remembers Black pontificating. "But what *does* the First Amendment mean?" Ab asks me, and then recites part of it: "'Congress shall make no law abridging the freedom of speech.' Look at the ambiguities. Freedom. Do you really mean that somebody can tip off troop movements during a time of war? Is that freedom of speech? Do you really mean that somebody can falsely holler 'fire' in a crowded theater? Is that protected speech? Of course not. So, therefore, with due deference to Hugo Black and with no deference to Nino Scalia, even the First Amendment cannot be an absolute. And that's what's wrong with *Citizens United*. The idea that money is speech, and that speech is absolute, is just ridiculous. Do we really want someone like Sheldon Adelson to be able to give $50 million or whatever it was in 2012? No, we can't allow that. Our founders weren't that stupid. Only Scalia is that stupid, or mad."

In the *Citizens United* case, Justice Kennedy wrote the majority opinion, and Scalia was only one of five "conservative" justices who wiped out a century of precedents prohibiting the use of corporate money to fund political campaigns. I think it's misleading and inaccurate to call the justices "conservatives" when it comes to the big political cases of the last two decades, beginning with *Bush v. Gore* and continuing through the Court's evisceration of the Voting Rights Act, *Citizens United*, and other cases. On cases that are about political power, the justices act as Republicans, not as conservatives who supposedly abhor judicial activism. Ab believes the Roberts Court is one of the most blatantly activist Courts in modern times. In fact, he goes even further, saying, "This is the most activist Court we have ever had, much more than the Court after the Civil War." But when I ask Ab if *Citizens United* was a partisan decision, I'm not entirely satisfied with his answer: "Not in terms of Republican versus Democrat, but it was definitely in terms of holders of power versus the common folk." To me, that seems like a distinction without much of a difference.

In 1984, while Bork and Scalia were on the Court of Appeals for the DC Circuit, they served on the panel that upheld the US Navy's dismissal of a chief petty officer for homosexual conduct. Bork wrote the decision in *Dronenberg v. Zech*, rejecting privacy and equal protection challenges to the navy regulation prohibiting homosexual conduct. Homosexuality in the military came up again nine years later, when Ab was chief judge of the court. He wrote the unanimous decision for the three-judge panel rejecting the navy's dismissal of Joseph Steffan, a homosexual midshipman at the Naval Academy. Steffan had been dismissed not because of his conduct but because, when asked by navy officials, he admitted to being homosexual. The Steffan case was one of the early pro-gay rulings by a federal court. It was one of Ab's last cases on the court and, he tells me, the one he's most proud of.

By coincidence, Ab and I were discussing the Steffan case just after the St. Louis Rams drafted the first openly gay football player, Michael Sam, in May 2014. TV coverage of the event showed an emotional, happy Sam crying after being drafted. There was also TV coverage of a party where Sam and his friends, including his significant other, were celebrating. Sam gently pushed a piece of cake with white frosting into his boyfriend's mouth and then kissed him on the lips, transferring some of the cake and frosting in the process. It was a familiar, playful, wedding-like scene, but for a lot of TV viewers, I imagined, it was unusual to see two men in those roles. I admit to Ab that I felt a little uncomfortable watching it. "I did not see it," he says. "But it reminds me of something that still bothers me, too. And it bothers me that it bothers me. If I saw two women kissing each other romantically, it wouldn't bother me. It's a bias, and I've got it."

Ab then recalls a seemingly small matter from the mid-1970s, during his time in Congress, but one that has tugged at his conscience. Ed Koch, a congressman from New York and a friend of Ab's, introduced "a bill to protect gay rights, and I hadn't cosponsored it," Ab says. "Ed came to me—we used to send around 'Dear Colleague' letters and we could see who had cosponsored our bill—and Ed said, 'Why aren't you on my bill?' And I said, 'Ed, I've got so many things to handle in my district. This one isn't worth it. You get it out of committee and I'll vote for it. You don't need me as a cosponsor.' Is that pragmatism? I suppose." For Ab, this kind of pragmatism was never a comfortable fit.

We talk about generational differences when it comes to prejudice and discrimination. "We've made such incredible progress," Ab says with great emotion, "in squelching what is an irrational reaction to the way people feel about Jews, blacks, Catholics. We've gotten rid of a lot of it. Hopefully, we've gotten rid of all the government implementation of these prejudices. But to say that we're now as pure as we're supposed to be, it ain't so." I mention that the younger generation, people in their teens and twenties, seem to have fewer of the old stereotypical attitudes. And Ab says: "You remind me of a song. I don't know if you remember *South Pacific*."

"Yes, I've seen *South Pacific*," I say.

"It is a great musical," Ab continues. "And one of the songs in it is 'You've

Got to Be Carefully Taught.'" We both recall the words. "In many respects," Ab says, "prejudice has to be carefully taught. If you grow up from birth without outside influences as to how you should feel about blacks or browns or Jews, you would grow up not feeling anything about them. Which is the way we want it to be. Much of the progress we've made is that we've at least gotten government out of the teaching. We don't allow laws segregating people. We don't allow discrimination against people based on other people's views of them. But that hasn't removed all of the prejudices."

As we return to our discussion of the Steffan case, Ab notes that, by the 1980s, "I had lost some of my homophobic attitudes, but I was never pro-gay. By the time of the Steffan case, I was somewhat sympathetic, but I never thought there should be any special laws for gays."

Joseph Steffan was an outstanding student at the Naval Academy, ranking among the top ten in his senior class. But he had told a few people at the academy he was homosexual, and an investigation followed. He was expelled just weeks before his graduation in 1987. This was six years before the "Don't Ask, Don't Tell" policy replaced an outright ban on homosexuals in the military. "That is why they were able to throw him out," Ab says. "They said, 'Are you a homosexual?' And he said, 'Yes.' He answered honestly. There was no evidence of any misconduct of any kind"—meaning there was no evidence Steffan had engaged in homosexual acts. But merely admitting his homosexuality, the Naval Academy maintained, required his dismissal.

Ab and his two liberal colleagues on the panel voted unanimously in favor of Steffan, ordering the US Navy to commission him as an officer and award him his diploma from the academy. For Ab, the heart of the case was that Steffan was being punished not for anything he did but for who he was. He recites the last line of his opinion from twenty-three years ago: "America's hallmark has been to judge people by what they do and not by who they are." As we're driving back to Ab's apartment, he tells me, "The Steffan decision was the best decision I ever wrote. I wasn't defying the Supreme Court because I had not staked out any new ground. I had very carefully kept it within the lines of the law of the land. But it didn't matter," he laughs. It didn't matter because the case was en banced, and Ab's decision was overturned by a vote of 7 to 3, the majority all Republican appointees. Ab was not one of the dissenters, however. By the time the decision was handed down in late 1994, he had left the court for the Clinton White House.

9

The Clinton White House and Hillary's Liberalism

The good news is that we Americans are living longer, or at least many white middle-class and wealthy Americans are. Access to good medical care is a big reason. I would not be having these conversations with the nearly ninety-year-old Abner Mikva if he didn't have access to medical care. It is certainly not his diet that has kept him alive beyond actuarial expectations for a man born in 1926, as I can see whenever we eat at The Bagel and his plate arrives loaded with delicious fats and tasty additives. "I had good health insurance for so long, ever since I entered Congress," he says, that he became oblivious to the cost of medical care. But now, "when I have a hospital stay and see the bill, I think, my God, this could wipe me out if I didn't have all the insurance that I have"—and he ticks off Medicare, governmental employees' health insurance, and Signa through the state of Illinois. It's no surprise that he favors a government-run single-payer system for all Americans. I do, too, although I try to avoid doctors as if I were a practicing Christian Scientist. What keeps Ab alive is a regimen of a dozen pills he takes every morning, he tells me. "That's a lot of pills," I say.

"Yes, it is," he agrees. "I take two heart pills. One thyroid pill. One digestive pill. Two eye pills. That's six. Two anti-pain pills for my arthritis. That's eight. Two vitamin pills. A water pill, a diuretic. That's eleven in the morning and three at night, plus two during the day," he laughs. "When I was in my fifties, I got my first permanent pills for blood pressure."

"You didn't say that you took a pill for high blood pressure every morning," I tell him.

"That is the twelfth," Ab says. "Back then, when the doctor said you're going to have to take this pill for the rest of your life, I thought, that's not so bad. One pill isn't so bad," and he laughs again. Now, all those pills "come with the territory," which is Ab's preferred phrase for describing—and accepting—his life in its ninth decade.

In the summer of 1994, when Ab was still chief judge, he told me there was something he wanted to talk to me about. We met in the judges' dining room at the courthouse, and he said he had been asked to be Bill Clinton's White House counsel. What did I think about it? Knowing Ab as I did, I tell him in a recent conversation, "I had the feeling you had already decided and you really wanted to do it, so I told you it sounded like a great idea." To which Ab replied, "Very smart."

But about a year earlier, I thought I had a better idea. Bill Clinton's first nominee for attorney general, Zoe Baird, had to withdraw from consideration when it was revealed that she had hired illegal immigrants as a chauffeur and a nanny and hadn't paid their Social Security taxes. That embarrassment for the new Clinton administration was compounded when Clinton's second nominee, Kimba Wood, also withdrew because of a nanny problem. The next nominee would obviously have to be someone with impeccable ethical credentials, and I decided it should be Judge Abner Mikva. Before I told anybody else, I went to see Ab at his Capitol Hill townhouse on New Jersey Avenue, a few blocks from the House office buildings. "How would you like to be attorney general?" I asked. I told him he didn't have to answer, unless the answer was no. He listened and didn't say no. So I made a few phone calls, and a friend of a friend who knew journalist Mark Shields told him about it. Shields floated the idea on the PBS *News Hour*. But before we got much further with a Mikva–for–attorney general campaign, the president nominated Janet Reno. I hadn't realized how determined Bill Clinton or Hillary Clinton or maybe both Clintons were to have the first woman serve as attorney general.

When Ab revealed that he was considering taking the job as Bill Clinton's White House counsel, I was lukewarm about the idea, despite what I told him. I could easily understand the thrill of being at the center of political action—and after all, this was our first Democratic president in twelve years. But I was somewhere between skeptical and doubtful about how compatible Ab and Bill would be.

Bill Clinton came to the White House with more than the usual amount of political baggage. His reputation for womanizing was legendary; his campaign for the White House was nearly derailed by stories of his alleged affair with Gennifer Flowers. And it wasn't hard to find people who threw more logs onto the fire.

Sometime after Clinton was nominated in 1992, my wife Joan and I were invited for dinner at Ab and Zoe's townhouse. There were about a dozen couples present, including Supreme Court Justice John Paul Stevens and his wife Maryan. The food was served buffet style, and after I placed a slice of Zoe's fork-tender beef brisket on my plate, I ambled over to where several women were standing and talking. The subject was the presidential campaign, and Maryan Stevens blurted out, with peppery disgust, "Everybody in Arkansas knows Bill Clinton is a bum."

Then, shortly after Clinton was inaugurated, my friend from Northwestern University, John McKnight, was in town. We went out for a late lunch and, by coincidence, found Al From and an associate sitting at an adjoining table. Al, a college classmate of mine at Northwestern, had made a big splash in Washington political circles as founder of the centrist Democratic Leadership Council (DLC). Bill Clinton had served as the high-profile chairman of the DLC, and he and Al had traveled the country pushing so-called New Democrat ideas. Al told us some Clinton stories, including how Al had to keep reminding Bill why he favored a national service program. Then Al smiled and said he was amazed at how "reckless" Bill had been when they were on the road together. He didn't have to spell it out.

So now I tell Ab what I really thought about his taking the job as White House counsel, characterizing it as something of an oil-and-water mismatch. He assures me that he saw it differently, largely because of Lloyd Cutler, who recruited him for the job. Cutler, nearly a decade older than Ab, was the quintessential Washington éminence grise, rotating seamlessly between a big corporate law firm and high-level public service. He had served as White House counsel for Jimmy Carter and temporarily reprised that role when the Clintons' good friend Bernie Nussbaum resigned after a difficult, controversial first year. "Lloyd and I had been friends for many years," Ab begins. "Talk about somebody having two personalities. In his law firm he represented some of the worst crooks of all time. But he was a purist about government service. I remember when he was with Carter. He blew the whistle on some of the things that some of the Georgia crowd wanted to do. I just felt that Lloyd would not encourage me—I felt that with Lloyd as the precursor, the White House counsel's office was clean."

Ab had made up his mind to take the job, but "before I said absolutely yes," he tells me, Leon Panetta, Clinton's chief of staff and Ab's former House colleague, took him to see the president. "It was a Sunday," Ab says, "and it was the first time I met with him. He said, 'I'll never lie to you,' and I was convinced that he was telling me the truth. And he never did. In all my dealings with him, he never lied to me. I was gone by the time . . ."—I interrupt and say, "by the time he lied to his wife, his staff, and the country about his affair with Monica Lewinsky." And Ab says, "Yes, he did lie to people. But he didn't lie to me." Ab knew that Clinton could be "curvy," as he put it, when it came to ethical considerations. But Ab liked the president's charm and personal style, and at least when it came to issues like civil rights, he believed Clinton was genuinely interested in doing the right thing.

As White House counsel, Ab's portfolio consisted primarily of judicial nominations, legislative issues, and ethics. "I was barely in the front door on a Thursday," he remembers, "when Leon Panetta told me we had to go after the secretary of agriculture, Mike Espy, who was an African American former congressman from Mississippi." Espy was being accused of a string of improprieties if not illegalities—using a government car for personal business, accepting gifts from private companies, and the like. "On Friday we were meeting with him," Ab recalls. "Leon and his aide John Podesta had put together all of the facts. Secretary Espy said at one point, 'What do you want me to do, Leon?' Leon said, 'I want your resignation on my desk by Monday morning.'" Then, over the weekend, Ab was at a social event and found himself in the men's room standing next to Vernon Jordan, the well-connected African American lawyer. "We were both at the urinal," Ab tells me, and Jordan says, "'Is there anything we can do for our friend?' And I say no. He says OK and walks out. Later on, that became a subject of a grand jury investigation when Jordan had to swear under oath that he asked me and I said no. So you have to be careful about pissing conversations."

The Espy episode was the first time Janet Reno appointed an independent counsel. She did the same with Secretary of Commerce Ron Brown and Secretary of Housing and Urban Development Henry Cisneros. "The president would rant and rave," Ab says, "that Janet was destroying his government. He'd say to me, 'You go tell her . . . ,' and so I'd have to arrange to see Janet, very delicately, because we were supposed to stay out of that area. It was no fun." According to Ab, his role as carrier pigeon between the president and the attorney general reminded him of a similar role he played as a child between his feuding parents. "The president would call me and say, 'You tell that woman da da da da.' And then I'd see her, and she was always much more polite. She'd say, 'Won't you ask the president if. . . .' It was a stupid role that I had to play. I didn't have that kind of rapport with the president, and I didn't really have it with Janet, although I grew very fond of her, and she was very fond of me. But I never knew her before I came to the White House. And she kept appointing all these independent counsels, and a couple were very bad ideas."

I ask Ab about his daily routine during his stint at the Clinton White House, and he says, "I was thinking about my schedule the other day. I usually got up around 5:00 and went over to the House gym. I had to get a policeman to let me in because it wasn't open yet. Usually I'd run and then I'd shower, shave, and get to the office about 6:30. Our first meeting was at 7:00. That was the senior staff. We met in Leon's office." There were about a dozen people at the senior staff meetings—Ab mentions Panetta; two deputy chiefs of staff, Erskine Bowles and Harold Ickes; and Robert Rubin, director of Clinton's National Economic Council. When Rubin became secretary of the treasury in January 1995, he was no longer officially part of the senior staff. "But Rubin recognized there was a lot of power at those senior staff meetings," Ab says. And then he tells me a story that reveals the political divide within the Clinton administration and the Democratic Party over economic issues, a divide that continued through the Obama administration.

Ab begins by saying that although he liked Bob Rubin, who could be gracious and charming, they were worlds apart on politics, priorities, and worldviews. "His whole idea was to defend the establishment," Ab says about Rubin, who spent more than twenty-five years on Wall Street with Goldman Sachs before joining the Clinton administration. "That's where he made it, and that's where he thinks the country has made it. And I remember how furious he got about the proposal to increase the minimum wage. He was outraged."

The episode Ab tells me about happened in the winter of 1995. Secretary of Labor Robert Reich, whom Ab calls "one of Clinton's few smart reformers and who came into the administration because he was an old friend of Bill's," went to see the president with a pointed agenda: Reich wanted Clinton to propose an increase in the minimum wage. In 1992 Clinton had campaigned for an increase but hadn't done anything about it yet. Later, Reich told Ab about his meeting with Clinton. Reich began by saying, "Mr. President, you know we haven't done anything for labor." According to Ab, Reich told Clinton that labor was getting restless, and it would be good for the economy to increase the minimum wage. "When Clinton doesn't like something coming from somebody he likes," Ab tells me, "he doesn't say, 'No, that's a bad idea.' He says, 'That's an interesting idea.' So, that's what Reich hears, and he knows the president well enough to know that his idea is going nowhere. But after he gets out of the Oval Office, he sees [Vice President] Al Gore in his office and says, 'Al, I was just talking with the president about increasing the minimum wage. And he said that he thought it was a good idea. Now, you're going to the AFL-CIO executive board meeting tomorrow in Florida. Why don't you tell them we're going to do something on the minimum wage.' So Al goes down to Florida and says, 'We're going to push for an increase in the minimum wage.' It's big news." After hearing Ab's story, I discover that Gore said much the same thing—"there's a very strong argument" for raising the minimum wage—on the Sunday news program *Face the Nation.*

"Monday morning at the senior staff meeting," Ab says, "Rubin is furious. He says, 'I thought we were going to have some discipline and that we agreed we weren't going to do anything about the minimum wage because it's going to hurt the economy. This is outrageous. How did this happen?' Everybody said, 'Not me, not me.' So finally, Rubin says, 'Leon, you've got to tell the president to disavow this immediately before the markets open because it's going to be a disaster on Wall Street.' Leon says, 'Before I go, let me see a show of hands to make sure that everybody agrees with Bob on this.' Everybody raises their hand except the two ultraliberals, Ickes and me." Panetta checks with the president and comes back to the meeting. "Rubin asks what's he's going to do," Ab says. "Panetta has a wry smile; he can be very sensitive to the drama of things. He says, 'Remember that story when Lincoln put something to his cabinet and they were all against it? And Lincoln said, "Well, the vote is 13 to 1, and you lose."' At that point, the fat was in the fire. We went ahead with it, and the economy didn't fall apart." It took more than a year for a 90-cent increase in the minimum wage to be passed by Congress and signed into law by President Clinton.

My initial misgivings about Ab taking the White House counsel job went beyond the ethical challenges he might encounter. I believed the mismatch between Ab and Clinton extended to substantive issues, both economic and constitutional. After all, the Democratic Leadership Council, with the help of its most effective front man, Governor Bill Clinton, had pulled the Democratic Party toward the warm embrace of corporate America and Wall Street and their ample campaign dollars. By the mid-1980s, with labor unions in decline and Democratic losses twice to Richard Nixon and twice to Ronald Reagan, the DLC essentially adopted a strategy of "If you can't beat 'em, join 'em." Liberal Democratic holdouts referred to the strategy bitterly as "Democratic Lite," and in the first Clinton administration, Robert Rubin may have been Exhibit A. Outside his administration, Clinton maintained a deferential relationship with the head of the Federal Reserve, Alan Greenspan, a Reagan appointee and devotee of conservative writer Ayn Rand. Men like Greenspan, whom Clinton reappointed, and Rubin were considered economic policy geniuses by New York and Washington elites. But by 2008, neither Greenspan nor Rubin seemed so smart when their pro–Wall Street policies contributed to the worst financial collapse and recession since the Great Depression.

Except for Ab's minimum-wage vote at the senior staff meeting, he didn't have much to do with economic issues as White House counsel, but he did have an important role when the Constitution was in play. One day during his tenure, Ab invited me to have lunch at the White House mess, and as we were finishing, he said with a spoonful of sarcasm, "I have to go now and remind the president why he's against a constitutional amendment to prohibit flag burning." Several years earlier, the Supreme Court had decided 5 to 4 that the First Amendment protected a protester's right to desecrate the American flag. But many in Congress wanted to override the Court's decision by amending the Constitution, a foolhardy misadventure that any good civil libertarian would oppose. So I was surprised when Ab told me that Bill Clinton, a Yale Law School graduate and Rhodes scholar, had to be educated about the First Amendment. In one of our recent conversations, I remind Ab about that lunch and about his observation that Clinton was not a liberal on those kinds of issues. "That's right," Ab says. "And on prayer in the schools, his instincts were to stay with God."

"That was the culture he grew up in," I say to Ab.

"Absolutely," Ab replies. "He had been educated on the separation of church and state at Yale and Oxford, but those weren't his views. On these God and flag issues, he was Arkansas through and through."

But it wasn't only through an Arkansas filter that Clinton viewed constitutional issues. Thoroughly political, he was always thinking about how it would play in Peoria, Ab tells me. "All through the time I was there, he didn't like being called a liberal. Even the word 'progressive' was not in his comfort zone." And then Ab tells me, with undisguised pain in his voice, about the time "Bill Clinton gutted habeas corpus."

In the aftermath of the Oklahoma City bombing of the Alfred P. Murrah Federal Office Building in April 1995, Congress was considering antiterrorism legislation. Some law-and-order Republicans, sensing a public relations opportunity, were pushing to limit federal judges' authority to grant writs of habeas corpus. Four former attorneys general from Democratic and Republican administrations, including Ab's old law school mentor Edward Levi, wrote to President Clinton and stated, "It is vital to insure that habeas corpus—the means by which all civil liberties are enforced—is not substantively diminished. . . . It has a proud history of guarding against injustices born of racial prejudice and intolerance, of saving the innocent from imprisonment or execution and in the process insuring the rights of all law-abiding citizens." According to Ab, the NAACP Legal Defense and Educational Fund had developed a "good alternative" to what Congress was considering. "I brought it to Henry Hyde," Ab says. Hyde, an

Illinois Republican and chairman of the House Judiciary Committee, had a friendly relationship with Ab dating to the 1970s and their days in Congress. "And Henry said, 'I can be for that if you have a client for it,' meaning the president. And I said, 'We're working on it.' Henry laughed." But when Ab went to the president with his alternative proposal, Clinton's response stunned him: "I'm going to let Congress do what they want to do. Habeas corpus is a bad idea and we ought to get rid of it." More than twenty years later, Ab still seems stunned as slowly, sadly he repeats Clinton's words to me: "Habeas corpus is a bad idea."

Gutting habeas corpus had a tough-on-crime appeal that may have played well in Peoria. But Clinton's crass political motivation on something of that magnitude was beyond the pale and a defining episode for distinguished *New York Times* columnist and constitutional scholar Anthony Lewis. "For Bill Clinton's natural supporters," Lewis wrote, possibly including himself, "the most painful realization of his presidency is that he is a man without a bottom line. He may abandon any seeming belief, any principle. You cannot rely on him." If Bill Clinton had any core beliefs, Ab tells me, it was about race. He was genuinely committed to civil rights and racial justice, despite what Ab calls the "despicable comments" he made about candidate Barack Obama during the South Carolina presidential primary in 2008, when Bill was campaigning for Hillary.

Bill Clinton was well aware, Ab says, of his reputation as a high priest of political expediency. "People do want honesty in their public officials," Ab notes as we're having breakfast one morning in the communal dining room at the Brookdale. "That was a big problem for Bill Clinton. Even though people love him, they don't trust him," Ab says with a chuckle. Then Ab tells me a story to illustrate Clinton's self-awareness of how he is often perceived. For some reason Ab doesn't recall, they were having trouble filling a vacancy on the DC Court of Appeals—Ab's old court. "I came up with the idea of Bill Cohen," he says. "Do you remember Bill Cohen?" I do. When Ab was at the White House, Cohen was a senator from Maine, a Republican. "We were locker mates in the gym when he was in the House," Ab says. "And he once said to me that he'd like to end up on the Court of Appeals in DC. He was a pretty good lawyer. So I proposed to the president that we appoint Bill Cohen because there was a Democrat who was the governor of Maine and the governor would then appoint a Democratic successor to Cohen in the Senate. We'd pick up a Senate seat. Well, Clinton thought about it for a minute or two and finally said, 'No, Slick Willie.' And he was right. The press would have denounced it as Slick Willie pulling one of his magic tricks again, because Bill knew he wasn't trusted." Smiling as he finishes the story, Ab adds, "Obama could get away with it."

The White House counsel's office was involved in the process of nominating candidates for federal judgeships. As a former judge, Ab, of course, had an especially strong interest in who was selected, but Clinton did not. "It was very hard to keep Clinton involved" is how Ab puts it. The occasional Supreme Court nomination was a different matter. But Clinton's high court nominations of Ruth Bader Ginsburg and Stephen Breyer came the year before Ab arrived at the White House. "On regular judges," Ab says, "every once in a while he'd stick his nose in, but it was very tough to keep him involved." Such presidential indifference was not unique to Clinton; most presidents don't pay much attention to judicial nominations, Ab says. "You don't score many points by appointing judges."

Then Ab shares an amusing story about a senator from our old home state, a judicial nominee, and an angry Bill Clinton. Typically, Ab and one of his deputies discussed judicial nominations at a weekly meeting that included attorneys from the Justice Department and the vice president's office. Usually the president had no objections to staff recommendations for district court nominees. Candidates for the appeals courts could be a little more complicated because the president might have to pick and choose among senators and their favorite judges. But the vacancy on the Seventh Circuit was not one of those potentially problematic situations, Ab tells me. Then he got a call from Herb Kohl, a Democratic senator from Wisconsin. Kohl was very enthusiastic about nominating Terrence Evans, a district court judge. The vacancy on the Seventh Circuit was traditionally a Wisconsin seat, so nominating Evans was not a problem. "But Kohl could be very determined, and he kept bugging me," Ab recalls. "I told him, I think you're all set, senator," and assured him that Evans was going to be supported by the White House. For unfathomable reasons, Kohl would not take yes for an answer. "He said, 'I've got to see the president, I've got to see the president.'" Ab replied: "The president, once he's made up his mind and he's agreeable, he doesn't like to. . . ." Kohl cut Ab off. "'No, I've got to see him.'" "Well," Ab says to me, "he's a senator. So I go to Erskine Bowles, who was a very good gatekeeper, and tell him he's got to put Herb Kohl on the list." Bowles asks why and is puzzled by the answer because he knows Clinton has no objection to the Evans nomination. But he puts Kohl on the schedule. Ab tells me, "Kohl spent twenty minutes in there. When the president was in a good schmoozing mood, my secretary would come in and cheerfully say, 'The president wants to see you.' But if he was mad when he called, my secretary would come in and say, 'You're wanted in the Oval.'

And then I knew to gear up. So after Kohl leaves, my secretary comes in and says, 'You're wanted in the Oval.' I come in and the president says, 'What the God damn hell. I had to spend all that time with that asshole. Who's the other senator from Wisconsin?'" Ab told him it was Russ Feingold. To which Bill Clinton replied, "'You tell him that he's got the next nomination, whoever he wants. I don't care if he wants a hyena.'" The next nomination for a judgeship in Wisconsin, Ab says, came from Feingold. The nominee was Lynn Adelman, and he's been a well-respected district court judge. "Every time I see Lynn," Ab says, "I tell him, 'You're the hyena judge.'"

I ask Ab why, over the last twenty-five years, liberals haven't put more pressure on Democratic presidents Clinton and Obama to nominate good liberal judges, compared with what the Federalist Society has done on the other side. He answers instantly: "Because the Federalist Society has been a very active agent in persuading their conservative base that the courts are dangerous places. Their remedy is to find people who are not going to do anything. It's sort of like the political Right elects congressmen now who promise to go to Washington and not do anything." And then Ab reminds me, "You told the story about my great success when I was in Congress, showing that I voted against more spending than anybody else in the Illinois delegation except for Phil Crane. It doesn't take a lot of thought to vote no."

Have we become a country of naysayers? Conservatives like to assert that we are a center-right country and that our natural feelings toward government are somewhere between suspicion and hostility. But mistrust in government is a relatively recent phenomenon. When Ab was first elected to Congress in 1968, trust in government was near its post–World War II high-water mark. From the Eisenhower through the Kennedy years and for most of the Johnson administration, approximately 75 percent of Americans told researchers they trusted government. But since the divisive Vietnam War, Watergate, and other government scandals, plus decades of growing income inequality, there has been a deep erosion of trust. Today, only about 25 percent of Americans have confidence in their government. Why then, in our disillusioned and polarized country, did Ab think that Hillary Clinton could have been an exceptional, transformational president?

What better place to talk about Hillary Clinton than in Park Ridge? It's late in the morning on December 10, 2014, when I pick up Ab and suggest lunch at a place in Park Ridge that's been there since the 1950s. "Let's go," he says. So we head up the Kennedy Expressway, forty minutes north, to Hillary's hometown and one of the worst suburbs for Ab when he represented the 10th Congressional District in the 1970s. Park Ridge was as solidly Republican then as it was when Hillary lived there in the 1950s and 1960s. Ab never cracked 30 percent of the vote.

We arrive at Mac's, a small breakfast-and-lunch place on Higgins Road, near O'Hare Airport. Whether Hillary ever ate there, nobody at Mac's seems to know. I interpret the historical indifference of our waitperson as a sign that she's not a Hillary supporter.

Ab got off to a rocky start with Hillary, he tells me. "It must have been my first week at the White House," he says, and he was the speaker at one of the breakfasts sponsored by the *Christian Science Monitor*, where journalists get to question a newsmaker. Years before, when he was in Congress, Ab had been a *Monitor* breakfast guest, and he remembered, incorrectly, that the sessions were off the record. "I didn't really say anything bad," Ab says of his appearance as the new White House counsel. But the president had recently established a legal defense fund to pay for the lawyers who were representing the Clintons in the expanding Whitewater investigation and in the sexual harassment lawsuit against Bill. Ab says, "Their legal bills were piling up, and Bernie Nussbaum and Lloyd Cutler and I said that you cannot use any of the White House counsel staff for personal problems. What was the name of that woman who said Bill showed her his penis?" he asks me.

"Paula Jones," I answer immediately, sounding like a contestant on a game show.

"Yes, Paula Jones," Ab says. "You can't use White House staff on any of that. So they were hiring outside lawyers. They weren't very good, but they charged a lot of money. Anyway, one of the reporters at the breakfast asked what I thought of the legal defense fund. And I said that I'm sure the president is uncomfortable about having to raise money for that, but he's not a rich man and he's got to pay these legal fees somehow. Well, the next day it was a page-three story, and the headline was, 'President Uncomfortable about Legal Fund.' Hillary was incensed. I think she felt that I was new and I'm already saying how the president feels. She didn't dress me down, but she let several people know that she thought I had been indiscreet."

I ask Ab if Hillary played the role of Bill's protector. "Absolutely. She was trying to keep people from getting him into trouble," he says. Throughout his White House tenure, Ab was fascinated with the Clintons' relationship, and he thinks he understands the basis of it. "I think my original analysis of who they were and how opposites marry was true. That she was very book smart but did not have the personality that he had. By the time they met, she was much more liberal than he was, even though she started out as a Goldwater girl." I ask Ab if Hillary has more candle power than Bill. "She has greater analytic powers," he replies. "Bill sees everything through political eyes." And, Ab adds, Bill knows Hillary is smarter. "He was clearly very dependent on her always. He sought her approval," is the way Ab puts it. "The last word on the pillow was the word that finally moved him"—and Ab ticks off some issues such as tobacco, the environment, and legal services, where he saw Hillary's liberal influence pushing Bill to the left. "Hillary saved the legal services program a couple of times," Ab says, referring to a liberal idea that Bill had little interest in. "Her ideas had much more of an influence on our country than anybody knows, except Bill Clinton. She made him much more of a liberal than he otherwise would have been."

In later conversations, Ab makes it clear that he is fond of the Clintons. As for Hillary, Ab tells me, "I think there is something that's overlooked about her: she has been all her life a very ethical person." Ab's aware that the current public perception is quite different—that if she had been elected in 2016, according to many polls, she would have been inaugurated as the least trusted president ever, except for Donald Trump. "I'm sure she's engaged in petty lies that anybody in politics has to do," Ab says, but he mainly thinks of her as a person of integrity when it comes to her commitment to liberal, democratic values.

I remind Ab that in 2008, instead of backing Hillary, he was an early supporter of the seemingly long-shot presidential campaign of young, inexperienced Barack Obama. What changed? Why was he enthusiastically for Hillary in 2016? First of all, he says, he wasn't anti-Hillary in 2008, but he was enthralled with Obama, who was his friend and had unexpectedly blossomed into a political star. "I had seen Obama in '04 come from nowhere to get elected to the Senate," Ab says, "which I considered much harder than getting nominated to be president." Suddenly, Obama seemed to have the magic touch. "He was the luckiest politician that I had ever seen. And of course, his keynote convention speech in '04 was spectacular." For Ab, helping to nominate and maybe elect the first black president was an exciting, irresistible prospect. But second, getting back to Hillary and 2016, Ab thought she had learned from her mistakes, such as her blunders as First Lady, when her leadership on health care legislation ended in failure. "The difference is that she has had enough experiences on her own, both as a senator and as secretary of state," Ab says. "I think she has finally developed the self-confidence that Bill has. You know, much of what makes a successful politician—Jack Kennedy once said, 'Why do you run for public office? You look around and you decide that you can do it better than anybody else and you run.' Bill had that when he was sixteen. I think it took Hillary much longer. Even the last time she ran, she really didn't have that self-confidence. I think this time she does."

As Ab and I continue to discuss Hillary Clinton that December day in Park Ridge and in later conversations, I reveal my own reservations about her: her vote for the Iraq War and her general hawkishness, her coziness with Wall Street, and her inclination to play ball with powerful interests. For instance, I ask Ab, when she was preparing to run for president in 2016, why did Hillary think it was a good idea to accept millions of dollars for private "speeches" to Goldman Sachs and other Wall Street firms? Ab's one-word answer: "Greed."

My reservations about Hillary Clinton were familiar among Democrats who yearned for a presidential candidate in 2016 with unquestioned populist, reformer instincts—like Elizabeth Warren. Ab has two responses to this: the country doesn't elect populists like Warren or Bernie Sanders, and there is a secret, more idealistic Hillary Rodham that Hillary Clinton has not forgotten. "One of the reasons I'm more enthusiastic about Hillary than a lot of people," Ab says, "and I don't talk about this, but she was very much influenced by your friend."

The "friend" he is referring to is Saul Alinsky. I wrote his biography nearly three decades ago. I'm caught off guard by Ab's comment, and I start to say, "You think there's still a lingering . . ."

And Ab cuts in: "Oh, absolutely."

"Why do you believe that?" I want to know.

"Did you ever read her college thesis?" he asks.

Hillary's thesis was about Alinsky, and I have read it. To my surprise, so has Ab, a long time ago. "It's very impressive," he says.

I remind Ab, "Not everything you did when you were twenty-one years old has a lifelong impact on the way you see the world. Why do you think this still does for her?"

"Because Alinsky was that kind of influence," he responds. "You don't forget somebody who influenced her as much as he did." And as Ab says that, I think of the framed photo of Clarence Darrow, young Ab's hero, that hangs on a wall in his apartment. "That's where a lot of her liberalism comes from," Ab continues. "Nothing in her background before Wellesley and Alinsky indicated any kind of progressive tendencies."

"So you're saying that Alinsky was an important part of her formative, young adult life, and when something like that happens, you never forget it and you continue to look at the world from that point of view?"

"Yes," Ab says. "It's what shaped her views on race, poverty, legal services. And it all came from Alinsky. I always found it fascinating, especially after reading your book, that Alinsky was not that doctrinaire about issues. To him, the goal was about organizing, and then we'll worry about the issues. But she perceived that community organization was a way to get at those issues and that those issues were important."

Whenever a politician loses a close election, like Hillary Clinton did to Donald Trump in 2016, pundits can concoct a laundry list of plausible explanations. One of the more compelling is that the 2016 election was about the voters' desire for change and that Hillary failed to project a credible, authentic narrative that she was robustly on the side of frustrated, angry, ordinary Americans. Her intentional avoidance of any connection with Saul Alinsky, an authentic advocate of power to the people, was symptomatic of her cautious political instincts, which served her poorly and helped doom her candidacy. Since Ab brought up the importance of Alinsky and his ideas about social change in Hillary's formative years, it's worth briefly revisiting that period of her life, which I can identify with.

In 1969 two college students were immersed in writing about Saul Alinsky, the father of community organizing: me, in Evanston, Illinois, and Hillary Rodham, in Wellesley, Massachusetts. I was a year away from completing my PhD dissertation at Northwestern University about Alinsky's theory and practice of social change. Hillary's topic was much the same for her senior thesis at Wellesley College's honors program in political science. She titled it: "There Is Only the Fight . . . An Analysis of the Alinsky Model." We both sought out Alinsky, a self-proclaimed radical, and were captivated by him. He was my hero and still is. Alinsky was Hillary's hero, too, but she stopped acknowledging it long ago.

By the late 1960s, Alinsky was a popular speaker on the college lecture circuit. Erudite, irreverent, and funny, he appealed to a swath of students who were pro–civil rights, anti–Vietnam War, and generally anti-establishment. They identified him as a kindred spirit, even though he was more than twice their age and the era's motto was "Don't trust anybody over thirty." To be sure, not all twenty-something activists were persuaded by Alinsky's distinctive blend of hard-headed organizing and his celebration of American democracy as a means of social change. Many New Left leaders started from the premise that the imperialistic, racist American political system was incorrigibly corrupt. A smaller number, such as Bill Ayers, who cofounded the Weatherman Underground, turned to violence. Alinsky's contempt for them was unequivocal because they were eliciting a political backlash and discrediting the antiwar movement. "Any serious radical organization would have executed the Weatherman bombers as a matter of course," he said. "The worst form of social treason is to stir up a reaction that is more damaging to you than to your enemy. The Weatherman should be getting paid by the extreme right for the work they do."

I met Saul Alinsky in the summer of 1966 after reading a fascinating two-part interview, "Conversations with a Radical," in *Harper's* magazine. I talked my way into a ten-day seminar he was leading at Asilomar, a rustic campground in Pacific Grove, California, and a short drive from Alinsky's small house in Carmel Highlands. As I recall, there were about thirty clergy of various denominations at the seminar and me, a graduate student at San Francisco State College. The *Harper's* interviews had drawn me in; the ten days with Alinsky hooked me.

He was an authentic American original with an unusual mix of intellectual and street creds—a brilliant graduate student in the famed Sociology Department at the University of Chicago; a well-read master of the Federalist Papers and the Great Books; an acquaintance of Chicago mobsters; author of the 1940s best seller about community organizing, *Reveille for Radicals*, and, later, a biography of his mentor and hero, labor leader John L. Lewis; and, most important, the organizer, along with his small band of talented associates, of low-income communities of eastern European immigrants, Mexican Americans in California, and American blacks. An influential article in *Fortune* magazine in 1962, "The City and the Negro," cited Alinsky's organizing work in Woodlawn and noted, "in many ways [it was] the most impressive experiment affecting the Negro anywhere in the U.S."

In the summer of 1966 at Asilomar, against the backdrop of recent urban riots, the prospect of more long, hot summers, and Dr. Martin Luther King Jr.'s emerging failure in Chicago, Saul Alinsky's ideas were powerful and hopeful. A few months later, I returned to Northwestern and began researching my dissertation on Alinsky. But I also started to think that rather than becoming an academic like Frank Haiman, I might want to become one of Saul Alinsky's organizers.

Hillary Rodham had a chance to work with Alinsky, or at least she had an opportunity to attend his new training institute for organizers in Chicago, after she graduated from Wellesley in 1969. Twenty-year-old Hillary met Alinsky in 1968 and started research on her senior thesis later that year. She interviewed him three times—once at Wellesley and twice in nearby Boston, where Alinsky's wife lived. She has never spoken publicly about why she was attracted to Alinsky, and the reasons are only implied in her thesis. But like me, she found Alinsky captivating and his work timely and important. Like many other young people in the second half of the 1960s, Hillary Rodham was profoundly affected and transformed by the social and political upheavals of those years. Before she went to Wellesley, her milieu had been staunchly Republican, white Park Ridge, a middle-class suburb bordering Chicago. Her father—a domineering, conservative Republican businessman—almost certainly would have voted for Donald Trump rather than a candidate like his daughter. Like her father, Hugh, young Hillary was a Barry Goldwater supporter in 1964, but she was an Alinsky admirer four years later. In that respect, she reminds me of my college roommate Jim Johnson. He, too, was a Goldwater enthusiast, but by the end of the 1960s, Jim was a draft resister and civil rights activist.

Although Hillary's senior thesis is sometimes critical of what she calls Alinsky's philosophical and strategic "inconsistencies," overall, she paints a portrait of a man she respects and admires and who personifies her own emerging search for social justice. "Much of what Alinsky professes does not sound 'radical,'" she writes. "His are the words used in our schools and churches by our parents and their friends, by our peers. The difference is that Alinsky really believes in them and recognizes the necessity of challenging the present structure of our lives. . . . The faith in democracy and in people's ability to 'make it' is peculiarly American and many might doubt its radicalness. Yet Alinsky's belief and devotion is radical; democracy is still a radical idea in a world where we often confuse images with realities and words with actions." In Alinsky, Hillary discovered a bold truth-teller in the tradition of Tom Paine and Sam Adams. For Hillary, Alinsky was an antidote for complacent Park Ridge and the politics and social values of Hugh Rodham.

I became aware of Hillary's senior thesis shortly after she became First Lady in the early 1990s. I asked a friend on her White House staff if I could read it. The answer was no. There was a copy of the thesis at Wellesley, but it was locked away, unavailable to anybody; this included curious journalists such as the conservative Peggy Noonan, a former speechwriter for Ronald Reagan. The secrecy only whetted the appetites of conservatives, who assumed the thesis contained damning revelations of Hillary's anti-American radicalism. Noonan wrote that the hidden thesis would turn out to be Hillary's "Rosetta stone." After the Clintons left the White House, Wellesley made the thesis available to the public. Although there were no damning revelations, Hillary continued to distance herself from Alinsky.

In her memoir *Living History*, published in 2003, she includes one short, misleading paragraph about her youthful hero, while otherwise going into great detail about her changing political views during her years at Wellesley. "Alinsky was a colorful and controversial figure who managed to offend almost everyone during his long career," she writes. "His prescription for social change required grassroots organizing that taught people to help themselves by confronting government and corporations to obtain the resources and power to improve their lives." This is a concise, accurate characterization of Alinsky's democratic populism that places him in the mainstream of the American tradition of fomenting social change from the bottom up—of working within the political system to make it more responsive to the have-nots. It might have—in fact, it should have—been a major theme of Hillary Clinton's 2016 campaign. But in 2003, in an apparent effort to distance herself from the "radical" Alinsky, she delivers this confusing non sequitur. "But we had had a fundamental disagreement. He believed you could change the system only from the outside. I didn't. Later he offered me a chance to work with him when I graduated from college, and he was disappointed that I decided to go to law school. Alinsky said I would be wasting my time, but my decision was an expression of my belief that the system could be changed from within."

That, of course, was pure baloney. One of Hillary's first jobs after law school was with the Children's Defense Fund (CDF), which was then a new organization that, like Alinsky, worked within the political "system" to change policies affecting poor kids and their families. The founding president of the CDF, Marian Wright Edelman, was a member of the board of directors of Alinsky's Industrial Areas Foundation.

What Hillary doesn't say in her memoir is that she continued to have a warm, adoring relationship with Alinsky after Wellesley. Despite his tough talk, Alinsky was a soft touch and generous with his time and attention when it came to smart college students like Hillary who were angry about injustice, not rigid ideologues, and not afraid to cause trouble. Saul would have loved the commotion Hillary stirred up with her Wellesley commencement address, which followed a bland speech by Massachusetts senator Edward Brooke. Extemporaneously, she chastised the senator for avoiding the controversial issues their student audience cared about. In a recently discovered "Dear Saul" letter from Hillary dated July 8, 1971, after her second year at Yale Law School, she wrote, "I miss our biennial conversations." She asked, "When is that new book coming out [Alinsky's *Rules for Radicals*]—or has it come out and I somehow missed the fulfillment of Revelation? I have just had my one-thousandth conversation about *Reveille [for Radicals]* and need some new material to throw at people. You are being rediscovered again as the New Left–type politicos are finally beginning to think seriously about the hard work of organizing. I seem to have survived law school, slightly bruised, with my belief in and zest for organizing intact." When I read about her "zest for organizing," I immediately think of the young Barack Obama, who came to Chicago twelve years later and was trained by Alinsky disciples to be a community organizer. His organizing experiences became an important chapter in the personal narrative he used to defeat Clinton for the Democratic Party's presidential nomination.

Hillary concludes her letter to Alinsky by thanking him "for the encouraging words last spring in the midst of the Yale-Cambodia madness. . . . The more I've seen places like Yale Law School and the people who haunt them, the more convinced I am that we have the serious business and joy of much work ahead—if the commitment to a free and open society is ever going to mean more than eloquence and frustration." Hillary, who was living in Berkeley, California, that summer and working at a law firm, wrote, "I would love to see you. Let me know if there is any chance of our getting together"—and she included her address and phone number. She received a prompt response from Alinsky's longtime secretary, Georgia Harper. Alinsky was out of the country, Harper wrote, but "since I know his feelings about you I took the liberty of opening your letter." Alinsky was going to be in San Francisco in late July, and Harper suggested that Hillary call him to see about getting together.

Who knows? Maybe Hillary Rodham, with her self-proclaimed "zest for organizing" intact, might have worked with Saul Alinsky after all. But less than a year after she wrote that letter, Alinsky dropped dead of a heart attack on a street in Carmel, California. I had bumped into him six months earlier, walking across the University of Illinois' Chicago campus. He looked like a ghost; he told me that he had been hospitalized with pneumonia and had stopped smoking. Then I knew for sure he was not well because Saul's public persona included an ever-present Benson & Hedges cigarette between the first and second fingers of his right hand. I had already talked with Saul about working with him, but he had said he was not ready to hire new organizers and suggested that my teaching for a few years at the University of Illinois made good economic sense. He was a very practical man. But he left the door open, and perhaps an idea or two he was massaging might lead to an organizing project. When he died, my interest in becoming an Alinsky organizer died, too.

"Your friend Ken Starr," Hillary whispered sarcastically to Ab. She had said it to him more than once. On this occasion, Ab remembers seeing Hillary at a fund-raising event; it was a few years after Bill Clinton's impeachment.

"She came to Illinois when she was running for the Senate in 2000," Ab says. "I went through the receiving line. I gave her a hug. She whispered to me, 'What do you think of your friend Ken Starr now?'"

Ab and Ken Starr, the independent counsel who tried to destroy Bill Clinton's presidency, had a friendly relationship when they served together on the Court of Appeals in the mid-1980s. Then, in the summer of 1994, Starr was appointed independent counsel at about the same time Ab agreed to be Clinton's White House counsel. Starr's appointment was a surprise to the Washington legal and political establishment, and his no-holds-barred pursuit of Bill and Hillary would be a big surprise to Ab. In retrospect, there had been warning signs.

Starr was the second independent counsel appointed to investigate allegations related to Whitewater, the failed Arkansas land deal the Clintons had invested in, along with a number of other controversial issues that surfaced, including the suicide of Vince Foster, a deputy White House counsel and friend of the Clintons. After Clinton's inauguration in 1993, media attention on Whitewater increased, and the president had to decide whether he should call for an independent counsel to investigate the allegations, which the Clintons vigorously denied. White House counsel Bernie Nussbaum, an old friend of the Clintons, argued vehemently against an independent counsel. He accurately predicted that it would lead to a long fishing expedition, a legal and political nightmare. The far better alternative, he said, was to give documents to the appropriate congressional committees and offer to have the Clintons testify. The president opted for an independent counsel. In his trenchant postmortem of the events leading to Clinton's impeachment, Professor Ken Gormley writes, "President Clinton would describe his decision to appoint an independent counsel as one of the greatest miscalculations of his entire presidency."

The first independent counsel appointed by Attorney General Janet Reno to investigate Whitewater and other issues was Robert Fiske, who had a reputation as a first-rate lawyer and a moderate Republican. Right-wing Republicans, however, were furious about the Fiske appointment. Fiske and his legal team concluded that Vince Foster's death had been a suicide, not, as some right-wingers recklessly charged, a murder arranged by the Clintons as some sort of Whitewater cover-up. Shortly thereafter, Fiske was abruptly fired and replaced by Ab's "good friend" Ken Starr. Well before Starr was appointed, conservatives had plotted and successfully maneuvered to take control of the independent counsel's investigation. Weeks before Clinton was elected, Chief Justice Rehnquist had quietly changed the composition of the obscure three-judge panel that oversaw independent counsel investigations. Rehnquist appointed two Far Right Republican judges—one of whom, David Santelle, became the presiding judge. Santelle had been appointed to Ab's Court of Appeals by Ronald Reagan in 1987. Ab held Santelle in unusually low regard.

Santelle's three-judge panel was technically part of the Court of Appeals, but it was so obscure that Ab knew nothing about it. In retrospect, Ab might have thought differently about Ken Starr's appointment, seeing it as part of a "vast right-wing conspiracy," as Hillary Clinton famously called the political assault on the Clinton presidency some years later. But Ab and Starr had had a good working relationship when they served together. Starr was a predictably conservative Republican, but Ab considered him intelligent, serious, and fair-minded. Starr had never been a prosecutor, and Ab thought of him as a mild-mannered, polite man who lacked the killer instincts that might prompt him to go for an opponent's jugular or engage in interpersonal warfare. Ab tells me about the time he and Starr were on a panel with Ab's contentious nemesis Laurence Silberman. "Silberman and I had a major dispute in conference, and he said that if I were ten years younger he'd punch me out. Starr was looking up at the ceiling, wishing he wasn't there."

So Ab told the press that Ken Starr would be fair, which angered Hillary. She had been against appointing an independent counsel, but apparently, that was an argument she lost at the pillow. She expected trouble. But in fact, the Clintons' first encounter with Starr was friendly enough. Starr wanted to take depositions from them, and Ab arranged for it to be done without fanfare. "I asked Ken if he would go through the back door at the White House so the press wouldn't be all lined up waiting to talk with him. And he agreed." So on a quiet Saturday, April 22, 1995, Starr began by deposing the president. It was civil, even friendly. When the deposition was over, Ken and Bill were chatting about White House history, and Bill turned to Ab and told him to show Starr the Lincoln Bedroom. But Ab recalls that "as Hillary walked by to take the witness chair, she whispered to me, 'Don't you dare show him the Lincoln Bedroom.'" Ab didn't, although another White House lawyer did.

For several months, Ab says, he had no reason to doubt Starr's motives. "I had this back-channel connection with somebody who worked in Starr's office. A good guy. He was telling me what was happening. He was sort of my Deep Throat. We would meet in out-of-the-way places. I think I told my deputy about it. I felt I needed somebody to know about it." Soon, however, Starr's attitude changed. Ab was stunned when Starr announced that he was going to reopen the investigation into Vince Foster's death. "It was one of the first things I had asked him to do," Ab recalls. "I said let's close this up because it's done. He clearly committed suicide. And Starr said, 'Yeah, we're definitely going to close that up.' Well, between the time he assured me it was going to be closed and his announcement he was reopening the investigation, they had hired a couple of junkyard dogs, and nothing was going well anymore." To make matters worse, Hillary had become unhappy with Ab. Jane Sherburne, an attorney who was technically on Ab's staff but really worked for Harold Ickes, was also monitoring Whitewater developments. She complained to Hillary that Ab was keeping her out of his secret meetings with his contact at Starr's office. "Hillary confronted me on it. I said to the First Lady that this is something that can only happen if it's back channel. Well, the First Lady said, 'You're keeping her out because she's a woman.'" After Ab tells me this, there's silence. I finally ask him whether Hillary knew he had three daughters. Ab laughs. "It didn't go well from there on in."

In January 1996, after the long-missing Whitewater billing records from Hillary Clinton's Arkansas law firm mysteriously appeared in the family's living quarters, Starr subpoenaed the First Lady to testify before a grand jury. It was an unprecedented event, which included the spectacle of a perp walk as Hillary waded through a phalanx of TV cameras and reporters at the front entrance to the old US Courthouse on Third and Constitution Avenue. The heretofore mild-mannered Starr was learning how to go for the jugular. "I was just furious," Ab says. "By then, Starr was out of control." But Ab's fury was expressed as a private citizen, because shortly before Starr served his subpoena, Ab resigned as White House counsel.

Ab insists that he left because he was exhausted after slightly more than a year of sixteen-hour days. "I was a list guy," Ab says. "Every night before I went home, I made a list of things I had to do the next day. But almost without exception, I could never get to the list because there were so many things that would come up at the senior staff meeting or the junior staff meeting that I had to get involved with. At one point, I had about three pages on my list of important things to do. Almost never did we do things according to plan. When we tried, the plan blew up." Just after he left the White House, Ab discovered he had walking pneumonia. But other factors contributed to his departure, and they slowly trickle out during our conversations.

A New York Times column written by William Safire after Bill Clinton's reelection in 1996 raised the issue of several White House improprieties, including sleepovers in the Lincoln Bedroom for wealthy contributors to the Democratic Party and fund-raising phone calls made from the White

House, despite Ab's directive, part of which Safire quoted: "Campaign fund-raising activities of any kind are prohibited in or from government buildings." Safire then wrote this about Ab: "The out-of-step old jurist added emphatically that 'no fund-raising phone calls . . . may emanate from the White House.'" I ask Ab about Safire's column, and he says, "I remember saying that and being furious at [Vice President] Al Gore, who was making calls from the White House, because he should have known better. I didn't expect any more from Bill Clinton." Ab tells me that the prohibition on fund-raising in government buildings was taken seriously by his former House colleagues, including the tough Phil Burton. "I remember that Phil, who was not exactly a do-gooder on this stuff, and I were in the Rayburn Room, and a lobbyist reached into his pocket and handed Phil a check. Phil said, 'Not here, you goddamn fool. Let's go outside.' And we never made fund-raising calls from our congressional offices."

Ab says that almost everybody on his White House counsel staff was first rate, "absolutely trustworthy." Ab brought in his prize law clerk, James Castello, as his deputy White House counsel. Elena Kagan, who was teaching at the University of Chicago, successfully lobbied for a spot on Ab's staff, too. There were also holdovers from Nussbaum's and Cutler's tenure. One was Beth Nolan. Ab liked her because she was smart, effective, and principled about the right things—at least usually. Then Ab tells me a story about Beth. One winter afternoon, they had meetings on Capitol Hill. It got to be late, after 6:00 p.m., as Ab recalls, and he decided to call it a day. "I lived a few blocks away on New Jersey. I said to the driver, 'Go down New Jersey and I'll get off at 442. It's not out of your way, and then you can go to the White House.' And Beth said, 'Judge, you can't do that.' And I said, 'What are you talking about, Beth?' And she said, 'You can't use the [government] car for personal privilege.' I said, 'Beth, why do I have to go to the White House to get my car and come back here?' And she said, 'Well, all I'm telling you is that you can do it, obviously, but it's wrong.' I said, 'That's crazy.' But I jumped out of the car and walked the three blocks. It was cold as hell."

As Ab tells me, again, about leaving the White House because he was bone tired, he adds, "This person was really getting to me." He's referring to Jane Sherburne, the lawyer who was technically on his staff but taking orders from Harold Ickes, one of Panetta's deputy chiefs of staff. Ickes was close to Hillary, and one of his specialties was knee-to-the-groin politics while fund-raising for Bill Clinton's reelection and riding herd on Whitewater-related scandals. Ab says, "Whenever I said something Sherburne didn't like, she would run to Ickes. Then Ickes would get involved, and we'd have shouting matches. I wouldn't have minded if it had been the president. But I didn't want Ickes, who as far as I knew never practiced much law, telling me what we should do about Ken Starr's investigation." On one especially rancorous occasion, Ab says, "I was complaining about Sherburne, and Ickes said, 'Then fire her.' And I said, 'Maybe I will.' And he said, 'Either fire her or shut up.' So I walked out of the office. I realized that I could fire her, but I didn't have anybody who knew as much about Whitewater. And it would really be a big hassle if I fired her. And it was about six months after the screaming match with Ickes that I decided to leave."

The Making of a (Possibly) Great President

It's two months before Ab's ninetieth birthday, and I say good-bye to him after an especially fruitful and enjoyable five-hour conversation—except for the very end.

When I picked him up for breakfast, I asked if he wanted to go to the Valois in Hyde Park, where he and Barack Obama met for meals and conversation. "No," he said, "let's go to The Bagel. I have a taste for salami." Our conversation that sunny, chilly November morning started with a postmortem of the previous night's televised debate in Milwaukee with the 2016 Republican presidential candidates. Ab was troubled, even appalled, by what he had heard. "I can't believe the Republican Party has declined to such a level, I really can't. None of them would I vote for dog catcher." But it wasn't only the candidates who unnerved Ab; it was also the raucous whooping and hollering of the audience. "The response to the anti-government rhetoric I heard last night is frightening," he said. "It was like Hitler speaking about the Jews."

We eventually got around to the topic of his old friend President Obama, as we often did, and myriad other topics, including Ab's reform agenda and the country's future. It was a thoughtful and optimistic conversation—so I wasn't prepared for the very end. We had gone back to his apartment after The Bagel, and as I was about to leave, I said, "I'm looking forward to celebrating your ninetieth birthday."

To which Ab replied, "I hope I make it to ninety."

He said it with a smile, but I wasn't smiling. For me, it was an unexpectedly sad ending to what had been another special day with my wise and fun-loving friend. On the elevator down from the seventh floor, I considered the sad possibility that Ab wouldn't be here tomorrow—and for that matter, I might not be here either. But I also kept thinking about that smile. It seemed incongruous at the time. But the more I thought about it, the better I understood it. I've come to understand that Ab had accepted that the end was near, whenever it might be, and he could live reasonably comfortably and peacefully with that. Maybe now, when my time comes, it will be easier for me to smile, too.

Ab and I met Barack Obama at about the same time. Ab was more impressed than I was, although neither of us imagined we had just shaken hands with a future president of the United States. But at least a few clairvoyant Chicago liberals would later say that's exactly what they envisioned after their first encounter with young Barack Obama.

I met Obama on a cold winter afternoon in 1998 at the headquarters of AFSCME Council 31 on North Wacker Drive in the Chicago Loop. He was thirty-six years old, just beginning his second year as an Illinois state senator and frustrated with his role of rookie legislator in the minority party. At least that's what I was told by my friend Henry Bayer, the director of Council 31, who brought us together. Henry thought we had something in common, apart from our interest in community organizing. Both Obama and I were interested in starting nonprofits that would promote progressive issues. In my case, I was inspired by the success of conservatives who had established a network of state organizations, smaller but energetic versions of the Heritage Foundation in Washington. They seemed to be influencing policy debates and public opinion with little competition from largely nonexistent progressive organizations. My strategy was to establish a headquarters in Chicago and develop a network of progressive legislators and activists in half a dozen politically competitive midwestern states, including Michigan and Wisconsin, where Donald Trump eked out victories in 2016. Obama, Henry told me, had talked about starting something similar in Illinois—something that would also give Obama a visible statewide platform, which he didn't have as a junior senator from Hyde Park. So Obama and I met for a couple of hours in Henry's office. Henry was away, but we were joined by his deputy at the time, Roberta Lynch.

I wish I could say I have vivid memories of our discussion, but I don't. Obama mentioned the book he had written, *Dreams from My Father*. I think we talked a little about Saul Alinsky and community organizing, which had brought Obama to Chicago in 1985. Obama expressed an interest in helping with my project, and he came to a planning meeting a few months later, held in a conference room at O'Hare Airport. After the meeting, the two of us had breakfast in Hyde Park near the University of Chicago Law

School, where he taught. We continued the conversation in his cluttered law school office while he opened a stack of mail. He volunteered to be on a fund-raising subcommittee for my project but didn't actually do anything. He seemed like a nice guy, but maybe a little self-absorbed.

Ab was chief judge of the Court of Appeals in 1991 when he first heard the name Barack Obama, he tells me. One of Ab's clerks, Sheryll Cashin, had been two years ahead of Obama at Harvard Law School and had worked with him on the *Harvard Law Review*. "She told me about him," Ab says. "She was going back to Cambridge, and I said that I would be interested in interviewing him. I was always interested in diversifying the staff, and as president of the *Harvard Law Review*, he was obviously a bright student. She came back and said he didn't want to clerk for me. I said, 'Oh, he probably wants to clerk for a black judge.' And she said, 'No, he would want to clerk for you, but he isn't going to clerk. He's going back to Chicago and run for public office.' I didn't know he had any history in Chicago; I didn't know about his community organizing days. So I thought, boy, he really has chutzpah. You just don't go to Chicago and announce that you're running for office. I kind of forgot about it. Well, about six years later, I came back to Chicago, and he was already in the state senate and teaching at the University of Chicago Law School. And I was teaching there, too, and we started having breakfast together regularly. He was an apt student." Ab became something of a sounding board and mentor for Obama, teaching him about the mores and characters in Springfield, much like Marshall Korshak had done for Ab. Barack and Ab became friends. As we're driving through Hyde Park one day, Ab says, "Somewhere around here Barack and Michelle had a little apartment, very tiny. Zoey and I went there for dinner. Malia had just been born. Michelle cooked the dinner and alternated between talking with us and looking in on Malia."

At the law school, Ab taught a course on the legislative process, while Obama was teaching constitutional law. Ab recalls, "I envied the grades he got from students. The students grade their professors and then post them. His grades were 9s and 10s. Everybody just fell in love with him."

"What did you think of Obama back then?" I ask Ab.

His immediate response, which I didn't expect, is that he thought of Obama in stark contrast to other black politicians in Chicago. "I had been very unhappy about the state of black politicians in Chicago," he says. In Congress, Ab had served with "some very distinguished blacks," and he mentions Parren Mitchell, Andrew Young, Shirley Chisholm, Barbara Jordan, Louis Stokes. But in Chicago, "there were few blacks of any distinction in the political scene," Ab says. Even Harold Washington, who became a beloved figure in the black community when he was elected mayor in 1983, was a pedestrian politician for much of his career. "I had known Harold for many years," Ab says. "He had been one of the machine guys. He turned out to be a much better mayor than I thought he would be. And he also turned out to be a real inspiration to the younger generation, and I realized how important that was. It was obvious from the first time I got to know Barack that he had those inspirational capacities."

Well, yes, Obama can be inspirational, I think to myself, but as we've all come to realize after Obama's years on the national stage, there have been long stretches when our often enigmatic forty-fourth president has been something other than inspirational. Again and again, as Ab and I rummage through a lifetime of memories in our conversations, we return to the mystery of Barack Obama.

In the summer of 2013, Ab and I are having lunch one day in Hyde Park at the Valois Cafeteria. I ask Ab about Obama's ill-fated campaign for Congress in 2000, when he challenged incumbent Bobby Rush. "He shouldn't have run," Ab says bluntly. "He didn't understand the role of the incumbent. A bad guy like Bobby Rush you don't knock off just because you're the good guy." I point out that Ab attempted something quite similar when he challenged incumbent Barratt O'Hara in 1966 and lost. "I think that I was a little wiser," Ab explains. "I already had ten years under my belt. I understood the ground game because that's how I got elected to the state legislature. I got 48, 49 percent of the vote the first time I ran against O'Hara because I had a ground game. Barack got shellacked by Rush." Indeed he did, losing by 31 points.

But Obama wasn't done in only by the absence of a strong ground game, which the former community organizer might have, well, organized. He was also dreadful on the stump. Ab recalls, "I went with him to several places. One was a black church, and he was awful. He was a dull University of Chicago professor lecturing the unwashed, who couldn't be less interested. I hadn't realized that as a campaigner he thought campaigning was like lecturing in a law school. But he realized out of that very disheartening loss that you've got to show them, you've got to be a showman. Boy, did he learn."

Well, yes and no, I think to myself. As a campaigner, Obama's oratory was better by the time he ran in the Democratic primary for US Senate in 2004, plus the campaign had good TV ads. But his upset victory in the primary had at least as much to do with his weak and ill-fated opponents. The front-runner's campaign imploded in domestic scandal. Then, after Obama won the primary, lightning struck again: in the early run-up to the general election in November, the campaign of his seemingly formidable Republican opponent ended abruptly—also because of a domestic scandal. After this once-in-a-blue-moon sequence of events, Ab called Obama "the luckiest politician I've ever seen." By then, however, Ab had also seen Obama's strength as a campaigner and his increasingly skillful political work in Springfield, validating Ab's early assessment of him. Obama was both lucky and good, and he had a unique, fascinating life story.

Proud and excited by Obama's win in the Senate primary, Ab, in a burst of extravagant praise, told our mutual friend Henry Bayer that Obama "was the most talented politician he had known in fifty years." Henry passed along Ab's assessment to his friend Jack Corrigan, who was in the midst of organizing the Democratic National Convention in Boston in the summer of 2004. (As a college student at Harvard in the 1970s, Corrigan had taken time off and worked in two of Ab's congressional campaigns.) Ab's enthusiastic testimonial was the first time Corrigan had heard of Barack Obama. When more pro-Obama appraisals came in from other sources, Corrigan called Ab to hear firsthand about Obama. Then, according to Corrigan, a consensus was reached in the John Kerry for president campaign "to take a leap on a state senator" as the convention's keynote speaker. Obama electrified the convention with perhaps the best political speech of his life, but he also introduced himself to the country as an exciting, distinctive young leader. In retrospect, it was Obama's first speech of his own presidential campaign.

For the last three years of Ab's life, he and I had some difficult discussions about President Obama's leadership, record, and likely legacy. I sometimes felt uncomfortable during these discussions because I knew—or at least I assumed—that Ab was going to be protective of Obama and less critical of him than I was. It started out that way, but over many hours and many months, we came closer to a shared vision.

Eight months into Obama's second term, Ab and Zoe, their Milwaukee friends Ruth and Len Zubrensky, and I were having dinner at Deleece, a North Side Chicago bistro. Len asked Ab to name the four or five greatest presidents. Before Ab could answer, Len said, "Roosevelt!" To which Ab replied, "Which one?" After a little more banter between the old college roommates, Len said, "On a scale of 1 to 100, what grade would you give Obama?" To which Ab replied, "80." Before Ab could explain, the waiter arrived, and the conversation shifted elsewhere.

The next day, Ab and I are having breakfast at The Bagel, and I ask him about his grade for Obama. "Last night you said you'd give Obama an 80."

And Ab says, "Would you give him higher?"

"I was thinking about that," I say. "It depends on what school you're attending. An 80 could be a B or less than a B."

Ab says, "At Chicago, it's an A. I graduated with an 80 average, third in my class. And that's about where I would grade Obama, a low A." Then Ab ticks off, in the laundry-list fashion of a State of the Union address, some of Obama's accomplishments: a vastly improved economy compared with what he inherited, a major expansion of health insurance, a new national commitment on global warming, gay rights, and so forth. "And his thoughtful approach will be given more credit," Ab says. "Right now, it often looks like he's being hesitant. In many respects, he's a minimal liberal, a minimal progressive. He doesn't strike aggressively, and that's part of his problem. But it will also be a plus for history." And then Ab stresses the truly historic meaning of Barack Obama's presidency: in fifty years, "it will become more significant that he was the first black president. Now it's so divisive. A lot of people think it's wonderful and a lot of people think it's terrible. But fifty years from now, it will be seen as a big breakthrough that the country elected a black man as president."

Yes, I suspect Ab is right. And I've suspected for a long time that Obama himself, perhaps more than anybody else, appreciates the unsettling symbolic power, for many Americans, of having a black man in the White House. But I had hoped for more in the summer of 2008 when I wrote this in the *Huffington Post*:

One year ago, on June 22, 2007, in Manchester, New Hampshire, Barack Obama told an audience that "we cannot settle for a second Gilded Age in America." Those were meant to be fighting words; they were preceded by Obama's paean to Teddy Roosevelt who, along with Wisconsin's Senator, Fighting Bob LaFollette, personified Progressive Era reformers reining in corporate power in America's first Gilded Age.

In Manchester last June, Obama spoke admiringly of TR's political courage, recalling that as New York governor "he had already begun to antagonize the state's political machine by attacking its system of favors and corporate giveaways." When Roosevelt became president after William McKinley was assassinated, "the greatest fears of all the entrenched interests came true," Obama said. "Over a century later, America needs this kind of leadership more than ever."

The New Hampshire speech is arguably Obama's most important. It transcends social issues such as race and goes to the heart of contemporary America's overarching economic and political inequalities and institutional failures. It also helps to place Obama in a larger narrative that Americans understand and can identify with.

A year ago, Obama saw a close parallel between the "robber barons, railroad tycoons and oil magnates" of the first Gilded Age, and today's powerful oil and drug company executives and financial interests that dominate "a new economy where more wealth is in danger of falling into fewer hands; where the average CEO now earns more in one day than an average worker earns in an entire year."

Is Barack Obama willing to shake things up in Washington if he is elected president, like the reformers of the Progressive Era?

There are doubters, in part because Obama has not consistently and forcefully employed the themes he struck in Manchester a year ago. Indeed, *Newsweek*'s Howard Fineman wrote recently that "in terms of policy, [Obama] is not looking to do the unexpected, or the radically new. He made an unspoken calculation long ago: that he, himself, is change enough."

Fineman proved to be largely right, I think, although I had reason to hope for more—and I think Ab did, too. Obama told us over and over again during the campaign that he wanted to "fundamentally change the way Washington works." In the Manchester speech, Obama sounded like a true reformer—like Bernie Sanders sounded in 2016. But by nature and calculation, Obama operated like he himself was all the boat-rocking the country could abide. Even President Obama's most controversial initiative, the Affordable Care Act (ACA), was a recycled conservative concept crafted years earlier by the Heritage Foundation and implemented successfully in Massachusetts under Republican governor Mitt Romney. Incongruously, the corporate-friendly ACA was tarred and feathered by congressional Republicans and branded derisively as Obamacare, an illogical lightning rod if there ever was one. Soon after the legislation passed the Senate without a single Republican vote, Mitch McConnell tossed red meat to his party's white conservative base in the South and elsewhere when he proclaimed, "The single most important thing we want to achieve is for President Obama to be a one-term president." That was the Republicans' game plan from the day the first African American was elected president, and they refused to negotiate with him on virtually anything.

So nearly from the start of his administration, the role Obama had enjoyed playing both at Harvard and in Springfield—conciliator between competing factions—was unavailable to him. "When he got to the White House, there was nobody to negotiate with," Ab says about the Tea Party—

fueled intransigence Obama encountered. In Springfield, Ab says, "He was just the master negotiator. He was LBJ without the club. So his great tool has been unusable for the most part. I think that in Barack's case, it's because he is black. There's too much inherent racism left in the country for him to overcome it."

But Ab and I also talk about self-inflicted wounds, especially in Obama's critical first year. Ab is unsparing in describing what he thinks were lasting blunders.

In my first conversation with Ab, I complained about the disastrous 2010 elections, when Democrats lost sixty-three seats and control of the House of Representatives, six seats in the Senate, and governorships and state legislatures throughout the country. The Democrats' massive midterm defeat was the worst for either party since the 1930s. Obama's legislative agenda was compromised by the results of the 2010 elections for the remainder of his presidency. And all this happened, I say to Ab, after the Republican Party had been thoroughly discredited only a few years earlier by scandal in the House of Representatives, the Bush administration's increasingly unpopular Iraq War, and the worst economic collapse since the Great Depression. How could a disgraced political party rise from the dead in the span of only two years and remake the political landscape? Ab says, "It was a total miscalculation of what Obama's priorities should have been. When he had a majority in both houses when he was elected, instead of health care, if he had done a big jobs program like Roosevelt's WPA, the political results could have been different." Indeed, in the 1934 midterm elections after Roosevelt took office, the Democrats picked up seats. "The difference was that Roosevelt really put things out there that excited his base," Ab says.

Obama's health insurance initiative did not excite the base. But it was worse than that. In young Barack Obama's world of community organizing, it was a cardinal sin to push an issue that creates a backlash and organizes a more powerful opposition. According to Ab, Obama and his aides also learned the wrong lesson from First Lady Hillary Clinton's failure to win congressional approval of health insurance reform in 1993. "Hillary, as you may remember, decided that the way to get it through was to come out with a full-blown baby and to present it to the papas in the Senate and say, this is it. A dumb idea, and it was dead on arrival. The Obama people took such a wrong lesson from that. They took the lesson that you had to let the Senate work its will; you would prod for the general idea but not get stuck on specifics. Keep telling them you've got to pass health care. It ended up with the Senate passing the worst sausage that you can imagine"—by which Ab means a complicated bill that was poorly understood by Obama supporters and therefore a political liability going into the 2010 elections. Still, Ab thinks that Obamacare, which has provided insurance coverage to some 20 million people, was an important, historic step in the right direction, imperfect as it is. Whether the extraordinarily high political cost was worthwhile remains to be seen.

When Barack Obama took office in January 2009, the economy was still sliding precariously toward the edge of the cliff, but his first inaugural address was much more cautious than FDR's. While acknowledging that the country was facing a "crisis," President Obama made only a quick, vague reference to the possible culprits and seemingly assigned blame to all of us. "Our economy is badly weakened, a consequence of greed and irresponsibility on the part of some, but also our collective failure to make hard choices and prepare the nation for a new age." Roosevelt had been blunt, placing blame and responsibility "primarily . . . [on] the rulers of the exchange of mankind's goods [who] have failed, through their own stubbornness and their own incompetence, have admitted their failure, and abdicated. Practices of the unscrupulous money changers stand indicted in the court of public opinion, rejected by the hearts and minds of men."

One day, I mention to Ab that after Obama was reelected in 2012, he gave a speech in which he said that income inequality was going to be the "lodestar" for the remainder of his administration. And then, as I begin to say, "Well, gee whiz . . . ," a despondent-looking Ab cuts me off. "Five years into it," he says sadly, referring to the tardiness of addressing income inequality. He then relates what he calls "one of the saddest stories I have to tell you about Barack." Ab says, "This is when he was running for the Senate, I think. We had breakfast or lunch. I used to call it 'the gap,' the gap between those who have and those who haven't. I said to him, 'You know, the gap is something that really is the overwhelming problem in our society, and you ought to be a closer of the gap.'" Then Ab stopped and didn't say another word to me. We sat in silence for several more seconds. I say, "Barack didn't say anything?" And Ab just shakes his head somberly.

In Ab's opinion, some of Obama's earliest and most surprising blunders involved a number of high-level appointments he made soon after the 2008 election. "I was shocked when Barack appointed Rahm," Ab says, referring to Rahm Emanuel, Obama's first chief of staff. "I remember hearing the rumor, and I called whomever and said, 'Is there any truth to that?' And he said, 'It's a done deal.' I said, 'You gotta be kidding.'" Ab knew Rahm from his stint in the Clinton White House, when Rahm had been a junior staffer. Emanuel prided himself on being a smart, aggressive tactician, but he was mainly a fixer and a deal maker, deferential to establishment power and money. For Ab, Emanuel personified none of the lofty possibilities Obama had evoked during the campaign. "I don't think of Barack and Rahm as being on the same page in terms of what the social contract is about or the role of government." When I ask why, Ab responds that Rahm's attitude is "help the rich and things will work out for everybody else. He's a trickle-down Democrat. That's different than a trickle-down Republican. A trickle-down Republican says that all you have to do is help the top and everything works out. Trickle-down Democrats say, no, you've got to help the poor, but part of the way you help them is by getting good guys at the top who will trickle it down. And Barack got a lot of those good guys."

Ab also had strong initial reservations about Obama's pick of Hillary Clinton as his secretary of state. We're having breakfast in February 2016, shortly after Ab celebrated his ninetieth birthday, when I ask him about a news story I remember in which he expressed concern about possible conflicts of interest between the Clinton Foundation's international fundraising and Hillary's role as secretary of state. "I got into lots of trouble," Ab says. "Obama had just gotten elected. It was the interim period before he took office. The rumors started flying about Hillary. The *New York Times* called and asked what I thought. I said that I'd worry that Bill and his foundation would cause serious conflict of interest problems. And that got printed."

"What happened next?" I ask Ab.

"Both Barack and his people and Clinton were upset about that," he tells me. I ask whether he heard about that directly or indirectly, and he says, "Directly from Axelrod," referring to a phone call from David Axelrod, Obama's top strategist.

I think that when Obama made his high-level appointments, he knew exactly what he was getting most of the time. Ab sees it a little differently. "Let me tell you what I decided is one of Barack's big problems," Ab says. "He has bad judgment about people." Among other appointments, Ab is critical of Obama's economic advisers, including Timothy Geithner, his first secretary of the treasury, and Larry Summers, director of the National Economic Council. Ab remembers Summers from the Clinton White House, where he and Bob Rubin were strong proponents of deregulating the financial industry. "If you rely on people like Larry Summers and Rahm Emanuel to be draftsmen of your agenda, what happens is that you get some good things and a lot of bad things. You miss a lot of opportunities." That reminds me of a conversation I had with my friend Julia Gordon, a lawyer at the pro-consumer Center for Responsible Lending. Early in his administration, President Obama reneged on a campaign promise to support a bankruptcy reform provision that Julia and other reformers estimated would save at least 1.5 million families from foreclosure. Julia, who had been hopeful about the new administration, was dumbfounded. As journalist William Greider later wrote, "The measure passed easily in the House, but was defeated by the Senate. The White House wouldn't let reformers include it in the stimulus package or in Obama's first budget."

When rumors circulated in the summer of 2013 that Obama was considering nominating Summers to head the Federal Reserve, Ab was appalled and wrote the president a letter. Ab says that when Obama was first elected president, he had encouraged Ab to communicate with him, especially about Supreme Court appointments, and had promised "he would read my letters carefully." Ab had written to Obama when he was considering his first Supreme Court appointment. "I didn't mention any names," Ab says. "I just said that this is the most important part of your legacy and you ought to think carefully about it and not worry about politics. Do what you think is right. He thanked me for the letter." In his letter about Summers, Ab says, "I recited conversations that I personally had with Summers when I was at the White House and Summers was at Treasury. I said that Summers's views were so antithetical to Obama's positions on minimum wage, Glass-Steagall, on the simplification of the tax code. I can't see how somebody who has such different views as you have should be appointed for a term of years that will extend beyond your term to be the most influential person on the economy." Ab didn't receive a response from the president, but a groundswell of opposition derailed the possibility of a Summers nomination. The vehement opposition was generated partly by Summers's widely criticized remarks as president of Harvard in 2005, when he had asserted that the underrepresentation of women in engineering and science was because women didn't have the intellectual aptitude for those professions. Ab, the father of three daughters, found those views appalling, too.

I ask Ab again about Obama's selection of Eric Holder as attorney general. Months earlier, we had talked about Holder's record of not vigorously prosecuting Wall Street and bank executives for their roles in the subprime mortgage disaster that brought the country to the edge of a financial meltdown. "Whose responsibility was it?" I ask Ab. "Was it Holder's Justice Department or President Obama's Justice Department."

"It is the president's Justice Department," Ab says.

To which I respond, "But isn't the attorney general supposed to be an independent operator? As I recall, one of the criticisms of President Kennedy when he appointed his brother, Bobby, as attorney general was that Bobby was going to do his brother's bidding. So help me out, Ab. You were a Supreme Court law clerk, chief judge of the appeals court for the DC Circuit, and a White House counsel. The attorney general is not a mere political appointment. It's the *Justice* Department. So how do you serve the president as his appointee and yet maintain an independent role as the attorney general?"

"Let me say this," Ab begins. "The president of the United States is the chief executive of the country. He appoints every one of those top-level people. It is his responsibility. During Watergate, the question was, could Nixon fire the AG and then the other AG because they wouldn't carry out his orders. The answer is clearly yes. If you're going to be the attorney general, you have to do what the president tells you to do. Having said that, the three departments in the cabinet that really have to have some measure of independence are Justice, State, and Treasury. Notice I didn't say Defense because the Defense decisions are much more political. But Justice, State, and Treasury have to be somewhat independent of the president but still under his control. So, when the attorney general is initiating a criminal investigation, the president should keep as far away from that as possible. You need a Chinese Wall. The White House doesn't talk to the attorney general about anybody being prosecuted."

I ask Ab where that position comes from, and he says, "It's been the practice historically, and that's the way it worked when I was White House counsel. I was the only one who could talk to Justice about a criminal investigation, with the understanding that I would merely call to find out what was going on and never to seek to influence the AG. I would call Jamie Gorelick, who was number two at Justice, and ask what's going on with so and so. And that was merely to avoid a situation—I remember, for instance, that Hillary was in Detroit and holding up the hand of a Teamsters official on the same day he was indicted. Other than things like that, the president was not supposed to get involved in a pending criminal investigation. That's the way it should work. But on the other hand, the attorney general is the president's appointee. If there is a policy not to indict white-collar criminals, that's the president's policy, not the AG's."

"So," I say, "you're suggesting that from day one, the policy on not prosecuting Wall Street executives was Obama's."

"Yes," Ab answers. "And he changed that policy when he appointed Loretta Lynch as Holder's successor after six years. She's a prosecutor." And then Ab repeated what he had told me months earlier: Holder was well qualified in most respects, but he was not a prosecutor. "He did not have a prosecutorial mentality," Ab says, "and he had been at this white-shoe law firm where the notion of sending executives to jail was unheard of.

And Obama appointed him knowing, or he should have known, that these things were true, and therefore it was Obama's policy not to prosecute white-collar crime. When Obama brought in Lynch, there was a change in policy, but it was way too late."

The Barack Obama that is indelibly etched in Ab's memory, and how he prefers to think of his friend's extraordinary political talents, is the inspirational Barack Obama he saw in September 2007 at Senator Tom Harkin's steak fry in Davenport, Iowa. Badly trailing his primary opponent Hillary Clinton in the polls, Barack put on a show. "The first time I saw him in action in the presidential campaign was when Zoey and I went out to Iowa for the steak fry," Ab begins. "I was still thinking of how miserably he performed in the campaign against Bobby Rush. We were standing in the front row; this was at the pre–steak fry rally for his people. I saw him standing offstage, looking like his usual pensive self." But when Obama was introduced, it was like a switch was turned on. "He jumped onto the stage, started waving his arms," and Ab mimics a high-energy Barack Obama stirring up the crowd with his impassioned rhetoric. "He was incredible," Ab says. "He had me awestruck. I remember at one point he asked if anybody had ever been to Greenwood, South Carolina, where Edith Child lived, the woman who started the chant 'Fired Up! Ready to Go!' I've been in Greenwood because it used to be represented by a congressman who was a good friend, and I went down there to campaign for him. So without thinking, I raised my hand. And Barack said, 'Ab Mikva's been there.' Then he jumped off the stage and started the chant, 'Fired Up! Ready to Go!' He led the procession to Harkin's steak fry. Sandy, I was eighty-one years old and I was chanting, 'Fired Up! Ready to Go!' This was not Barack Obama as I saw him in the Rush campaign. This was major domo Barack Obama."

But for whatever mystifying reasons, Obama turned on that switch only periodically during the eight years of his presidency. I say to Ab, "He's a bit of a puzzle, isn't he?"

"A lot of a puzzle," Ab answers. And then, reaching for an explanation, Ab says, "I used to think that being a professor, as good a law professor as he was, would be a plus. I was wrong." Ab laughs at his miscalculation, indicating that he should have known better. So I ask Ab why he thought being a good professor would make Obama a good president, and he answers, "Communicating, being able to parse out problems, being able to listen while you talk. But there's also this very careful thoughtfulness and desire to be absolutely sure that you're right before you go ahead. Most of the professors I know, or I knew in my day, are not risk takers. They don't want to be caught speaking from the heart. They want to have thought about it." And here, there's a tinge of ridicule in Ab's voice: "Parse it, weigh the pros and cons, and then come out with a considered judgment. And that's Barack."

"But that's not really you," I say, and I remind Ab that his mentor, the scholarly Ed Levi, hadn't thought Ab would be happy or suited to the scholarly world of the law.

"Right," Ab agrees.

"And you," I point out, "have strong, passionate feelings about issues, which isn't typical of law professors as you describe them."

"Let me put it another way," Ab says. "I think law professors have passions, and I think Barack Obama has passions. But their main priority is to keep those passions in check and always speak from up here [the head]. And that's not what I do."

Millions of Americans were passionate about our first African American president and excited by the bold optimism captured in the title of his book, *The Audacity of Hope*, written in the run-up to the presidential primary campaign. But by the summer of 2009, only six months into the Obama administration, an op-ed appeared in the *Washington Post* by two Obama supporters, Marshall Ganz and Peter Dreier, with the headline: "We Have Hope; Where's the Audacity?" Like me, they were disappointed that the Obama administration had failed to mobilize millions of supporters to push for more progressive health care legislation and other reforms.

The 2008 Obama campaign created the largest, best-organized army of volunteers in the modern history of electoral politics. More than 2 million volunteer foot soldiers were recruited by some 3,000 paid campaign organizers and thousands of volunteer organizers trained in basic community organizing at scores of Camp Obamas. The philosophy, programs, and workshops at these Camp Obamas were shaped to a large extent by Marshall Ganz, a student of the great organizer Fred Ross. Both Ganz and Ross worked with Cesar Chavez, leader of the United Farm Workers Union; Chavez and Ross were disciples of Saul Alinsky and worked for him. But Organizing for America (OFA), the post-campaign entity established by Obama operatives, was not engaging citizens in political action. As Ganz and Dreier noted, Organizing for America was encouraging supporters "to work on local community service projects, such as helping homeless shelters and tutoring children. That's fine, but it's not the way to pass reform legislation."

By the summer of 2009, President Obama's health insurance initiative, including a controversial public option, was already facing strong political headwinds. In Milwaukee, the Wisconsin director of OFA organized a pro-health insurance rally by a coalition of groups at Serb Hall. It was a roguish, atypical political use of OFA. At the rally, elected officials were asked whether they supported a public option. Many did. But when a representative of Senator Herb Kohl, a Democrat, said the senator had not taken a position on the public option, there was booing. The next day Senator Kohl called the White House, angry about the public pressure exerted by OFA.

It certainly would have been audacious for Obama and his team to lead or actively support a popular, organized movement for progressive legislation, but we'll never know if it might have succeeded. OFA was mothballed until Obama's reelection campaign. In the 1930s Franklin Roosevelt was able to pursue progressive policies because there was organized popular pressure from an ascendant labor union movement, Huey Long's "Share the Wealth" adherents, and millions of senior citizens in Townsend Clubs. Barack Obama had no comparable political base on the Left. We tend to forget that fundamental political change almost always starts from the bottom up, not in the Oval Office.

After Obama was reelected in 2012, Ab read Jonathan Alter's book about the campaign, *The Center Holds*, which clarified some things for him. We're in the car driving to the South Side when Ab says, "As far as Alter is concerned, the Democratic Party is the center, and Obama is the center. There's not much of a Left, and there's the crazy Far Right. And most people are where Obama is on most issues. He doesn't please us a lot of the time"—a reference to liberals like the two of us—"like not closing Guantanamo, on some civil liberties, and so forth. But he's a centrist. When I first knew Barack, he was a lot younger, of course, and he was probably more liberal than he is now. With these responsibilities he has, things don't look as easy as they did when you were twenty-five. But he is basically what I hoped he would be, very thoughtful, very bright."

As Ab and I continue to talk, I recall the headline in the satirical website *The Onion* the day after Obama was elected in 2008: "Black Man Given Nation's Worst Job." With the economy possibly heading toward a depression, Barack Obama took the oath of office not only as the country's first African American president but also as one of the least experienced presidents in modern times. He hadn't been in the Senate long enough, as Ab observes, to learn from his legislative failures or to develop close ties with congressional leaders. Ab's former House colleague John Dingell, the longest serving congressman in American history, said that when Obama was elected, he had the thinnest Rolodex of any president he had known. When I mention this to Ab, he says, "Obama made a pretty good inaugural speech and then went about finding where the men's room was." Perhaps if Obama had served a term or two in the Senate before becoming president, he wouldn't have surrounded himself with Wall Street–friendly establishment types and would have been more of the reformer Ab had hoped for, especially in the fateful first two years.

"It could have been so much better," Ab says about Obama's first term. But he is quick to add, "I still think that he's going to be one of the great presidents, his legacy is going to be so good." Ab is "gleeful" that African Americans, who turned out in unprecedented numbers to vote for Obama, can take credit for his electoral victories. "It wouldn't have happened without them," Ab says. And Ab is pleased with Obama's Supreme Court nominations, starting with Sonia Sotomayor, the first Hispanic on the Court. Before Obama announced his second Supreme Court nominee, Elena Kagan, he called Ab. "She had been my clerk, and I liked her, and she will be a great justice," Ab says. "But at the time, I thought Merrick Garland would be better." Ab had known Merrick even longer than he had known Elena. As a college student, Merrick had volunteered in Ab's congressional campaigns in 1972 and 1974. When the president called, Garland was a respected judge on Ab's Court of Appeals. "I told the president how good I thought Elena was and how smart she was, but I also said, 'I hope you're keeping in consideration Merrick Garland.' He said, 'I'm considering Merrick, but let's talk about Elena.' Obviously, he had made up his mind." And then, six years later, Ab was thrilled when the president nominated Garland to fill the vacancy on the Court after Justice Antonin Scalia's death.

So where do Ab and I stand on Obama? Like me, Ab wishes Obama had "seized that enthusiasm that he brought in with him, the enthusiasm of kids, minorities, progressives, and taken on some really major cause, some institution-deserving cause." Although Obamacare may turn out to be a historic achievement, Ab thinks it's too early to know. "I wish he had done something about political corruption instead of making it worse," Ab says, referring to Obama's decision to opt out of the presidential public financing system when he ran in 2008. "But I still think he's going to go down as a great president because he was reelected, the country is better off economically compared to where we were, and I'm glad he's shown restraint in foreign affairs. For almost eight years, we haven't gotten into a new war." And with a big smile, Ab says, "I don't want my money back."

Ab's overall grade of a "low A" is higher than I would write on Obama's report card, at least for now. Like Ab, I think Obama was too cautious on domestic policy and politics but properly, wisely cautious on military and foreign affairs, despite some missteps. He inherited a gigantic mess in a destabilized Middle East, thanks to the recklessness of the Bush-Cheney administration. As Thomas Friedman wrote toward the end of Obama's presidency, "This is absolutely the worst time in 70 years to be managing U.S. foreign policy." But Obama is a historic two-term president who broke through the biggest barrier in American society and confronted a relentless, mean-spirited, often racially motivated opposition and the feverish, often crazed voices of a dying order. Despite the aberration of Donald Trump, Obama, who personifies the new, more inclusive, more diverse America that is slowly emerging, will ultimately triumph. In fifty years, Barack Obama may well be regarded as a heroic figure of Mount Rushmore proportions.

II

Mikva's Challenge for Democracy's Next Generation

Summer is over, but the determined maples are still clinging to their leaves. It's been two years since Ab, Zoe, and I shared a meal and a spirited political conversation with Ruth and Len Zubrensky. On this early fall day in 2015, Ab and I are driving from Chicago to Milwaukee, where Ab is going to speak at Len's memorial service. Ab's dearest friend and college roommate was seven years short of his goal of living to 100.

Ab tells me that most of his family—his grandfather and grandmother, aunts and uncles, his father and sister—are buried in a cemetery on the outskirts of Milwaukee. I inquire about Ab and Zoe's final plans. "Our original preference was to be cremated, but Rachel objected to that." I ask if Rachel, their Reform rabbi daughter, objects for religious reasons. "No," he answers. "Rachel says it's not a religious concern but that the Holocaust was just too recent for her to be comfortable about being burnt. We had wanted our ashes to be strewn over Lake Michigan, where we spent so much of our lives in the Dunes and enjoyed it. But I can understand Rachel's feelings. It really won't matter to me." Ab and Zoe have burial plots west of Chicago in a cemetery affiliated with KAM, their old Hyde Park synagogue.

Ab and Zoe had been members of KAM for decades, Ab says, until recently. They first joined in 1956 when he decided to run for office because somebody said it would be a good idea if he belonged to a synagogue. Ab has some interesting family influences when it comes to religion—his father was an atheist and his daughter is a rabbi—so I ask him to tell me about his faith. "Well, it's confused," he laughs, suggesting it's not a topic he takes too seriously. "I have great respect for Rachel, her intellect and integrity. And part of my faith, and I'm not sure it's even worthy of that name, stems from the fact that there must be something to it or Rachel wouldn't be that committed. There must be something more to it than I can see," he says.

I interrupt and say, teasingly, "For somebody who finished third in his law school class and went on to a great intellectual career as a jurist, what you just said is not very convincing."

Ab laughs again. "No, and I realize that. I have all the same rational questions I've had all my life. It's easier for me to make the necessary assumptions and explanations of how the world came about than it is for me to attribute it to some kind of ephemeral thing that is responsible for all these things yet isn't responsible. If it goes right, thank God. But if it goes wrong, it's not His fault." That's just not something he can happily accept.

"So, at this point in your life," I say, "how far away from your father's position are you?"

"Well, my dad was very anti-God. For him, religion was the opiate of the masses. It was harmful, evil and kept people oppressed. I don't feel that way."

"So, when it comes to your faith, are you an agnostic?" I ask.

"Yeah," he says a little reluctantly, as if that label doesn't seem adequate. "I feel that I'm more of an agnostic than anything else."

"It only gets better," Ab says, when I tell him how much fun Joan and I are having with our young grandchildren, Lila and Vivienne. Weekends and summers at the Mikvas' house in the Dunes had been a regular gathering place for their children and grandchildren, especially after Zoe and Ab left Washington and moved back to Chicago in 1997. Professionally, Ab continued to teach, mostly at the University of Chicago Law School, and until we started our conversations, he also worked on big, complex arbitration and mediation cases for JAMS (Judicial Arbitration and Mediation Services). "A nice part of the arbitration work is it's as varied as you can imagine," Ab says. His cases ranged from sex discrimination at an auto company to tobacco company settlements with the states to an international dispute in the funeral home industry involving provisions of the North American Free Trade Agreement.

But as Ab's eyesight continued to decline, reading legal briefs and documents became more difficult, and he began to phase out the arbitration work. And just before he turned ninety, he reluctantly gave up driving. Ab discovered he had macular degeneration about fifteen years ago. "I've had various treatments to slow it," he tells me. "I can still see you, both of your heads," he jokes. "Fortunately, the technology has come along which allows me to hear so much of the stuff that I can't read. I get the *New York*

Times every day on my iPod, orally. I read books on my iPod. I'm finishing the second book in a series about Henry VIII," he says.

"How do you happen to be reading that?" I ask.

"My sister-in-law, Paula, told me about it. That's how I get all my books. Somebody says this is worth reading." In fact, Ab says, he's "reading" more now, both fiction and nonfiction, than he has since college—or maybe since he won "Book Worm" awards from the Milwaukee Public Library as a kid. He takes me into his office and shows me his magnifying machine, which he uses to read medical bills and letters, and his computer, which has a big yellow keyboard. Although he doesn't use the computer much, he says, "I can still write a letter to the president."

When Ab and I started our conversations in the spring of 2013, about 70 percent of Americans thought the country was on the wrong track. And so did Abner Mikva. Ab and I had our last conversation shortly before he died in July 2016, five months before Donald Trump was elected president. Although the economy had been improving, albeit slowly and unevenly, the mood of the country remained deeply gloomy. Even Ab, with his naturally sunny disposition, could not escape the gloom.

How bad was it? Well, about a year before he died, Ab and I are talking about Congress, an institution he loved. The high-water mark of his public life was the day he was elected to the House of Representatives, where he served for nine years. We discuss how different the House is now—the gridlock, the polarization, the acrimony. I mention that when Ab was in the House, only about 3 percent of the members who left became lobbyists; today, it's nearly 50 percent. "That's part of it," he says, "the kind of people who run. I was attracted to politics and running for office because it gave me a great deal of psychic income. I never felt that I was short-changed by the fact that most of my law school classmates made a lot more money than I did because I got more satisfaction out of my career than most of them got out of theirs." But these days, he says, members of Congress don't get that kind of psychic income because government has been disparaged.

"I thought of this many times," Ab says, and what follows is something I never dreamed I'd hear from him. "I can't imagine aspiring to the Congress, given what it is now. I don't know what I would have done because I enjoyed government, but I don't think I could have stood the embarrassment of identifying myself as a congressman." Does he really believe this? I ask myself. It's so unlike him.

To an extent, the polarization in the House of Representatives reflects a more polarized electorate in which there are fewer ticket-splitting voters. But aggressive gerrymandering in recent years, especially after the big Republican victories for governor and in the state legislatures in 2010, has resulted in fewer competitive congressional districts. I mention to Ab that when Obama was reelected in 2012, Democrats running for Congress received a majority of the votes, but it was only the second time in seventy years that the party that won the majority of the votes didn't win a majority of House seats. "That's an indication of how gerrymandered the congressional seats have become," Ab replies.

Ab's career in the House was highly unusual because first he was elected in a district that was lopsidedly Democratic, and then he represented another district that was just about evenly split between Democrats and Republicans. What's better, I want to know, having safe districts or competitive districts? "Clearly, competitive districts are better, better for the people and better for Congress," he says. "Congress functions better with competitive seats even though it means a lot of Sturm und Drang. I think every congressman ought to be nervous about his or her reelection. It means that members can be persuaded by popular opinion. It better reflects what the House of Representatives is supposed to be, especially when you have the cooling saucer of the Senate to slow things down if there's too much popular passion involved. But no legislature is going to vote for competitive districts. Whichever party has the majority is going to try to take advantage of it and carve up the districts in their favor. Those are the facts of life."

But when Ab was in the Illinois state legislature in the 1950s and 1960s, he thought he had devised a pretty good alternative to the excesses of gerrymandering, if not a perfect solution. He and his reformer friends pushed for a system whereby a bipartisan committee of legislators, appointed by the legislature, would draw the map of state legislative districts whenever reapportionment came up. If they failed to agree on a map, there would be a coin flip, and the winning party would draw the new district lines. "We were sure that no savvy politician would let it go to the luck of the draw," Ab tells me. "They'd reason together. They'd sit down and cut a deal. But that's not what happened," Ab laughs. "Every time, it ended up with a coin flip. And of course, once one party wins, then they really make sure the districts go their way."

Despite his experience in the Illinois legislature, Ab still thought, until recently, that politicians could do a better job with reapportionment than the courts, mainly because most judges are naïve about politics. "I didn't like the idea of people who didn't understand politics dividing towns and districts without being aware of the political consequences," Ab says. But racial and partisan gerrymandering, abetted by sophisticated computer programs, has become so extreme and widespread that Ab has reconsidered. I ask Ab whether there is a constitutional issue at stake when extreme gerrymandering diminishes the impact of black voters or when lines are drawn to diminish the impact of Democratic or Republican voters. "The standard is," Ab says, "you start with Brennan's decision in *Baker v. Carr*, one man, one vote," referring to the landmark 1962 decision in which the Court found that constitutional protections are at risk when voters are disadvantaged by state redistricting decisions. "And then it really comes down to a question of intent." That is, it depends on whether cramming African Americans, for example, into one legislative district, or dispersing them into multiple districts, is intended to diminish the importance of their votes. If it is, then the process is inconsistent with the finding in *Baker v. Carr*. (Four months after Ab died, a three-judge federal district court panel ruled that Republican legislators in Wisconsin had unconstitutionally gerrymandered the state's legislative districts, drawing numerous boundaries that deprived Democratic voters of fair representation. The decision was appealed, but the Supreme Court recently avoided addressing the issue, sending the case back to a trial court and leaving the ultimate decision on partisan gerrymandering unclear.

While Ab is disheartened about the institutional demise of Congress and the disparagement of government, he's furious about some recent Supreme Court decisions. He says to me, "This Supreme Court has done more damage in the last half dozen years between *Citizens United*, the *Heller* case, and the voting rights decision than any Supreme Court in history." Ab is visibly angry about the Court's 5-to-4 decision in 2013 that gutted the landmark Voting Rights Act of 1965 (VRA), calling it "just so disgraceful."

In fact, seven years earlier, Congress had reauthorized the VRA with overwhelming bipartisan support. The vote was 98 to 0 in the Senate and 390 to 33 in the House. "Since when does the Court decide what evidence Congress should use for its decisions?" Ab asks contemptuously. He's talking about the Court's high-handed, contrived rationale for eviscerating section 4 of the VRA, which required states with a history of voter discrimination to seek approval from the Justice Department or a Washington court before making any changes to voting procedures. Once again, he says, "This is the most activist Court we've ever had, much more than the court after the Civil War, which was the other famously activist Court." I observe that we don't hear conservative commentators talking about activist courts these days. "No, you don't," Ab replies. "Activism is in the eye of the beholder. That's what I used to say. But this was total contempt for Congress." And of course, the VRA decision will have an adverse impact on minorities and young voters, key parts of the coalition that elected Barack Obama twice.

Because of the country's changing demographics, today's increasingly conservative Republican Party is hard-pressed to win national elections without changing the voting laws. Donald Trump's "victory," despite losing the popular vote to Hillary Clinton by 2.8 million votes, illustrates the Republicans' problem. The Supreme Court's VRA decision conveniently provides new opportunities for Republicans to implement more voter suppression laws. In that sense, it's not difficult to think of the Court's decision as partisan.

Similarly, the *Citizens United* decision in 2010, which overturned a century of prohibitions on corporate campaign contributions, skews the playing field in favor of wealthy, mostly Republican partisans. Corporations are people, the Court argued, and those "people" can contribute as much as they want because they have a right to express their political views. To which Ab says, "That's what's wrong with *Citizens United*. The idea that money is speech and speech is absolute is just ridiculous." Historically, there have been limits on political campaign contributions because of the possibility of corruption or even the appearance of corruption. "I suppose you could say," Ab observes, "that everybody has a price. My favorite Abe Lincoln story—I'll give a shortened version. When he was practicing law, Lincoln was closeted with a client and after about an hour—the office was on the second floor—he opens the door, he's got the client by the scruff of the neck, and throws him down the stairs. Lincoln's partner comes in and says, 'What was that all about?' And Lincoln says, 'That son of a bitch tried to bribe me.' And the partner says, 'But Abe, you were in there with him for an hour. Did the bribe just come up at the end?' And Lincoln says, 'No, but he was getting close to my price.' So, do we really want a system of legalized bribery where the Koch brothers and Sheldon Adelson can give unlimited millions to political campaigns? No, we can't do that. As I said before, our founders weren't that stupid. Only this Court is that stupid."

Well, I point out to Ab, it's not really stupidity. The Republican-appointed Court majority in *Citizens United* and other recent campaign finance cases knew exactly what they were doing but pretended that legalizing large political contributions wasn't partisan and doesn't taint the democratic process. "Faux naïveté" is what the Court employed in these cases, according to liberal columnist E. J. Dionne. In a flagrant example of the practice, Justice Anthony Kennedy asserted in his *Citizens United* opinion that wealthy donors' large, unlimited campaign expenditures are permissible in part because the "appearance of influence or access . . . will not cause the electorate to lose faith in our democracy." That's preposterous, I say to Ab. How can the Court majority possibly believe or justify that? To which Ab says, in the "social bubble where the Republican justices live," there is virtual unanimity that "the more we keep those Democrats down, the better. The more we make it harder for them to get elected, the better. And they think that's good for the country."

Until Scalia's death, the dominance of the Court's conservative Republican majority was just "the luck of the draw," as Ab calls it. For example, Jimmy Carter made no Supreme Court appointments during his term, while Ronald Reagan made three. Although he has always supported an independent judiciary, Ab tells me he's ready to consider term limits for justices. "An idea that's been proposed is that each justice is appointed for a nonrenewable eighteen-year term. That would mean, eventually, that every president would get two appointments during his or her term, which is the part of the proposal I like. That would provide a little more balance to the Court and counter the political winds that are blowing."

We talk more about corruption. I ask Ab, on a scale of one to ten, with one being akin to a corrupt banana republic, where he would place our political system today. "About a four," he answers. "I've thought a lot about this. For a while, I thought we were making such progress," he says, referring not only to the post-Watergate federal reforms but also to the caliber of people entering politics in Illinois, for example. "With people like Paul Simon and Dick Durbin and later Obama, I thought honest people were getting more influence and power and that there wasn't as much corruption. But now I realize that it's just gone to a higher level. Fifty years ago in Illinois, Paul Powell was a two-bit crook. Now you've got these multimillion-dollar crooks. And you've got the banks; they own Congress. It's not like they're buying Congress, they own it."

A big part of the problem, he says, is the soaring cost of political campaigns. "When I ran against Sam Young in 1976, we each spent about $250,000, and that was a record. Now you can't even get on the ballot for $250,000." That's not much of an exaggeration. Forty years later, in Ab's reconfigured 10th Congressional District the candidates and outside groups spent a total of almost $20 million in 2016. Even adjusted for inflation, that's twenty times greater than in Ab's campaign—an astonishing increase. "Money has gotten completely out of control," Ab says. "It's just mad. I wanted to keep my seat, and I fought very hard for it. Obviously, people who gave me contributions had more access. That happens. But I never voted differently than I believed was the right vote, nor was I tempted to." But these days, with campaign costs so much greater, Ab says, "It's harder for members of Congress to avoid the pressure from industry lobbyists if they want to stay in office and are running in close districts or states." Ab mentions his old House colleague Max Baucus of Montana. In 1975, Ab recalls, Baucus was an idealistic first-termer who "was so progressive we had to restrain him." Thirty-five years later, when he was chairman of the Senate Finance Committee, Baucus's industry-friendly negotiating performance on health insurance legislation was roundly criticized by progressive groups. "If anyone had gotten chewed up by the system," Ab says, "it was Max Baucus."

Public financing of political campaigns is one of the two issues at the top of Ab's reform agenda. He knows it's a steep hill to climb, but it's critically important because the growing perception of corruption has contributed to the public's disaffection with and cynicism about government. "Public financing is the only real answer, there is no other. I've toyed with all kinds of ethics and disclosure and contribution limitation laws, and the more you put in, the more lawyers you need. Those laws don't work. There would still be corruption no matter what system you developed, but I think public financing is the only way you can minimize it to a bearable amount."

I note that the politics of public financing seems to be just as difficult as the politics of gun control, and Ab agrees. "When I mention public financing to somebody who's not involved in the system, they say, 'So your cure is to give more money to government?'" Moreover, the political class has learned to thrive in the current system. Some years ago in Illinois, Ab tells me, Obama helped pass a bill in the state senate that provided for public financing in judicial races. "Electing judges is a bad idea," Ab says, "and raising money for judicial campaigns is a bad idea." So Ab and Paul Simon went to see the powerful Democratic leader in the Illinois house, Michael Madigan. They had a friendly relationship with Madigan and tried to persuade him to pass Obama's bill in the house. Ab says, "He wouldn't budge. He didn't say so, but he was worried that the bill was a camel's nose under the tent. If we got public financing for judges, pretty soon it would be for legislators, and that's a bad idea from Madigan's perspective." Why, I ask Ab, expecting a version of the answer he delivers. "Because then Madigan doesn't have any influence," Ab replies. "He was spending maybe a million dollars in some state representative districts to get Democrats elected. That's where his power came from. In many of those districts, he raises most if not all of the money. And when those guys come to Springfield, they're completely beholden to him."

So how does the country get out of the corner of corruption? I ask Ab. We talk about the possibility of a new Supreme Court majority overturning *Citizens United* (this was before Donald Trump was elected). But that alone would probably not produce enough cleansing. Public financing of political campaigns was supported by 50 percent of Americans in 2013, according to a Gallup poll. Perhaps the base of support is larger now. But the political pros are inevitably skeptical about good-government reforms being voting issues, and so far, there are no signs of a robust citizens' reform movement for public financing. Even Bernie Sanders, running for the 2016 Democratic presidential nomination as a populist reformer and a critic of the *Citizens United* decision, offered only tepid support for public financing of congressional campaigns. "So how do we get from here to there?" I ask Ab.

His answer is inferential and Mikva-hopeful. The country has achieved legislative breakthroughs that were far more unlikely, even miraculous, Ab says. He mentions overturning Jim Crow laws, women's suffrage, malapportionment. "We cured it," he says about these seemingly intractable undemocratic institutions. "I can't believe we can't cure one that is ridiculously small by comparison. Don't ask me how it's going to be done or who's going to do it." As Ab momentarily pauses, I recall one of my favorite Tocqueville quotes: "The great privilege of the Americans is not that they are more enlightened than other people, but that they have the capacity to correct mistakes they commit from time to time." Before Ab responds, I say to him that if the system is too corrupt, the capacity for change can diminish or disappear. "That's right," he says. "If the capacity to change is squeezed off too hard or for too long, we can lose it."

"What you're suggesting," I say, "is that if corruption were at a one or two on my scale, then you would be less optimistic. But we're not yet at a tipping point."

"No," Ab agrees. Then he says that he can imagine the next president making campaign finance reform a big issue, a cause. This is when we both thought Hillary Clinton was going to be the next president. And I ask, with undisguised skepticism, "Do you mean Hillary Clinton?"

He's ready with a pretty convincing retort: "If you were sitting there in 1960," he says, "could you have predicted that several years later, Lyndon Baines Johnson would stand at the Speaker's rostrum and say to the country, 'We Shall Overcome'? Absolutely not. You would have been locked up. So who knows? Hillary may, at the end of her first term, when the system will probably be worse, decide this is going to be her moral crusade." With Donald Trump as president, this seems highly unlikely. But, as Ab might have pointed out, a reform Democrat running in 2020 could make public financing his or her "moral crusade" and win the election.

Ab's second big issue is tax reform. In the 1970s, when he served on the House Ways and Means Committee, he asked the General Accounting Office (GAO) to review a set of tax policy proposals. One of the GAO's findings some forty years ago was that most Americans paid more in regressive payroll taxes than they did in federal income taxes. And today, the federal tax burden is even more regressive. "The problem is that our system is so screwed up; it's so bad with all these regressive taxes—sales taxes, property taxes, marriage license taxes, toll road taxes, the list goes on," Ab says. "Everybody feels oppressed; taxes are unpopular. But the fact is we're not paying anywhere near enough taxes to run our government. We're running on empty and not doing even the basic things we need to do. Our infrastructure is in terrible shape. We have bridges that are going to collapse. Every time I go downtown, I look at the 'L'"—the rapid-transit system. "I think of how underexamined and undersupported it is. It was built in flush times when you put in all the money you needed for a safe, solid structure."

Ab concedes that anti-government conservatives have been winning the tax debate. "Starve the beast" is their credo, he says. "They have successfully sold the notion that the more money you put into government, the worse off we are. You can't run the country that way." I mention the conservatives' assault on the estate tax, one of my favorite examples of our wrongheaded tax policies and how anti-government conservatives have bamboozled many of my fellow middle-class citizens. The estate tax was enacted in 1916, during the country's great Progressive Era. Its main purpose was not to raise revenue but to limit the political power of the rich. The estate tax was intended to keep the society more fluid, open, and democratic. But over the last thirty years, anti-government conservatives have successfully rebranded the estate tax as a pernicious "death tax," dishonestly asserting that it hurts mom-and-pop businesses and small family farmers. "That's bullshit," Ab exclaims. "We should be redistributing the wealth. We shouldn't want this 99 percent and 1 percent kind of society. There is only one fair way to tax, and that's a tax that takes more from the rich and less from the working class and middle class and redistributes the wealth."

As for Ab's other tax reform priorities, he would raise the limit on income subject to payroll taxes and plug the carried-interest loophole that allows billionaire hedge-fund managers to escape paying taxes. "That's such an obvious one," Ab says. "There are others like forcing corporations to bring their money back from overseas and prohibiting them to do these inversions. An increasing problem is that more corporations are using their huge profits to buy back their stock. That's bad for the economy because those are basically disinvestments. Instead of using profits to expand, they use profits to pay off stockholders, and of course, stockholders don't pay any taxes until they sell their stock. It's a great way for corporations to disinvest and avoid taxes." The problem with achieving any of these reforms, Ab says, is that "the lobbyists have such control." And so we're back to the necessity of changing the way political campaigns are financed.

Another tough problem our county has not yet solved, and that neither Ab nor I have given up on, is the tragedy of gun violence. I spent twenty-five years working in the gun control movement after Ab left Congress. Nobody is talking these days about a federal law banning the sale and manufacture of handguns, such as Ab proposed in the 1970s. But the Republican Party banned all firearms from its national convention in Cleveland. If, as the NRA contends, we would all be safer if virtually everybody were armed, shouldn't all the Republican delegates have been packing heat in Cleveland?

Short of banning handguns, Ab and I both favor universal background checks, much longer waiting periods to buy guns, and a ban on assault weapons. In the coming years, new smart-gun technology seems like a promising method for significantly reducing firearms-related homicides, suicides, and accidents. Ab is enthusiastic about it, and so am I. The technology exists, and it is being refined. Through fingerprints or other means, it prevents anybody except the lawful owner of a firearm from shooting it. This technology might have prevented the young shooter at the Sandy Hook Elementary School from using his mother's gun to kill twenty schoolchildren and six educators. The technology is opposed by the NRA, and gun dealers have been pressured not to sell smart guns. But a profitable market could be established if the federal government began purchasing smart guns for the military and law enforcement. Even the NRA might have a tough time stopping the Defense Department and the FBI from purchasing thousands of smart guns. My friends at the Industrial Areas Foundation (IAF) organized a coalition of police chiefs, other public officials, clergy, and concerned citizens to prod the Obama administration to persuade the largest gun manufacturers to produce smart guns for local, state, and federal law enforcement agencies—and, eventually, for the retail market. The Obama administration flirted with the idea but waited too long before acting in the waning months of Obama's presidency. The IAF coalition continues to press gun manufacturers to adopt smart-gun technology and other anti–gun violence measures.

Ab grew up in the 1930s and 1940s, and I came along a little later, when gun violence was rare and city neighborhoods were safer. It was also a time when Americans trusted one another. Not so much anymore. For decades, social scientists have been asking Americans the same survey question: "Generally speaking, would you say that most people can be trusted or that you can't be too careful in dealing with people?" A majority of Americans used to say that people could be trusted, but today, only 19 percent of millennials feel that way. The sources of our distrust are multiple, from presidents lying and getting us into wars to the bowling alone phenomenon, in which Americans are much more likely to be disconnected from one another.

The decline in trust—the fraying of our social fabric—and the decline in confidence in government, I say to Ab, are inevitably linked. "That's the point," he says. "The whole notion of government is on the basis of trust." Some months after we first discussed this generational decline in trust, Ab surprises me when he says he favors mandatory national service for post–high school youth. "Everybody should serve a year or two of service, either military or civilian," he says. He sees this as a way of strengthening the social contract with a shared experience for the common good. "I think of it almost like a tax. Just as everybody ought to pay taxes to run the government, everybody ought to pay with their skills to help run the country." He began to consider mandatory national service when he thought about how successful the Peace Corps has been. When I mention that the number of Peace Corps volunteers—and AmeriCorps volunteers—has been modest over the years, he doesn't miss a beat. "But think how much more could be done if there were five million in a national service program. Think of all the things that need to be done in this country, all the poor kids that could be tutored, and the rivers that need cleaning, and the neighborhoods that need fixing."

12

The Mikva Challenge

The end came quickly, suddenly, unexpectedly. Well, not really, unless your ears were closed to death's heavy breathing. Mine were. I knew, intellectually, that my last conversation with Ab could come at any time, even after our first conversation three years ago. As I mentioned earlier, the Mikva Google alerts that popped up on my computer screen were instantly unnerving and ominous. I suppose I should be grateful that Ab was able to share his wisdom and friendship to the very end. I am grateful, but I'm also sad we didn't have more time. Despite his many chronic health problems and then bladder cancer, somehow, I thought we would.

I phoned Ab on Wednesday afternoon, June 22, 2016. "How are you?" I asked.

"I think I'm getting a little better," he said. He had recently been discharged from the hospital. I told him I would be coming to Chicago next week. "When?" he asked. Wednesday or Thursday, I replied. "My days are open, so if I'm feeling okay, let's get together," Ab said. I promised I would call him on Monday.

Before we said good-bye, I asked Ab if he knew about the remarkable sit-in demonstration under way in the House of Representatives. He did. Congressman John Lewis, a civil rights icon, was leading scores of Democratic members in a noble exercise in civil disobedience in the well of the House floor. They were demanding that House Republicans allow a vote on legislation to curb gun violence. It was ten days after the then-largest mass shooting in US history, when forty-nine people were killed in an Orlando nightclub. I asked Ab, "If you were back in the House, would you be sitting down with Lewis and the others?"

"I would, I would," he responded enthusiastically if a bit weakly. "I think I still remember the words to 'We Shall Overcome.'"

I didn't know "We Shall Overcome" were going to be just about the last words I heard my friend speak. When I phoned on Monday, an aide in his apartment told me Ab was back in the hospital. On Wednesday, I arrived in Chicago and made my way to Ab's room at the Rush University Medical Center. I stopped in the doorway. The room was dimly lit. Ab's daughters Mary and Rachel and one of his granddaughters were there. Ab was not up for talking. Mary took me out in the hallway and asked if I would begin working on her father's obituary. I was stunned, close to paralyzed with disbelief and sadness. "How long does your father have?" I asked quietly. Mary didn't know. A month, a week, maybe only days.

In 2014 President Obama presented Ab with the Presidential Medal of Freedom, the nation's highest civilian award, at a White House ceremony. Other honorees that day included actress Meryl Streep, broadcaster Tom Brokaw, and, posthumously, the three civil rights workers who were murdered in Mississippi in 1964—James Chaney, Andrew Goodman, and Michael Schwerner. "They got the most sustained applause," Ab says. "They deserved it." After the White House ceremony, many of us from Ab's congressional staff, his law clerks, and his old friends gathered to celebrate with him at The Monocle restaurant on Capitol Hill. That venerable, unfancy political hangout was, fittingly, Ab's choice. Among the happy crowd of Mikva disciples were Supreme Court Justice Elena Kagan and chief judge of the US Court of Appeals for the DC Circuit Merrick Garland.

Ab, of course, was thrilled to receive the Medal of Freedom from his friend. A photo of President Obama standing behind Ab and draping the medal onto his chest is prominently displayed on a table in the Mikvas' living room.

When Ab stood up to receive his Presidential Medal of Freedom, a White House announcer briefly summarized his career and contributions—his service in three branches of the federal government, his reverence for the rule of law, and so forth. But the last sentence was this: "He has imparted a sense of civic duty to a new generation." More than anything else he's done or been associated with in his public life over the last sixty years, that's what Ab is proudest of. The most concrete manifestation of that, apart from the role model he's been for countless young lawyers and others engaged in public service, is the Mikva Challenge.

"That is absolutely the best thing that Zoey and I ever did in our lives," he says to me, referring to the civic education organization the Mikvas shaped and supported after they returned to Chicago in 1997. Ab says this when I tell him about the CNN series *Chicagoland*, which cited the Mikva

Challenge as one of the five ways the city could become safer and stronger. "I don't know if you remember," he says, "that we got off to a shaky start." I do. Although we started with the right impulse—to engage disconnected high school students in the civic and political process—we hadn't developed a set of compelling programs, nor had we identified the capable Brian Brady to run the nonprofit. But within the first five years, the pieces came together. By now, thousands of Chicago students, with support from Mikva Challenge staff and their teachers, have volunteered in local and national election campaigns, served as election judges, and worked on neighborhood and citywide issues that are important to them. These have been transformative experiences for many students, a powerful realization of what it means to have a public voice and how to make a difference in the larger world. It's the best kind of experiential learning and the most hopeful way to counter the troubling evidence that the majority of democracy's next generation is unprepared and uninspired to become engaged, effective citizens. If our country took citizenship and democracy seriously, rather than giving it collective lip service, we'd elevate civic education to the top of our educational priorities. The Mikva Challenge, which is now being implemented by teachers and school districts in California, Washington, DC, and elsewhere, is a timely, important Mikva legacy. (In Washington, Mikva Challenge high school students played a role in mobilizing support for the national protest against gun violence on March 24, 2018, in the nation's capital. Ab would have been proud and thrilled.)

The sad news came five days after my visit to the hospital. It was not a Google alert.

When I picked up the phone at my house in Arlington, Virginia, on that peaceful Fourth of July morning, Mary Mikva told me. She asked if I had written an obituary the family could give to the media. I had just finished it. The first sentence began: "Long known in Chicago and Washington political and legal circles as a liberal reform leader and a man of unassailable integrity…." Yes, I think as I read these words again in 2018. Given the calamitous reign of Donald Trump, integrity and political courage are more important than ever.

I was inspired by Ab Mikva when we met more than four decades ago, and I feel newly inspired by our conversations over the last three years of his life. Even at ninety years old and with all those pills he had to take, his determination to make a difference, to fight for a more just society and country, was never compromised. Maybe that's the best medicine for the unkind encroachment of old age. Here's a small but important example: Near the end, despite his failing health, Ab agreed to help his lawyer friend Mickey Gaynor with a case. More than two decades ago, fifteen-year-old Adolfo Davis had been given a mandatory life sentence without parole in a murder case. But in 2012 the Supreme Court ruled that mandatory life sentences for minors were unconstitutional. Ab visited Davis at Stateville, a maximum-security prison in Joliet, where Davis had been a model prisoner for many years, and Ab testified at Davis's resentencing in a Chicago courtroom. It was an exhausting marathon from morning until late at night, and Ab was there for it all. "The judge's decision was just awful," Ab said with disgust. "She resentenced Davis to another life term." According to her, Ab said, "none of the witnesses were credible. Not me, not a priest who testified for him or an ex-warden. Can you imagine? He's been there for twenty-four years, he has this resentencing, and nothing changed." The verdict was appealed, and a year after Ab died, Davis's sentence was reduced. He is scheduled to be released from prison on October 1, 2020.

As for our gloomy political times, only once did it seem to me that Ab Mikva might have succumbed to the darkness. That was when he told me, if he were starting over, running for Congress would have no appeal for him. The lack of public respect for the institution and the frustration of not getting anything done would be too depressing. At the time, I wondered if he really meant it. But then he asked, "Did I tell you about my dream that involved you? Zoey and I had just moved into the Hallmark. I got a call from the New Trier committeeman [in the northern suburbs]. He said, 'Ab, there's an open seat up here and we think you ought to run for Congress.' I said, 'I can't do that. We just moved and Zoey would kill me if I talk to her about moving again.' And he said, 'You don't have to move until you win.' I thought about that, and it's true. So I called you, and we wrote up a press release and called a news conference, and I announced that I'm running for Congress. One of the newspaper reporters said, 'Aren't you the same age as Barratt O'Hara was when you beat him?' I looked around for you, and you were gone. Then I woke up."

"Ab," I said, "I can assure you that even at my advanced age, I'm fired up! Ready to go!"

ACKNOWLEDGMENTS

In thinking about my journey that resulted in this book, I'm reminded of the immortal words of philosopher and Hall of Fame pitcher Lefty Gomez: "I'd rather be lucky than good."

After three years of monthly reflections with my friend Ab Mikva, I realize anew how lucky I've been throughout my life filled with loving family and caring friends. In so many ways my good fortune is encompassed in this book—a book that would not be possible without the help and support of family and friends, old and new. Among the latter is the gifted David Congdon, my editor at the University Press of Kansas. David recognized immediately that a book based on conversations with Ab Mikva was important and timely and has been enthusiastic from the beginning. He is part of a stellar team that I have been privileged to work with at UPK—Michael Kehoe, marketing and sales director; Larisa Martin, production editor; and freelance copyeditor Linda Lotz.

I was lucky to have crossed paths with Ab Mikva in 1974, and I'm grateful he wanted to share his end-of-life wisdom and feelings about everything from impending death to his hopes for our country and democracy's next generation.

I was moved by Ab's vivid memories of a long-ago Milwaukee schoolteacher who made a big difference in his life. Thank you, Ellen Hardgrove. And thank you to my Milwaukee teachers who made a difference in my life, especially Mary Donovan, Jennie Brodi, Maxine Sawtelle, and Bob Spicuzza.

I am also grateful for the support and friendship of Zoe Mikva and her family in addition to the help Mary and Rachel provided in rounding up all the wonderful Mikva family photos.

One of the joys of working for Ab when he was in Congress was that he attracted a staff of women and men who shared his values and characteristics: high ideals and integrity, humor, and collegiality. Many have been my friends for decades. The acclaimed attorney Ken Adams, one of Ab's first legislative assistants, helped me with his wise counsel throughout the book-writing process, from critiquing one of my early drafts to representing me with my publisher. Ken is a great, cherished friend, as are other old Mikva colleagues who helped with this book: Henry Bayer and his wife Jackie Kinnaman, Zoe Gratsias, Linda Imes, Greg Kinczewski, Jack Marco, Dick Meltzer.

A special thanks to James Castello and Sheryll Cashin, two of Ab's favorite law clerks, for sharing their insights and stories, and also to Jonathan Baum, Brian Brady, and Bob Hercules.

I appreciate the assistance I received from Susan Saller and Tina Just at the Milwaukee Public Schools administrative office and from Linda Durrenberg, a graduate of Washington High School in Milwaukee, who shared her encyclopedic knowledge of Ab's and my old high school. Also in Milwaukee, I'm very lucky to have dear friends like the uncommonly generous and gracious Lynn Krebs and Ruth Zubrensky.

For help translating and spelling Ab's Yiddish stories, I benefited from the expertise of Eddie Portnoy at the YIVO Institute for Jewish Research, Rabbi Michel Twerski, Howard Karsh, and Paul Melrood.

Luckiest of all, I am in close proximity to three of the most talented writers and editors: my wife Joan and sons Dusty and Jeff. As they always do, each has made the storytelling in this book better than it was at the beginning. I'm proud to say that among Joan, Dusty, and Jeff, I am the fourth best writer.

INDEX

civil rights issues and movement, 34–35,
53–58, 72–73, 81, 121–122, 136, 140,
185
Clinton, Bill
Abner Mikva as White House
counsel to, ix, 6–7, 60, 67, 134,
135–142, 143, 151–155, 167
Abner Mikva on, 134–136, 137–142,
143–144
and capital punishment, 124–125
Democratic Leadership Council and,
135, 138
habeas corpus, 139–140
and health care reform, 76
Ken Starr investigation of, 150–153
and minimum-wage increase,
137–138
reputation of, 134–135
Clinton, Hillary Rodham
Abner Mikva on, 1, 5, 142–146,
·150–153, 163, 165, 181
and health care reform, 76, 163
Saul Alinsky's influence on, 145–146,
147–150
and 2008 Democratic primary, 168
and 2016 election, 1, 144–145, 146, 149,
178
Cochran, Thad, 98, 101–102
Cohen, Bill, 140–141
Collin, Frank, 83, 87
Conable, Barber, 92–93, 117
Corrigan, Jack, 160
Coyle, Marcia, 96
Crane, Phil, 82, 142
Cutler, Lloyd, 135, 143, 154

Daley, Richard J. "Dick"
Abner Mikva's relationship with, 33,
34, 44–45, 74, 91–92, 128
black vote and, 40–41
Chicago Film Review Board and, 44,
45–46
in Chicago machine politics, 44–45,
53, 54–55, 56, 61, 62, 91–92

and 1968 Democratic National
Convention, 74
and 1975 redistricting scheme, 91–92
Danforth, Jack, 101–102
Darrow, Clarence, 18, 125, 145
Davidson, Claire, 126
Davis, Adolfo, 188
Davis, Leon, 72
Dawson, Bill, 40
Decker, Bernard, 87
deGrazia, Victor, 28, 29, 30
Democratic Leadership Council
(DLC), 135, 138
Democratic National Convention
(1968), 74
Democratic Study Group (DSG), US
House, 74, 76
Derwinski, Ed, 34, 64
Despres, Leon, 29, 34
Dingell, John, 170
Dionne, E. J., 178
discrimination. *See* civil rights issues
and movement
Douglas, Paul, ix, 25, 72, 80
Douglas, William "Bill," 48
Dreier, Peter, 169
Dronenberg v. Zech, 130
Dunne, Finley Peter, 124
Durbin, Dick, ix–x, 179

Edelman, Marian Wright, 149
Edwards, Don, 71, 74
Edwards, Harry, 126
Eisenhower, Dwight, 122, 142
Emanuel, Rahm, 164–165
Espy, Mike, 136
Evans, Terrence, 141
Everett, Marge, 38
Exon, James, 101

family life, politics and, 62, 78–79
Fannings, Helen, 55, 56
Federalist Society, 121, 142
Feingold, Russ, 142